GLORY DAYS

GLORY DAYS

Forty Years of One-Day Cricket
1963–2003

EDWARD GRIFFITHS

VIKING
an imprint of
PENGUIN BOOKS

VIKING

Published by the Penguin Group
80 Strand, London WC2R 0RL, England
Penguin Putnam Inc, 375 Hudson Street, New York, New York 10014, USA
Penguin Books Australia Ltd, Ringwood, Victoria, Australia
Penguin Books Canada Ltd, 10 Alcorn Avenue, Toronto, Ontario, Canada M4V 3B2
Penguin Books (NZ) Ltd, Cnr Rosedale and Airborne Roads, Albany, Auckland,
New Zealand
Penguin Books India (P) Ltd, 11 Community Centre, Panchsheel Park,
New Delhi – 110 017, India
Penguin Books (South Africa) (Pty) Ltd, 24 Sturdee Avenue, Rosebank,
Johannesburg 2196, South Africa

Penguin Books (South Africa) (Pty) Ltd, Registered Offices:
Second Floor, 90 Rivonia Road, Sandton 2196, South Africa

First published by Penguin Books (South Africa) (Pty) Ltd 2003

ISBN 0 670 04788 0

Typeset by CJH Design in 10.5 on 14 pt Charter
Cover design: Mouse Design
Printed and bound by CTP Book Printers, Cape Town

Dedicated to the Saints,
David, George, Christian, Oscar N, Alex, Hamish,
Casper, Oscar R, Tolly, Henry, Julius, Owen and Kate,
with the message that . . .
opportunity plus hard work equals glory.

Contents

Introduction

The eighth Cricket World Cup final was played under an African sun, between Australia and India at a jam-packed Wanderers Stadium in Johannesburg on Sunday 23 March 2003.

One of the finest teams ever to play one-day cricket amassed the highest total ever scored in a World Cup final, the eighth-highest in one-day internationals, utterly dominated the match, took home a cheque for US$2 million, the largest winner's reward in the history of the game, and, according to the team's captain, most importantly, retained the prized title of 'world champions'.

For Ricky Ponting and his all-conquering Australian team, the eighth World Cup final had been the triumphant culmination of four years' hard work and 14 boyhood ambitions.

For 31 000 people at the Wanderers and a television audience in excess of two billion viewers, the final had been an opportunity to observe the awesome brutality of Australia's batting, the wonderful atmosphere and the sheer scale of the event.

For the game, indeed, it had been another glory day.

Through four decades since its inception, one-day cricket has provided its fair share of 'glory days', and unsatisfactory days, and unforgettable days, and dull days as well.

The limited overs game has produced exhilarating stroke play, heart-stopping finishes and sensational atmosphere, but it has also yielded anti-climax and results distorted by rain.

It is, by nature, a mongrel, a truncated version of the original sport. It is not a pedigree contest, like football, golf or, indeed, Test cricket. The one-day game is innately contrived and manufactured, a pragmatic compromise between the traditional first-class contest and modern public demand for relentless action and a clear result, all packaged in a sharp, compact seven-hour product.

In consequence, this game is fickle. Some days, it can shine like a diamond, appearing as dramatic and fabulous as any kind of entertainment; other days, it seems fatally flawed.

This book traces the development of the one-day game from its nervous inception in 1963 to Ponting's World Cup final in 2003, a genuinely global sporting event. It follows the evolving strategies and celebrates the game's greatest heroes.

Reaching far beyond simple scorecards, it seeks out the heart and soul of the game, relives the feats and drama, focussing on the development of the World Cup, the showpiece event.

'I would love to have played one-day cricket,' remarked Len Hutton, the fine England batsman of another era, 'because I would always have had an excuse for getting out.'

For him, 'one-dayers' were an ugly parody of the old game he had known and loved; and this annoyed scepticism was echoed by many, including cricket's greatest writer. 'Call it snicket or slogget,' wrote Sir Neville Cardus, 'but don't call it cricket.'

In the face of such hostility, limited overs cricket took time to establish itself, but it had become so popular by the mid-1970s that it was essentially subsidising the rest of the game. They could call it snicket or slogget, but they were happy to bank it.

The World Cup has evolved from an experiment in 1975 to an extravaganza with US$5 million prize money in 2003.

Of course, the one-day game has some shortcomings: it often lacks variation, it can sometimes be pedestrian, and it might reward improvisation and foster bad technique, but, around the globe, many millions of people love it. This book tries to explain why.

I am indebted to Penguin South Africa for the commission, to Alison Lowry, Pam Thornley and Claire Heckrath for the professional help and thoughtful encouragement, and, not for the first time, to Owen Hendry, for his sensitive and expert editing. Writers are fated to work in the dark, often alone, and a few words of timely support can fall like the most dazzling shaft of sunshine.

Finally, as ever, I am grateful to Bridget, David, Kate, Harry and Dennis for their forbearance and patience.

Edward Griffiths
March 2003

Chapter One

The Idea

The day dawned predictably damp and overcast over Manchester, but on time, just before eleven o'clock, the established Leicestershire captain, Maurice Hallam, led his team out to field at Old Trafford. It was a Sunday, the first day of May 1963, and cricket was shuffling quietly into a new age.

Hallam tossed the new ball to Charles Spencer, who would open the bowling; and within moments Brian Booth and Robert Entwhistle, both wearing long-sleeved jerseys to withstand the morning chill, emerged from the famous redbrick Victorian pavilion, on their way to open the innings for Lancashire.

A mood of excitement and anticipation rippled around the ground as several thousand people settled in their seats and wondered what to expect. The atmosphere seemed undeniably different; it was keener and sharper than usual.

'Ah well,' said one wizened, flat-capped Lancashire County Cricket Club member to another, sitting beside him on the white benches in front of the pavilion, 'it'll be a bit of fun.'

'Aye, but it's not cricket,' replied his friend.

'Well, it's still batting and bowling, isn't it?'

'Aye, but it's not cricket.'

'Let's wait and see.'

'Aye, but it's not cricket.'

In fact, this was the first preliminary qualifying match of the Knock-Out Cup, contested by the 16 county cricket clubs in England and sponsored by Gillette, a razor manufacturer. This match in Manchester was the first officially recognised game of one-day cricket ever played.

In terms of its appeal across the globe, in terms of its public image, in terms of its financial viability, this historically conservative and cautious game would never be the same again ... although to have suggested as much to any of those people struggling to stay warm on that grey Sunday at Old Trafford in 1963 would have been regarded as nothing but nonsense.

Booth and Entwhistle put on a brisk 42 for the first wicket, but it was Peter Marner's innings of 121 that enabled the home side to reach 304 for nine from their allotted 65 overs.

Leicestershire's reply stuttered into life when their opening batsman Harold Bird, who was destined to become a world-class, much-loved umpire, was bowled by the legendary Brian Statham for only seven. However, the heavens opened soon afterwards, forcing the players to leave the field.

The rain persisted, and umpires Aspinall and Yarnold had no option but to call 'stumps' soon afterwards; so it was that the celebrated Manchester weather forced the first-ever one-day match to move into a second day.

Fewer than a thousand spectators returned to witness the game's conclusion on the Monday morning and, although Hallam dug out a defiant 106, Leicestershire never seriously threatened to reach their target. Not long after lunch, the Lancashire players were back in their changing room, celebrating an emphatic 101-run victory.

'Well, that was fun,' said the flat-capped member as he packed away his binoculars.

'Aye, but it's not cricket,' replied his friend grimly, remaining at least consistent in his view.

For better or for worse, the 'Knock-Out Cup sponsored by Gillette' was under way. One-day cricket was a reality, the culmination of a long and painstaking process that had started no fewer than 89 years before.

It was then, during the first weeks of summer in 1873, when William Gladstone was serving as Prime Minister, that officials of the Marylebone Cricket Club, the ruling body of the game worldwide, decided to launch a new knockout tournament in which county clubs were invited to compete for a newly acquired Silver Cup.

Supporters of this event argued the game would benefit from the introduction of a competition that was shorter and less drawn-out than the standard Championship. They were not proposing a limited number of overs, or that matches should necessarily be completed within one day, although they often were, but their basic theme – that cricket needed to be played in a form more digestible than the traditional three-day matches – would echo in years to come.

The Silver Cup did not prove a success.

Only six counties were persuaded to enter the tournament, and, once Kent had beaten Sussex in the opening match at Lord's, the rest of the field reached a decision that, set aside the Victorian standards of noble, genteel, almost effortless athleticism, such a knockout event seemed vulgar and unworthy. They immediately withdrew and went home. The Silver Cup was left on the shelf, and cricket's structure was left almost untouched for 80 years.

Championship followed upon Championship as summer followed summer, and every once in a while this basic diet of the first-class game in England was bejewelled by the excitement of an Ashes series against Australia. The game thrived and somehow straddled old English divisions, appearing equally cherished by privileged boys at the great public schools and by shrewd, chiselled veterans working in the Yorkshire minefields.

There seemed no need to alter anything. Cricket felt perfect exactly because it did not change. Cosy images like the neatly creased whites, the satisfying clunk of willow on leather, freshly mown grass, salad for lunch and scones for tea, last man in and one to get … these were revered by almost every Englishman and woman as precious, as being quintessentially English. Mere mention of change was scorned.

As time passed, enthusiasts of the summer game propagated national teams in the far corners of the British Empire, and soon South Africa, the West Indies, New Zealand, India and Pakistan were emerging to challenge not only the mother country but also one another. An international cricket community took shape, great players appeared around the globe, and all seemed well.

This sense of prosperity peaked during the seasons after the Second World War. Amid the grey austerity and hardship of daily life, cricket appeared to many people as a gleaming white beacon of exhilaration and interest. During the 1947 season, an astounding 2 200 910 spectators paid at the gate to watch first-class cricket in England. Committeemen started to hail a 'golden age' to compare with the famous prosperity between 1895 and 1912.

It didn't last.

Even as people flocked to the grounds, the balance sheets of many county clubs were already starting to look distinctly vulnerable. Their finances had been underpinned for generations by a benign and un-demanding patronage, but these funds started to wither when England's richest families faced up to the debilitating effects of two World Wars in the space of three decades, and the introduction of punitive death duties.

Under the surface, this 'golden age' was forged not of the shining, 24-carat variety but of straw; and when attendances tailed off – as they inevitably would in a world in which an ever-increasing number of leisure activities began to compete for the public's attention – financial alarm bells started to ring.

At the end of the 1956 season, with crisis looming, the MCC moved to take action; and, in characteristic fashion, such 'action' took the form of creating a sub-committee to investigate the issue and propose a remedy. The group gathered under the energetic chairmanship of Mr H.S. Altham and set to work.

Their enquiries quickly confirmed a general consensus that something needed to be done, and almost everybody was keen to outline their own solution. Many favoured some or other tinkering with the laws to bring back the crowds, but the England captain of the day, Peter May, was altogether more radical, steadfastly insisting that standards needed to be raised, which could only be achieved by scrapping the Counties and replacing them with no more than eight new regional teams.

The sub-committee delivered its report in January 1957, a document that included a wide variety of recommendations relating to the Champion-ship. These were all implemented. However, Altham's gentle suggestion that a shortened version of the game be devised and launched was left to gather dust on the shelf. MCC seemed reluctant to embrace a concept that many of its diehard members regarded as no less than heresy.

Unfortunately the malaise remained, and as the game limped into the 1960s, reality became harder to ignore: for English cricket, the game simply needed to reform or go bankrupt.

The total attendance at first-class matches in the 1961 season dipped below a million, to only 969 382, and leading minds at Lord's were duly concentrated. There was no alternative. A motion was finally placed before the MCC Advisory Committee: to introduce a one-day knockout competition for the county clubs.

On Wednesday 20 December 1961, the eve of the shortest day of the year in England, perhaps the longest discussion in sports history reached its conclusion. MCC passed the proposal by a majority of just two votes, and it was declared that limited overs cricket would start 18 months later, in 1963.

Several of the more conservative committee members sat solemn in their seats immediately after the vote, sadly wondering what hounds had been let loose in their game. For these gentlemen, there was to be no respite from change and reform: two months later, the traditional distinction of amateurs and professionals was abolished, and it was decided that all players would be referred to as 'cricketers'. To those conservative committee members, nothing seemed sacred.

In contrast to such caution, the young, imaginative secretary of Leicestershire County Cricket Club could hardly contain his excitement that the MCC authorities had grasped the nettle. 'At last,' Michael Turner later noted, 'we had found the courage and determination to take our game forward.'

However, as he drove home to Leicester, back up the M1 motorway, Turner felt frustrated that the new event would not be launched until the 1963 season. It seemed a long time to wait, and the impatient club secretary conceived a plan whereby his county would stage a trial one-day tourna-ment at the earliest opportunity in the forthcoming season.

So, from 2 May until 9 May 1962, Derbyshire, Nottinghamshire and Northamptonshire joined Leicestershire in the Midlands Knock-out Cup, an event comprising two semi-finals and a final. Innings were limited to 65 overs, and there was no restriction on the number of overs allowed to each bowler.

Respectable crowds gathered for both semi-finals, but they watched in some bewilderment as all four teams persisted with their pace bowlers throughout each innings, effectively ruling spinners out of the game. Turner saw that this was wrong and quickly convened a committee meeting, where it was decided that a restriction of 15 overs per bowler would be introduced for the final. The standard rules of one-day cricket were evolving.

The Grace Road crowd enjoyed a balanced contest between bat and ball in the final, even though their Leicestershire side was emphatically defeated by Northamptonshire, and the trial was generally acknowledged a success.

Almost a year later, appropriately, Turner took his place among the crowd at Old Trafford on that chilly Sunday when the first official one-day match was played, and, even though his Leicestershire team lost again, the secretary remained positive that limited overs cricket would safeguard the future of the game.

As the inaugural Knock-out Cup ran its course, his optimism was increasingly shared around the country, and encouraging attendance figures at the various venues were noted with pleasure and some relief at Lord's.

A bandwagon was starting to roll, and an enterprising promoter named Harvey Bagenal was quick to meet the public's new-found appetite for one-day cricket. He began to arrange 40-over matches on Sunday afternoons, played between county sides and an International Cavaliers XI that variously featured such heroes as Denis Compton, Tom Graveney, Bobby Simpson, Graeme Pollock, Garfield Sobers, and even the Nawab of Pataudi.

The games started at two o'clock and, in a smart move that almost guaranteed public support, profits were paid to the various local county players celebrating their benefit year.

Bagenal also recognised the commercial opportunities. He guaranteed financial viability by signing Rothmans to sponsor his all-stars, and he goaded the BBC into broadcasting the matches live on BBC 2. Such efforts to promote a special atmosphere, even a bit of razzmatazz, hardly compare with the gimmicks that Kerry Packer's marketing men would introduce 15 years later, but they appeared revolutionary in their time.

And they worked. Cavaliers matches on Sunday afternoons spawned a new generation of armchair cricket fans.

Through the 1963 season the English cricketing public – and many others who had been oblivious to the sport – developed a taste for the one-day game, and few were surprised to see the 'Ground Full' signs hanging outside Lord's during the days before the first Knock-out Cup final on 7 September.

A crowd of 22 500 packed into 'headquarters', and watched Sussex struggle to score what most believed would be an inadequate total of 168 all out. However, Worcestershire collapsed in a stumbling pursuit and finished 14 runs short.

Norman Gifford of Worcestershire was named Man of the Match for his bowling figures of four for 33 in 15 overs, although the raw 21-year-old Sussex fast bowler, John Snow, had also played his part, ripping through the Worcestershire tail and finishing with three wickets for 13 runs in eight overs.

'Supporters wore favours and banners at Lord's,' Wisden reflected at the end of the year. 'The whole scene resembled an association football cup final more than the game of cricket, and many thousands of supporters invaded the pitch at the finish to cheer Ted Dexter, the Sussex captain, as he received the Gillette Trophy from the MCC President, Lord Nugent.'

The game's authoritative almanac continued: 'The Knock-out Cup has been a great success, but there are two valid criticisms of the new format: firstly, despite the restricted number of overs per bowler, the majority of counties seem loath to include even one slow bowler in their sides, and rely mainly on pace.

'Secondly, the placing of the entire field around the boundary to prevent rapid scoring – Dexter used this tactic in the final – became common, and should be discouraged. However, there is no doubt that, provided the Competition is conducted wisely, it will attract great support and benefit the game accordingly.'

Notwithstanding any aesthetic misgivings about it not being 'proper' cricket, the editor concluded by recognising that one-day matches brought spectators pouring through the gates in a way that the Championship could not.

People could debate and discuss the niceties as much as they liked – respected cricket writers such as E.W. Swanton expressed doubts about what he called 'the most fundamental change to the face and image of cricket since the legalisation of over-arm bowling the best part of a century and a half ago' – but the improvement in the various CCC balance sheets ended the argument.

It was the economics, stupid.

Gillette, the event sponsors, were pleased by the inaugural season. The American razor company had been motivated to invest in cricket by a desire to support something truly English to stimulate sales, and their prolonged exposure through the course of 1963 enabled them to sustain their strong position in the market at a time when their most serious rivals, Wilkinson Sword, introduced a brand-new stainless steel blade.

Henry Garnett, the managing director of Gillette, attended the final at Lord's, and it was during the Sussex innings that he casually remarked to Lord Nugent: 'I just wish people used our name more often when they referred to the competition.'

The MCC president did not respond.

'Maybe,' Garnett persevered, 'we should just call the thing the Gillette Cup next season.'

Nugent arched his eyebrows, smiled, and, without diverting his eyes from the cricket, declared: 'First-class idea, Garnett.'

Thus it was done, and the renamed Gillette Cup held its place on the English cricket calendar every season from 1964 until 1980, when the NatWest Bank took over as sponsors.

Innovations flowed thick and fast.

The winners of the 1963 competition, Sussex, were invited to host a special one-day match against the West Indies at the end of the touring team's long tour of England. So, Wes Hall, Lance Gibbs, Rohan Kanhai and Garfield Sobers starred in what was the first ever one-day match involving a full international side, but Dexter's team eked out a notable four-wicket victory.

Ahead of the Gillette Cup in 1964, the number of overs per innings was reduced to 60, and five Minor Counties were allowed to enter the preliminary stages of the competition, but nothing could prevent Sussex winning through to the final again, and emerging as Gillette Cup winners for the second season in a row.

Dexter, urbane and popular, was praised as the architect of this success, and it is hard to exaggerate the impact of successive triumphs on a county that, for all their long and colourful history, had never won the Championship. The impact of one-day cricket was reflected in the wild euphoria on the south coast.

So it continued through the decade until, in 1969, the MCC incurred the wrath of Harvey Bagenal and Rothmans by annexing Sunday afternoon cricket and introducing a new competition, the John Player League, to be played at that time of the week. Rothmans certainly did not deserve to have their pioneering efforts rewarded by the sudden emergence of their commercial rivals as title sponsors, and Bagenal was left powerless and frustrated when his Cavaliers were forced to disband because their county opposition was now committed to the Sunday league format.

MCC had flexed its muscles and resolutely regained control of an important part of the game, although the new competition was only launched once prolonged discussions with the still-influential Lord's Day Observance Society had led to an accord that Sunday matches would never start before 2 pm, thereby ensuring that cricket did not become an alternative attraction to church.

The John Player League proved an instant success, attracting 280 000 people to 120 days of play in its first season. In that same year, 330 000 spectators paid to watch almost three times as many days' play in the traditional Championship.

Despite such overwhelming statistical evidence of the public's preferences, traditionalists were still not content. 'The life of a county cricketer has changed forever,' wailed one, 'but it's hard to feel much pity. The fact they have agreed to play in these Sunday bashes on the middle day of a proper Championship match merely shows the players will do anything for money.'

Swanton developed a more cogent argument when he suggested that these encouraging attendances at one-day cricket did not tell the whole story because, far from benefiting all elements of the game, they seemed to have been achieved solely at the expense of the Championship, where crowds continued to decline.

One-day cricket may have solved a short-term financial problem, he argued, but the long-term consequences for the game would be serious because limited overs competitions undermined broad affection for the traditional form of the game.

His point was made, but it was hard to escape the fact that, week after week, the spectators were voting with their feet. The public was demanding one-day cricket, and the authorities were in no position to do anything but increase the supply.

Wisden again sought the middle ground. 'Limited overs cricket is a vital part of today's sport,' the editor wrote in the 1969 edition. 'The batsmen have to sharpen their strokes and the majority of these games produce wonderful fielding as well as superb catching. There is a feverish tempo and something no one could expect in three-day Championship matches.'

The leading article then concluded with a thunderous warning: 'None-theless, this instant cricket must never, ever be regarded as any kind of substitute for genuine first-class cricket.'

Perhaps it was this widely held conviction – that, despite its popularity, one-day cricket should never be 'elevated' – that meant eight long years elapsed between the first one-day match at county level, and the first one-day international … and when it did take place, on 5 January 1971, it happened by accident.

Raymond Illingworth's touring England team had drawn the opening two Tests in the Ashes series against Australia, and were in optimistic mood ahead of the third Test match to be played at the Melbourne Cricket Ground over the New Year holiday, on 31 December and 1, 2, 4 and 5 January.

However, the first and second days were washed out, and as the relentless rain continued on the third day, the umpires decided to abandon the match. A conference was called between members of the Australian Board of Control, led by Sir Donald Bradman and the MCC manager, D.G. Clark, and two visiting MCC officials, Sir Cyril Hawker and Gubby Allen. These men decided to rearrange the tour schedule to include an additional

Test in Melbourne during the fourth week of January; and that seemed to be that.

'But what are we going to do on Tuesday?' asked Bradman.

'What do you mean?' Hawker replied.

'Well, the weather forecast is pretty good, and I reckon we could sell a decent number of tickets.'

'All right, Don, but the Test has been abandoned.'

'I know, but what about having a one-day match?'

The MCC men asked for a few moments to discuss the issue among themselves. After some time, they said they had found no reason to object. So, following the impulsive and unexpected suggestion of probably the greatest batsman of all time, Australia and England emerged on a warm Tuesday morning in Melbourne to contest the first-ever one-day international.

By coincidence, the match was played on the very ground where Test cricket had started 94 years earlier. Some officials had feared an underwhelming public reaction, particularly since Melbourne was recognised as one of the most conservative cities in Australia, but the ACB was staggered when an enthusiastic crowd of more than forty-six thousand spectators arrived at the MCG, paying receipts of $33 894 to watch this historic limited overs game.

Bill Lawry was an experienced cricketer playing in only the second one-day match of his career, but the Australian captain soon set the tone of a thrilling day. After sending England in to bat, he dived sharply to catch a full-blooded hook from Geoffrey Boycott, dismissing the opener for eight. John Edrich studiously compiled a substantial score, but his 82 stood alone in a paltry England total of 190 all out. Of the rest, only D'Oliveira, Hampshire, Fletcher, Knott and Extras managed to reach double figures.

The Australians launched their pursuit with gusto, and when Doug Walters had cracked 41 from 51 balls, and Ian Chappell had scored a careful 60 from 103 balls, the home team cantered to an emphatic victory, overhauling their target in the 35th of their 40 eight-ball overs, with five wickets still standing.

'England's know-how had been tipped to get them home against opponents less wise in the tricks of the one-day trade,' reflected Brian Chapman in *The Guardian*, 'but the tremendous firepower of these uninhibited Australian batsmen carried them to a comfortable and surprising victory.'

It should perhaps be noted that Illingworth and his team bounced back from the disappointment of defeat in grand style. A week later they won the fourth Test at the Sydney Cricket Ground by an innings; then victory in the seventh Test, also played at the SCG, secured their place in history as one of the few England teams to have won the Ashes on Australian soil. In the light of such glory, the side's participation in the first one-day international match ever played was reduced to an incidental footnote.

Bearing in mind the insatiable enthusiasm with which various national bodies would schedule endless one-day internationals in seasons to come, it is worth noting that, through these early years, it was only the supposedly staid English administrators who seemed remotely interested in promoting limited overs cricket.

Elsewhere, caution reigned.

Asian officials appeared utterly indifferent to the advent of limited overs cricket. Oblivious to the potential of the new format, neither the Indian nor the Pakistani Board of Control hosted any one-day international matches on their own grounds until after the first World Cup had been completed in England.

The Australian Cricket Board did launch the domestic V&G Australasian Knock-out Competition in 1969, when they invited New Zealand to compete alongside the various State teams – and the Kiwis responded by winning the event in its inaugural season. And yet, despite obvious signs of public interest, the ACB felt no need to include any one-day internationals in the itineraries of incoming international tours for the next four years.

The Australian team, in fact, did not play another one-day international at home until January 1975 when, in a strange twist of fate, England successfully chased a target of 191, both reversing the result and duplicating the exact score of the first game.

Across the Tasman Sea, the cricket authorities in New Zealand proved quicker off the mark than the ACB, hosting their first-ever one-day international on Sunday 11 February 1973, when an evidently exhilarated crowd saw New Zealand defeat the touring Pakistan team by 22 runs in Christchurch.

Eighteen months later the West Indians recognised the appeal of one-day cricket, and Clive Lloyd's team won the first-ever limited overs international played in the Caribbean when they defeated Pakistan by four wickets at the Albion Sports Complex in Berbice, Guyana, on 4 November 1974.

Beyond England, the South African Cricket Union seemed most eager to seize the opportunity. They moved to establish their own Gillette Cup as an important domestic event for the provincial teams, but by now the country's apartheid policies had provoked complete international isolation and the Springboks had to wait until 1991 to play their first one-day international.

While others dithered, the MCC and the Test and County Cricket Board (TCCB) moved forward. One-day cricket was conceived in England and developed in England; now, through the early 1970s, it was being matured in England.

Prudential, an insurance company, were secured as long-term sponsors of international limited overs cricket in England; and, year on year, compact series of two or three one-day matches were played between England and a touring side.

In 1972 the Prudential paid £30 000 to sponsor three games between England and the Australian tourists, to be played over the August bank holiday weekend. The series of matches replaced a sixth Test on a schedule that had previously been agreed between TCCB and the ACB. England won the first game, Australia won the second at Lord's, and Tony Greig steered the home side to a narrow victory at Edgbaston to win the third and the series.

The following year England beat New Zealand in Swansea, and when a second match was interrupted by rain at Old Trafford, they duly retained the Prudential Trophy. Six weeks later they played two further one-day internationals against the West Indies, winning by one wicket at Headingley, but then losing at the Oval when Roy Fredericks smashed a memorable 105.

India and Pakistan were scheduled to tour England in 1974, and after some persuasion both agreed to play two one-day internationals against the home side. As novices, India subsided to an emphatic 2-0 series defeat, but the Pakistanis seemed to relish the limited overs format. Majid Khan scored 109 at Trent Bridge as the tourists overhauled a decent England total, and the touring bowlers reduced the home side to 28 for seven on a damp pitch at Edgbaston before tying up a surprise 2-0 win.

Runs, wickets, action . . . the Gillette Cup and the John Player League were, in 1973, joined on the domestic calendar by a third limited overs competition, the Benson and Hedges Cup. Together with the annual Prudential Trophy matches, this represented a full package of one-day cricket to meet public demand.

Peter Ecker, of Derby, wrote a letter to *The Guardian* newspaper that seemed to reflect the general mood.

> Sir, – Your report begins 'It was just short of nine o'clock and the street lights were going on all round Old Trafford . . .' This before a crowd of 23 520 and with 459 runs scored in a single day.
>
> I understand that there is a similar game played at other times where only 100 runs may be scored in a day before a mere sprinkling of onlookers, and the players insist on coming off the field when a cloud passes over the sun in broad daylight.
>
> Is there any known connection between the two?
> Yours sincerely,
> Peter Ecker

One-day cricket was thriving in England, and it seemed only a natural progression that TCCB representatives should sit down with their commercial partners, Prudential, and mention the idea of inviting all the world's established international cricket teams to England to compete in one integrated event.

'But what would we call it?' asked the man from the Pru.

The TCCB official thought for a moment.

At length he said: 'The World Cup.'

'How about the Prudential World Cup?'

Both men smiled.

It was a deal.

Chapter Two

The First World Cup

One-day cricket came of age during two weeks of brilliant sunshine and magnificent action in June 1975. Any misgivings about the limited overs format, any remaining doubts about whether it would catch on around the world, quickly evaporated in the excitement and drama of the first World Cup.

The draw may have been flawed and some tactics may have been amazingly naïve, but the spectacle of the world's finest players assembled together in one event, thrilling capacity crowds in the grounds and millions of television viewers around the globe, exposed the game to something new.

Almost a century of traditional Test cricket had produced many unforgettable heroes and moments, and enshrined the game in many hearts, but this blissful fortnight offered a first glimpse of the potential popularity and prosperity to be generated by one-day cricket and its showcase, the World Cup.

A gastronomic analogy might be instructive: five generations of cricketers had grown up to love the taste of roast beef with all the trimmings, but now the same meat was being refined into a product that would appeal to an ever-wider audience, and the sport began to gorge itself on hamburgers.

Many people continued to argue, with good reason, that three-day cricket – the roast beef – still offered a much more satisfying and wholesome experience, but few denied the easy access, the pleasing taste and the simple fun that made one-day cricket – the hamburgers – so popular so quickly.

The discovery of this new-found pleasure, in England in 1975, left officials and players alike asking one another: 'Why on earth didn't anyone think of staging a cricket World Cup before?'

In fact, they had.

The two mighty oaks of international sport had been planted earlier in the 20th century, with the modern Olympics being inaugurated in 1896 and football launching its own World Cup in 1930. The evolving success of these events, each contested to global acclaim every four years, prompted ambitious cricket officials to wonder whether their own sport could support the same kind of quadrennial jamboree.

They wondered a lot, but did little . . . until 1966, when England won the football World Cup. Encouraged by the flag-waving euphoria sweeping the land, the MCC agreed to host three teams – England, West Indies and a Rest of the World XI – at Lord's to compete in an event billed as 'The World Cup'.

Rothmans were secured as sponsors and the sun shone for three days in September, but the event failed to capture the public's imagination. Even though Colin Cowdrey's England won the Cup, the total attendance of 13 000 spectators at three matches left the famous ground less than a quarter full.

The organisers persisted and held the event again in 1967, but another poor public response appeared to confirm the cricket World Cup as an idea ahead of its time. Some observers suggested that a World Cup of five-day Test matches would prove a more authentic and appealing contest, but the logistics of such an unavoidably long and drawn-out competition condemned the idea as plainly impractical.

It became clear that, if such a tournament was ever going to succeed, all the established cricket nations needed to take part; and, for this to happen, two obstacles needed to be cleared.

First, each of these countries had to accept the legitimacy of one-day cricket as an appropriate format for what would be marketed as the 'world championship' of the game. Second, an appropriate timeslot would have to be found on an international calendar already packed with traditional Test match tours.

The first hurdle was gradually overcome in the early 1970s, as national team after team experienced the atmosphere of Prudential Cup matches during tours to England. Once the Australians, West Indians, Pakistanis, New Zealanders and Indians had been exposed to one-day international cricket, they began to feel more at ease with the prospect of contesting a World Cup under similar conditions.

And the second issue was resolved when a proposed South African tour to England in 1975 was cancelled for political reasons, leaving the first part of that summer free for a World Cup.

Representatives of the Test and County Cricket Board held discreet discussions with Prudential, hit upon the idea of the Prudential World Cup to be played in June 1975, and tabled a full proposal for the consideration of the International Cricket Council – a compact, 60-overs-per-side event involving six Test-playing countries and two ICC Associate Members, divided into two round-robin groups of four with the first and second sides in each group advancing to contest the semi-finals, followed by a final at Lord's.

On 26 June 1973, meeting at Lord's, the ICC gave its formal approval to these plans. Donald Carr, the TCCB secretary, overflowed with enthusiasm. 'The Prudential World Cup will be a great success,' he declared. 'Sponsorship and television rights will cover all expenses. Gate receipts should be satisfactory, and we believe a substantial profit will be available for distribution to member countries of the ICC.'

Early estimates set the likely revenue from television broadcast rights and other promotional activity at £750 000 with a further £100 000 to be paid by Prudential, as the event sponsors. These amounts might seem minuscule by modern standards, being scarcely enough to pay a top Premiership footballer for two months, but in the early 1970s they were sufficient to fund the first Cricket World Cup.

An organising committee was established, and it was quickly agreed that associate members Sri Lanka and a composite side known as East Africa, largely drawn from Asian expatriates, would be invited to join the six major cricket nations. The official draw ceremony was held at Lord's in June 1974, and moments after the names had emerged one by one, the World Cup's first controversy erupted.

'It's a fix,' declared several outraged journalists.

MCC officials affably shrugged off the suggestion, and offered the reporters a sandwich.

The cause of complaint was that Group B looked extremely strong – Australia, West Indies, Pakistan and Sri Lanka – while England appeared every inch the home nation in the pound seats, well placed in Group A alongside the ostensibly weaker opposition of New Zealand, India and East Africa.

All allegations of bias were strongly denied at the time, although it did subsequently emerge that England and Australia had been discreetly seeded to keep them apart at the group stage.

The TCCB worked hard to bedeck the stage for the inaugural tournament, but they had no control of the English summer weather and their worst fears seemed to be realised when, five days before the World Cup was due to start, the second day of the county championship match between Derbyshire and Lancashire was abandoned after a sudden snow storm had swept across the ground at Buxton.

As it turned out, the first World Cup was blessed with unremitting warm sunshine from the opening day when four matches were played simultaneously on Saturday 7 June, through to the final at Lord's on 21 June. Through a schedule of 15 games, not one minute of play was lost to rain.

The tournament was launched by an elegant reception at Lord's where each of the 112 competing players was personally welcomed to the inaugural World Cup. Such a gathering of the world's greatest cricketers in one place was unique in the history of the game, and left a deep impression on those present. 'It started as just an idea,' reflected Jim Laker, the former England spin bowler, 'but it was wonderful to peer around a room and see Lloyd, Lillee, Gavaskar and the rest. The vision had become a reality.'

In line with most predictions, and to the relief of the organisers, England eased through Group A, winning their three round-robin matches and qualifying for the semi-finals as group winners.

The host nation's opening match, against India at Lord's, featured some powerful batting as England put together a score of 334 for four wickets in 60 overs (at the time the highest ever in one-day cricket), but then exposed a straightforward lack of understanding of the game in the Indian team.

Sunil Gavaskar, one of the world's leading batsmen, apparently concluded that his team would not be able to reach the England total and therefore decided not to try. The opener resolved to focus his sights on ensuring his side were not dismissed and batted through their full 60 overs.

More than 20 000 spectators watched in bemused confusion as the Indian batsmen blocked and blocked, eventually finishing their innings at 132 for three. Gavaskar had batted through all 60 overs and ended on 36 not out from 174 balls. 'Maybe Sunny thought he could play for a draw,' suggested an MCC member sitting in the pavilion. He was only half joking. England strolled to victory by 202 runs.

New Zealand crushed East Africa on the same day, winning by 181 runs at Edgbaston. The East Africans seemed to have used selection for their World Cup squad as a way of thanking veteran players for long service to the game in that part of the world. Ten of their 14 players were older than 30, and these geriatric underdogs managed totals of only 95, 120 and 128 in their three round-robin defeats.

England maintained their encouraging form, defeating New Zealand by 80 runs in Nottingham. Yet the Kiwis soon recovered composure and, in what had become their decisive last group match, against India, Glenn Turner's second century in three innings enabled them to overhaul the target of 231 with seven balls to spare, and thus secure second place in Group A and a place in the semi-finals.

Group B produced cricket that was more competitive, more exciting and more controversial, as three fine teams – Australia, Pakistan and the West Indies – scrambled for two semi-final places.

Australia approached the tournament with a confidence founded on the threat of their celebrated pair of intimidating fast bowlers, Dennis Lillee and Jeff Thomson. Even if this form of cricket restricted them to bowling 24 six-ball overs between them, they were regarded as potential match-winners.

Ashes to ashes,
Dust to dust,
If Lillee doesn't get ya
Thomson must.

The popular refrain proved more than an empty boast in Australia's opening match, against Pakistan in Leeds. Once his batsmen had compiled a respectable score of 278 for seven from their 60 overs, Lillee hurled himself into action and clean-bowled Sadiq Mohammad in his second over. Headingley thrilled to the spectacle of a great fast bowler in full cry, an exhilarating blur of fine technique and raw guts.

Clear blue sky, balmy sunshine, a fast outfield, the Headingley gates closed on a capacity 22 000 crowd for the first time since 1966, world-class bowlers and world-class batsmen: this was the essence of the 1975 World Cup, and the cricketing world soaked it all up and purred with pleasure.

Lillee finished with an analysis of five for 34 runs in his 12 overs, and helped to ensure Pakistan finished 73 runs short of their target. The robust

Australian challenge was up and running.

The West Indians also hit the ground running in Manchester, rattling through the Sri Lankan batting order and reaching their target of 87 in 20.4 overs. Fearing the Old Trafford crowd would feel short-changed by such a one-sided match, the players agreed to play a further 20-over match just for fun.

These opening results piled the pressure on Pakistan, who now needed to defeat the West Indies in their second match to retain any hope of progressing in the tournament. Enjoying the bulk of the crowd's support at Edgbaston in Birmingham, the Pakistanis posted a score of 266 for seven and appeared poised for victory when Sarfraz Nawaz took his fourth wicket, reducing the West Indians to 203 for nine.

Andy Roberts joined wicketkeeper Deryck Murray at the wicket in what seemed a hopeless position: 63 runs were still required with 14 overs remaining and one wicket standing. Sporadic boundaries and scrambled singles reduced the target until, amid amazing tension, five were required from the last over.

Roberts scuttled two off a leg bye; then Wasim Raja produced a dot ball; then an overthrow enabled the batsmen to run another two; and finally, with two balls remaining, Roberts dabbed the winning single into the off side and the West Indian spectators were celebrating a remarkable recovery.

'In all my days of playing cricket,' Clive Lloyd, the West Indian captain, would later reflect, 'I have never known such elation in a dressing room as there was that day at Edgbaston. Men with years of experience were jumping up and down and hugging each other. Several were sobbing uncontrollably.'

Murray finished unbeaten on 61 from 76 balls, and Roberts unbeaten on 24. For all their fine cricket, the Pakistanis found no consolation in such an exciting match, only a flight home.

Meanwhile, the Australians had been expected to confirm their semi-final place by overcoming Sri Lanka at the Oval, but their victory was not secured without controversy.

Sent in to bat, the Australians seemed in control as they amassed an imposing score of 328 for five in 60 overs. Some feared for the amateur Sri Lankan batsmen as they prepared to face Lillee and Thomson, but the underdogs stuck to their task and seemed in contention at 150 for two in the 32nd over. The Australian captain, Ian Chappell, was growing concerned, and he summoned Thomson for a second spell.

'OK, Thommo mate,' Chappell muttered. 'Do something.'

'What?'

'Anything!'

The paceman sloped back to his mark, slicking hair back from his forehead, long arms swinging, and he moved in with a purpose. The inevitable bouncer rose and struck the batsman on the forehead. Duleep Mendis had thrived in reaching 32 in 45 balls, but now he was dazed, and being taken to hospital.

Four overs passed, the score moved on to 164 for two, and Thomson was moving in again. This time, his sizzling yorker struck Sunil Wettimuny on the foot. As the crowd roared its fury, the Sri Lankan captain hopped around the crease in agony, but he was getting no sympathy from the fast bowler.

'Look, you weak bastard,' Thomson snarled. 'It's not broken.'

Wettimuny summoned a runner from the pavilion but remained at the crease. In his next over Thomson produced another fast yorker, striking Wettimuny on the instep of the same foot. The batsman stumbled two steps forward and fell to the ground. Thomson picked up the ball, threw down the stumps at the receiver's end, and unashamedly claimed the run-out. Sections of the Oval crowd started to jeer.

Thomson later recalled: 'The ball came straight back to me, and the boys were yelling at me to run him out. My first reaction was 'no', but then I thought 'bugger it'. Anyway, I hit the stumps and shouted an appeal but no other bastard moved. My team-mates had done me stone cold, on purpose!'

The Sri Lankan was given not out because his runner had not moved, but Wettimuny was clearly unable to continue his innings and, like Mendis, he was forced to retire hurt. Tissera and Tennekoon kept up a gallant chase, but Sri Lanka eventually finished 52 runs short, with their pride intact.

Both teams happened to be staying at the same Kensington hotel, and when Thomson joined the queue for breakfast the following morning, he found himself surrounded by Sri Lankans, most of whom were wearing some kind of bandage. Suddenly, the story goes, the fast bowler lost his appetite.

With both teams already qualified for the semi-finals, the final match in Group B, between Australia and the West Indies, was only relevant because the winner would advance to play New Zealand while the loser was going to face England, and the Oval crowd witnessed a curious kind of sparring.

Sent in to bat, Australia lost Rick McCosker before a run had been scored, and only a fighting sixth-wicket stand between Ross Edwards and Rod Marsh enabled them to reach 192.

Now the cricketing world held its breath, waiting to see how the talented Caribbean batsmen would fare against Lillee and Thomson. The answer could not have been more emphatic. First Roy Fredericks hooked and cut his way to 58; then Alvin Kallicharran launched an amazing assault on Lillee. In the space of ten balls from the fast bowler, the rampant West Indian crashed 4, 4, 4, 4, 4, 1, 4, 6, 0 and 4.

The Australian icon finished with a bruised ego and an analysis of one wicket for 66 from ten overs, and the West Indians cruised to victory by seven wickets with 14 overs to spare.

Briefly humbled by this reverse, Chappell took his team to face England in the semi-final. Having taken one look at the green pitch, the Australians dropped the spinner, Ashley Mallett, and called up a stocky, almost unknown all-rounder named Gary Gilmour to play his first match of the tournament.

Chappell won the toss, asked England to bat first, gave the new ball to Lillee, and declared Gilmour would open the bowling from the other end. Thomson was relegated to second change. The decision took everyone by surprise and yet, within an hour or so, it was being hailed as a stroke of genius.

Bowling left-arm over the wicket, Gilmour settled on a steady length, moving the ball in to and away from the batsmen, off the pitch and through the air, and suddenly looked unplayable.

He lumbered in, trapped Dennis Amiss LBW with the opening ball of his second over, and proceeded to annihilate England's World Cup ambitions. Barry Wood gone for six, then Keith Fletcher for eight, Tony Greig for seven, Frank Hayes for four and Alan Knott for a duck: all dismissed by the no-name brand.

The capacity crowd of 22 000 that had squeezed into Headingley were now staring at the scoreboard in silent disbelief. But there it was in black and white. England was reduced to 36 for six wickets. Gilmour eventually completed his 12 overs, delivered in one spell, with an analysis of six for 14.

The home team looked unlikely to reach 50 but Mike Denness, the only recognised batsman left, held his ground and somehow managed to rally the innings, wrenching the total to 93 all out in 36.2 overs. It seemed wholly inadequate, but the captain had fought hard and it could have been worse.

It was supposed to be a great day . . . 93 all out? People shook their heads.

After this drama, the nature of the game seemed to return to normal as Alan Turner and Rick McCosker cantered to 17 without loss. Then, to everybody's surprise, Australia collapsed.

Once Turner had fallen LBW to Arnold, John Snow ran in and sensationally removed both Ian Chappell and Greg Chappell. With his opponents struggling at 32 for three, Denness sensed a chance. Chris Old took the ball and, amid uproar, clean-bowled McCosker, Edwards and Marsh in quick succession.

Australia was staggering at 39 for six, still 55 runs short of the target. The famous Western Terrace was bellowing its approval of the England fight-back when Gilmour emerged from the pavilion and made his way to join Doug Walters at the crease. To paraphrase the words of Sir Alf Ramsey, the all-rounder had won the match once for his team; now he had to go out there and win it all over again.

That's exactly what he did. In a situation when many would have panicked, Gilmour attacked. He bashed five boundaries in a brisk innings of 28 runs from 28 balls, and won the game without further alarm. Named as the Man of the Match, he left to celebrate the greatest day of his career . . . by far.

Chappell was ecstatic. 'We take huge satisfaction from this win,' the Australian captain said afterwards. 'Everyone here seemed to think England were the one-day kings and we were not able to adapt properly to the demands of one-day cricket. Well, it doesn't look that way on the scoreboard.'

In a bleak home dressing room, Denness said the pitch had been inadequate. Considering 16 wickets had fallen for 187 runs, and the match had lasted only 67 overs, he seemed to have a point, although groundsman George Cawthray argued it was the atmosphere that had made batting difficult.

For the England captain, at least, the day ended with a smile. Eager to get home, he left Leeds straight after the match, driving south with Alan Knott. Denness eased his foot down, accelerated into the fast lane and inadvertently passed a police patrol car, travelling at exactly 70 mph.

'Just my luck,' he sighed as flashing blue lights appeared in his rear-view mirror. The captain pulled over to the kerb, resigned to accepting the consequences of speeding.

The police officer arrived at the driver's window.

'I thought it was you two!' he declared, grinning.

'Yes,' Denness replied.

'Well, what on earth went wrong at Headingley today?'

'Surely you didn't stop us for an inquest on the cricket.'

'No,' said the policeman. 'We do get a little upset when we're doing 70 and someone overtakes us, but let's not worry about that now. What do you think of Gilmour?'

Denness smiled, shrugged and said something about people having their day. He was eventually allowed to make his way home, left to contemplate that even on such a desperately disappointing evening, the position of being the England cricket captain still carried a few welcome privileges.

That same day, in the other World Cup semi-final at the Oval, New Zealand had seemed to be mounting a reasonable challenge to the West Indies. Batting first, they reached 98 for two in 22 overs, but then lost the key wicket of Glenn Turner, their icon, for 36, and subsided to 158 all out.

Gordon Greenidge and Kallicharran led the swift pursuit of this modest target, and by tea the apparently carefree West Indians had cruised through to the final with 20 overs to spare.

In advance of the tournament, organisers had hoped for a 'dream final' between England and the West Indies, the home side against the favourites. But now that this largely experimental event had unfolded as such a success, nobody was complaining about the prospect of a contest between Clive Lloyd's richly gifted, apparently unbeatable team and the courageous never-say-die Australians.

And nobody was disappointed.

The game of cricket has relished many memorable occasions, but in terms of setting and quality of play, sustained excitement and dramatic conclusion, few compare with the inaugural World Cup final. Saturday 21 June 1975 is enshrined as a great day in the history of cricket . . . indeed, of any sport.

Soon after six o'clock in the morning, brilliant blue skies and bright sunshine welcomed MCC members arriving early to queue outside the Grace Gates. Amid the quietly excited line of blazers and egg-and-bacon ties, newspapers were avidly read and the day's prospects discussed. All seemed well.

'Can anyone contain the West Indians?' asked one.

'Well, if anyone can, it must be Lillee and Thomson,' replied his son.

'Or even Gilmour,' said another.

'Exactly!'

The two teams arrived at Lord's soon after nine, with each captain hoping more keenly than usual to win the toss. It had become evident during the course of the tournament that both the West Indians and Australia preferred to bat second and chase targets, rather than bat first and set them.

So, when it was announced over the public address system that Chappell had won the toss and asked the West Indies to bat first, the excited murmur that spread around the grandstands reflected a general conviction that Australia, the underdogs, had quickly redressed the balance of expectation.

Dennis Lillee led the Australian attack with raw speed and rare skill, but even he could only stand back in admiration when Roy Fredericks, the West Indian opening batsman, effortlessly rocked on his heels and hooked the last ball of the third over into the main grandstand for a wonderful, soaring six.

'What a magnificent shot,' murmured Lillee, as his eyes followed the ball.

'He's out!'

Lillee turned to face umpire Dickie Bird.

'What?'

'He's out,' Bird repeated in his broad Yorkshire accent.

Fredericks had opted to wear rubber soles rather than spikes, slipped in the morning dew, and trod on his own wicket. Blissfully unaware West Indian supporters were still cheering the 'six' when the unfortunate opener tucked his bat under his arm and started making his way back to the pavilion.

Kallicharran and Greenidge both gave catches to Marsh behind the wicket soon afterwards, and the West Indians suddenly looked vulnerable at 50 for three in the 18th over. As Clive Lloyd purposefully loped out to join Kanhai, excited Australian fielders were buzzing with enthusiasm. Chappell immediately called up Lillee to bowl his second spell and examine the opposing captain before he settled.

Lillee pounded in. Lloyd let the ball go by. Lillee pounded in again. Lloyd leaned forward, and powerfully guided the ball to the boundary in front of square leg. Lillee was muttering as he returned to his mark, but he turned and ran in again, perfectly side-on, high elbow, and bowled . . . and Lloyd imperiously hooked the ball into the tavern for six. A single off the last ball took the total to 11 off the over.

Lloyd moved into his stride, and ruthlessly savaged the Australian bowling with a barrage of sweet hooks and powerful off-drives. As the runs started to flow, John Arlott told his radio listeners: 'Forget about bowling a maiden over, it now appears almost impossible to bowl a maiden ball.'

The irrepressible West Indian did offer two chances, hard and low to Edwards at square leg when he had only 26, and spiralling beyond Lillee's reach at long leg on 62, but these were minor blemishes on a magnificent innings that Bird later described as 'the greatest I have seen in 30 years'.

Lloyd cantered to 50, then galloped into three figures. He reached his century in only 82 balls, and soon afterwards, with his score on 102, was unfortunate to edge a leg-side catch to Marsh. At one stage, batting to the relentless 'long-short-short' calypso rhythm of Caribbean supporters clanking empty cans, Lloyd and Kanhai plundered 73 runs from eight overs; in total, they added 149 for the fourth wicket.

Kanhai's crucial contribution of 55 runs proved to be his last innings for the West Indies. The grey-haired master had wisely dropped anchor, content not to score a single run in 12 overs while his captain ran riot, but Keith Boyce, Bernard Julien, Deryck Murray and Vanburn Holder hit out in the closing overs and took the West Indian innings to an imposing total of 291 for eight from their allotted 60 overs.

'Come on, guys, we can get these runs!' Chappell was not giving up. 'If we can score at around four an over for, say, the first 40 overs of the innings,' he told his players, 'and not lose many wickets, I reckon we'll then be in pretty good shape to accelerate and get past 291 towards the end.'

Few in the capacity crowd gave the Australians much chance, but once McCosker had gone cheaply, Ian Chappell and Alan Turner started to thrive, guiding the fast bowlers through the gaps, almost keeping up with the required run rate, and taking the score to 81 for one in the 16th over.

Australians in the crowd needed little encouragement to become more vociferous, but their heroes were batting under the constant pressure of a demanding run rate, and through the hottest part of the day. This may explain why, in three decisive moments, three errors of judgement were exploited by three pieces of brilliant fielding. Cricket of the highest standard, on the finest stage, presented an exhilarating spectacle.

Turner was called for a quick single but hesitated. Viv Richards pounced at mid-wicket and, in a blur of athleticism, threw down the stumps. The opener was run out.

Greg Chappell joined his brother at the crease and, as they added 26 in four overs, the innings appeared to have recovered. Then, as Richards and Greenidge appeared to hesitate on the leg side, the batsmen tried to run a misfield. Richards hit the stumps again, and Greg Chappell was run out.

Ian Chappell remained, and in tandem with Walters took the score to 162 for three, ready to launch the final assault in the last 20 overs. The captain prodded a stolen single into the leg side, but Richards burst into life once again, whipped the ball to Murray, and Chappell was run out for 62.

Richards had only scored five runs earlier in the day, but his devastating fielding had ripped the heart out of the Australian innings. The West Indians tightened the noose, claiming wickets at regular intervals, and it all seemed over when Australia limped to 233 for nine with only six overs remaining. Thomson strolled out to join Lillee in the middle, with their team still 59 runs short of their target.

Many spectators were by now assembled around the boundary, poised to dash onto the field and hail the West Indians as cricket's first world champions. But Lillee and Thomson were not done yet.

Edging singles and scampering twos, they began to chip away at the target. Eating an elephant can seem an impossible task, until you start chewing chunk by chunk, and even if their running between the wickets was far from exemplary, the two Australians were making steady progress.

'They can never make it.'

'No.'

With four overs remaining, the last-wicket pair needed another 35 runs.

'Surely, they can never make it.'

'Well, you never quite know.'

Holder moved in to bowl. Thomson drove uppishly into the off side where Fredericks held the catch, finally triggering the long-awaited invasion of Lord's by jubilant West Indian supporters.

'No ball!'

Umpire Tom Spencer stood unmoved at the bowler's end, his right arm outstretched. Thomson was therefore not out, and the match was not over. Fredericks shied at the stumps, missed, and the ball sped past mid-wicket, disappearing in the flood of stampeding spectators.

With hundreds of people now milling around the square, generally unaware of what had happened, Lillee quickly assessed the situation, burst out laughing, and started running. 'Come on, Thommo,' he shouted at the top of his voice. 'They've lost the bloody ball. Come on! We can run 17 here.'

'Don't be stupid,' Thomson yelled back. 'One of them could have the ball in his pocket.'

'Run,' Lillee bawled.

Police and stewards began to restore order, ushering people back behind the boundary rope, and leaving the umpires to decide how the game would continue. Umpire Dickie Bird had been struck on the head during the commotion, and had been ransacked by the mob, being relieved of a spare cricket ball, spare bails, Thomson's jersey that had been tied around his waist, and his trademark white cap. While Bird readjusted his clothing and tried to compose himself, umpire Tom Spencer was approached by Thomson.

'Hey, how many runs are you going to give us for that?' the batsman asked.

'Two,' Spencer replied abruptly.

'Pig's arse!' Thomson declared.

'What?'

'You're kidding! We've been running up and down here for the last five minutes!'

'So what?'

'So you've got to give us more runs than that.'

Spencer withdrew to consult with Bird, and eventually emerged to declare that three runs had been scored. At last, the match was ready to continue. Now, 24 runs were required from three overs.

Andy Roberts took the ball and produced perfect discipline, line and length amid the pandemonium. Only three runs conceded left Lillee and Thomson requiring 21 runs from 12 balls. Holder was called to bowl the 59th over of the innings: single off the first ball, leg bye off the second, single off the third.

It was not enough. The Australians needed boundaries. Holder bowled; Thomson swung and missed, but seemed to be carried forward by momentum. Wicketkeeper Murray rolled the ball towards the wicket and, with the batsman stranded out of his crease, umpire Bird slowly raised his finger. The fifth run-out of the Australian innings had finally concluded the match; the West Indies had won by 17 runs.

Thousands of spectators swarmed onto the field all over again, and the players dashed for the sanctuary of the pavilion. Most arrived safely; others were not so lucky: when Boyce was tackled to the ground, his boots became someone's prized souvenir; Lillee was stripped of his pads, gloves and bat.

Even if the situation occasionally verged on chaos, it seemed happy chaos. It had been one of those days when most people in the ground sit back for a moment and congratulate themselves on having been present at an unforgettable occasion. The World Cup final had started at 11 am, produced sensational batting, fine bowling and breathtaking fielding, and ended at 8.42 pm: in every respect, a full day.

In fading light the players from both sides gathered on the middle balcony of the pavilion, and the Duke of Edinburgh, that season's President of the MCC, presented the Prudential Cup to Clive Lloyd. The captain took the trophy in both hands and, as the world's cameras flashed, raised it aloft.

Lloyd sensed the emotion of the moment. As he glanced at the hundreds of West Indians celebrating on the field under the balcony at Lord's, his mind wandered to the hundreds of thousands partying at home in the Caribbean, and to what the title 'world champions' would represent in the islands.

'I will never forget that experience,' the captain reflects, 'but I was very disappointed by the West Indies Cricket Board's response, or its lack of response, to our success. It was unfortunate that the squad received no recognition at all from the Board, apart from the agreed fee of £350 per man. I can imagine how the players of India, Pakistan or Australia would have been fêted at home had they won the World Cup.'

It was left to the government of Guyana to get all the players to Georgetown and organise a triumphant motorcade through the streets. A series of stamps was later issued to mark the World Cup win, but Lloyd's side was neither the first nor the last West Indian team to feel unappreciated.

Notwithstanding a small group who still denigrated the one-day game, the first World Cup was generally regarded as a success, above all because it had unfolded as 15 days of tremendously entertaining cricket. Huge crowds had flocked to the grounds and, almost without exception, had gone home happy; and at the end of it all, the West Indians were universally admired as worthy 'world champions'.

The event was also proclaimed as financially viable. A total of 158 000 people paid to watch 15 games in the tournament, raising total gate receipts in excess of £200 000. This sum equated to the net profit, of which £4 000 was paid to the winners, £20 000 to the TCCB as hosts, and £15 000 to the other competing nations, the remainder being held in reserve for the following World Cup in 1979.

The World Cup had arrived, and it would remain on the cricketing calendar. A tournament conceived as an experiment almost immediately became treated as a quadrennial part of the game.

With hindsight, the weakness of the 1975 tournament – and it was not really apparent at the time – was that it could scarcely claim to be an authentic World Cup when the reality was that only seven countries and, in East Africa, an artificially created region, had been invited to take part.

As an international cricket community evolved, the ICC qualifying tournament was created to ensure that future World Cups would be contested by more teams and from a broader base.

Nonetheless the memories of the 1975 World Cup have gradually been gilded into the game's history, and the small scale of the event does not in any way diminish the achievement of Lloyd's team.

Fredericks, Greenidge, Kallicharran, Kanhai, Lloyd, Richards, Boyce, Julien, Murray, Holder, Roberts . . . in the eyes of many who saw them, they remain the greatest of all cricket's world champion teams.

Clive Lloyd

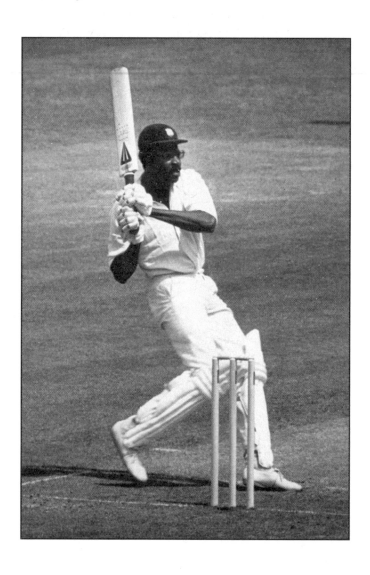

The school playground had once again been transformed into a seething, angry arena; and as their chanting classmates gathered in a tight circle, the pair of ten-year-olds launched into each other.

Nobody believed this was a violent school, established on the outskirts of Georgetown, British Guiana, but nobody minded a scrap now and then. It was viewed as relatively harmless and, within reasonable limits, the teachers were content to keep their distance and let the boys be boys.

'Stop this! Please stop it!'

Heads turned. A tall, 12-year-old boy, quickly recognised as the school's outstanding athlete, had worked his way into the middle of the circle and was trying to hold the fighters apart.

'What's the point in fighting? Break it up,' he said.

Just as calm appeared to settle over the mob, somebody lashed out, someone else reacted, and a brawl erupted. The athlete was hit in the face. He left clutching his right eye, and was then sent on his way to hospital. The doctor's verdict was simple: Clive Lloyd would wear glasses for the rest of his life.

As the years passed, he channelled his athletic ability into cricket, maturing into a wonderfully powerful batsman, one of the finest cover fielders ever seen, and a useful medium-paced bowler.

And the leadership qualities that prompted him to interrupt that playground fight in 1956 equipped him to become the most successful, most respected West Indies captain of all time, a towering figure who welded disparate talents from around the Caribbean into one genuinely great team.

Aged 17, he made his debut for British Guiana. Aged 22, he scored 82 and 78 not out in his Test debut against India in Bombay. Aged 23, he travelled to play for a club in Manchester, and the next year launched his long, profound association with Lancashire. Aged 27 he was named Cricketer of the Year. Aged 30 he was appointed West Indies captain, and led his new team to a series victory in India. Aged 31 he scored a famous century in the final and guided his side to victory in the inaugural World Cup.

This list of achievements alone would have represented a great career, but Lloyd was only just starting. Five months after winning the World Cup, his West Indian team suffered a 5-1 series defeat in Australia. For all their flair, the Caribbean batsmen were repeatedly routed by Lillee and Thomson.

Out of humiliation, Lloyd resolved to build the future of West Indian cricket on a pace attack every bit as intimidating and ruthless as Australia's. One of the great sporting conveyor belts began to roll . . . Andy Roberts, Malcolm Marshall, Colin Croft, Wayne Daniel, Michael Holding and Joel Garner.

He harnessed the batting talents of Gordon Greenidge, Desmond Haynes and Viv Richards, and insisted upon high standards of discipline and professionalism. He armed a tradition of entertaining 'calypso' cricket in iron, and made his team seem almost unbeatable. Above all, he swept aside inter-island rivalries and united the far-flung nations and supporters that combine to make this unique cricketing entity.

The West Indies had often produced great individuals. Lloyd produced its first great team, and the records flowed: an unmatched 26 Tests without defeat, including 11 Test wins in succession.

In his agile youth, Lloyd resembled nothing so much as a cricketing panther, prowling around the covers, and even if passing years turned him into more of a polar bear, he remained a massive force in the game past his 40th birthday. On his final tours in 1984/5 he averaged 67 as his team completed a famous 5-0 'blackwash' over England, and 50.85 in leading his team to a 3-1 series win against Australia.

He retired in 1985, an acknowledged all-time giant of the game, his features – 6'5" of stooped shoulders, moustache and black-rimmed glasses – instantly recognised wherever cricket is played.

It was inevitable that a man of such stature should remain close to the game, and Lloyd became a highly respected ICC match referee.

In 1996 he was persuaded to return to the fold as a team manager expected to re-establish the prestige and playing fortunes of a struggling West Indian team. He applied himself to the task with typical resolve, eagerly campaigning for Caribbean unity, but his role became clouded by confusion. Ultimately frustrated when he became an administrator with no say in team selection, he resigned at the end of the team's 1999 tour to New Zealand.

Today he remains revered as an elder statesman of the game, grey, benign and wise, working hard, still ready to intervene and resolve any fights in the school playground of international cricket.

Chapter Three

Evolution and Revolution

The County Ground at Hove nestles snugly between rows of terrace houses in a civilised town on the south coast of England, but any sense of comfort among spectators is often disturbed by a chill breeze that whistles up from the English Channel, only 400 yards away.

Gerald Hartley-Campbell, 61, had been a Sussex member for as long as he could remember and, on time as usual, he unpacked his cushion, binoculars and scorecard, and took his place in the front row of the pavilion to watch the John Player league match between Sussex and Yorkshire. The rural estate agent didn't particularly enjoy the 40-over bashes, but loyalty to his team outweighed any reservations.

It was Sunday 8 May 1977, and as the players fanned out onto the field, Brian Smith, 26, excused his way along the row and took his seat beside Hartley-Campbell. Wearing the blue-and-white vertical stripes of Brighton and Hove Albion, the hotel porter loved cricket. He had never played the game as a boy, but the 1975 World Cup sparked his enthusiasm, and now he never missed a one-day match.

'Afternoon, Gerald. You all right?'

'Very well thanks, Brian. And you?'

'Ace!'

The two men appeared to have little in common beyond their shared interest in cricket, but as the season had worn on they had grown to enjoy each other's company and the gentle banter.

'So, how's the three-day match going?' Brian asked, smirking, knowing full well that Gerald would have sat resolutely through the previous day when, on the second day of the championship match between the same two teams, only 187 runs had been scored in 94 painstaking overs.

'The game is finely poised.'

'I don't know how you can watch that stuff. It's so boring.'

'Well, these one-day matches are not perfect. It's fun when there is a close finish, but there's nothing more tedious than a limited overs game when the team batting first makes such a big score that the target is out of range. And if either side is dismissed cheaply, the game is virtually over.'

One of the Sussex opening batsmen took two steps down the pitch and lofted a drive over cover which clattered into the boundary, prompting Brian to declare: 'There you are! I bet you didn't see very many shots like that yesterday! At least batsmen go for their strokes in one-day cricket.'

'Perhaps,' Gerald conceded, 'but not all the strokes are good strokes. All this slogging has encouraged bad habits. In my day, batsmen were taught to get behind the line and play straight, but nowadays everybody seems preoccupied with angling the ball through the slips. It's poor technique.'

'Well, it works for the West Indians,' Brian noted.

Gerald fell quiet, and reached for a cheese and pickle sandwich. He understood the game had changed since his playing days, but he often found the modern wisdom difficult to accept.

'You must feel sorry for the bowlers,' he said, carefully venturing into discussion again. 'They have been brought up to take wickets by varying line, length and pace, but in the one-day game all they're told to do is contain batsmen and restrict the run rate. Spinners are discarded as an unacceptable risk, and the most sought-after bowlers – the just-short-of-a-length medium-pacers – are also the dullest.'

Brian was struggling to stifle a yawn. 'Bowlers?' he pondered. 'Who cares about them? I come to watch people score runs. It's the big hitters, the fours and sixes that turn me on.'

'Turn you on? Yes, I suppose so,' Gerald said, sensing it was time to talk about something on which they could agree. 'Well, one-day cricket has improved the general standard of fielding.'

Brian smiled: 'All that diving around? Yep, that's good.'

'It's all about fitness and athleticism these days,' Gerald continued. 'I think modern players spend more time lifting weights in the gym than they do practising their technique in the nets.'

As he spoke, a Yorkshire player held a remarkable catch, diving full length at cover point to grasp the ball inches from the turf. Gerald stood to applaud an outstanding piece of cricket.

Brian was not so happy. 'That didn't carry!' he yelled, his face contorted with rage. 'He didn't make that catch! That umpire is blind. It's a joke. I've never seen anything like it!'

Gerald sat down, resolving to keep his thoughts to himself. He began to contemplate how one-day cricket had changed the character of the game: how everyone seemed more fixated with winning than anything else; how players were more competitive and less courteous than ever; how so many supporters, like Brian, seemed more partisan, more quick to criticise, and more belligerent.

He wondered if the game was somehow harsher, or if it was just him. He remembered cricketing days of his distant youth when Sussex supporters were enthralled by a Hammond century or a magnificent spell of fast bowling by Larwood. It didn't matter then that their team was on the receiving end; people were delighted to be watching great players in their prime. Nobody seemed to feel like that any more.

'Everything's changed,' he eventually said out loud.

'What?' Brian asked.

'Everything.'

'Right.'

The two men glanced at each other quickly, then turned their focus back to the middle where the Sussex batsmen put Yorkshire to the sword. Gerald clapped, Brian cheered, and cricket's past more or less managed to find common ground with cricket's future. The game continued, and all seemed well.

In fact, on this particular day in 1977, at this particular ground on the south coast of England, the game of cricket was about to be plunged into the most serious crisis of its history.

Brian first realised something significant was happening when, while buying himself a pint of beer during the break between innings, he saw an agitated club steward in conversation with two reporters. 'All right,' the steward had said, 'Tony Greig promises he will be available in ten minutes.'

That seemed odd. What could be so important that it needed to be said in the middle of the game? Brian returned to his seat and explained what had happened. Gerald listened, shrugged, could think of nothing to say, and carried on double-checking the Yorkshire bowling analysis on his scorecard.

'It's something big,' Brian murmured, still standing, his eyes darting this way and that.

'You think so?' mused Gerald.

'Yeah, I do.'

Perhaps ten minutes later, a breathless, flushed member emerged from inside the pavilion and sat down beside his friend in the row immediately behind Gerald and Brian.

'Have you heard?'

'What?'

'Greig apparently had a party for a group of players at his house, and he was telling everybody that the world's top players are going to play in some kind of rebel circus.'

'What do you mean?'

'I don't know. There's someone from the *Daily Mail* standing at the back of the pavilion.'

'When did Greig say that?'

'At the party, and I think he's talking about it now.'

'Where?'

'Over there.'

Brian was bewildered, wondering what a circus had to do with cricket. Gerald hardly blinked: nothing in the modern game surprised him any more, and his extras column didn't tally . . .

✳

The news that broke at the County Ground in Hove on Sunday 8 May 1977 – and was exclusively reported by the energetic Ian Wooldridge in the *Daily Mail* the next day – shook the game of cricket to its foundations. It was announced that 35 top international players, drawn from every Test-playing country except India and New Zealand, had committed themselves to participate in an unofficial series of five-day and one-day matches, to be staged in Australia during the imminent 1977/78 season.

Cricket was facing a full-scale mutiny.

Disgruntled because Test cricketers were earning as little as £6 000 per year, the leading players in the world had been persuaded *en masse* to abandon the official structures and sign contracts worth a minimum of £12 000 per year with an organisation backed by Kerry Packer, an Australian businessman.

Officials and supporters around the globe were shell-shocked: if cricket had been a garden, it seemed as if this reviled tycoon had walked in and cut off all the largest, most colourful blooms. Packer had executed an audacious raid.

Convinced that international cricket would provide a strong and enduring revenue stream for his station, Channel Nine, in 1976 he had bid to buy the rights to broadcast cricket in Australia, but the Australian Cricket Board was committed to his rivals, the ABC, until 1979.

Feeling as if he was being barred from the restaurant, Packer simply decided to buy the ingredients and do the cooking himself. He was angry and frustrated, and determined to show the Board he would get his way in the end. So he effectively bought the top players, and planned his own events.

He carried out his strategy with clinical efficiency: as news travelled from Hove around the world on this spring Sunday, the establishment seemed to be caught completely unaware. Greig, the England captain and a central agent in Packer's recruitment process, had leaked the news and was under pressure to confirm or deny the rumours. It didn't matter, because by then the 35 contracts were signed.

On 11 May an anonymous advertisement appeared in *The Times*, deploring the death of international cricket in a style that echoed the famous 'obituary' of English cricket in the *Sporting Times* after Australia had won their first Test on English soil, and which gave rise to 'The Ashes'.

It read: 'In affectionate remembrance of international cricket which died at Hove, 8 May 1977. Deeply lamented by a large circle of friends and acquaintances. RIP. NB: The body will be cremated and the ashes taken to Australia and scattered around the studio of Channel Nine in Sydney.'

Packer, an impatient, quick-tempered, resolute man, had opened a window on his soul when he most infamously declared, 'There's a little bit of the whore in all of us,' and he had emphatically proved that the maxim applied to international cricketers who, probably with good reason, felt seriously underpaid.

Having assembled his high-quality ingredients, mostly purchased from Australia, England, Pakistan and the West Indies, with some South African seasoning, the magnate started to cook. His recipe was simple: to serve the players to the public with heaps of razzmatazz and loads of fun, fun, fun.

Old, fundamentally English traditions of reserve and elegance were ruthlessly discarded and replaced by an aggressive, brash and unashamedly vulgar brand of American marketing. The game was being repackaged to attract a new, younger audience, and nothing was sacred any more.

'Nobody wants to watch a boring cricket game where 22 people stand around for six hours doing virtually nothing,' declared Tony Skelton, general manager of Packer's marketing and promotions operation. 'We aim to make this sport exciting. Our matches will be genuine entertainment events.'

Such remarks were received with disbelief and horror at Lord's. Traditional enthusiasts of the game, from Barbados to Bombay, had grown accustomed to change, and accepted a gradual evolution towards commercial viability as a fact of life, but this dollar-drenched revolution was too much to bear. They had now lost control of the elite area of the game, and were left only with a bewildered sense of sadness.

Bill O'Reilly, one of Australia's most distinguished former Test players, reflected the sentiments of many when he raged against the Packer project: 'It's not cricket as I know it. It's an Americanisation and they must not be allowed to call it cricket. This is not sport any more. It's a big business now.'

World Series Cricket lasted two seasons in Australia, overcoming teething problems in 1977/78 to deliver an obviously successful product in 1978/79. Peace was eventually announced in April 1979, when the ACB sold Channel Nine the rights to broadcast and promote international cricket in Australia.

The establishment had continued to organise 'official' tours, fielding second-string teams, but they soon reached a stage at which giving Packer what he had wanted all along seemed a price worth paying to regain sole control of the elite level and re-establish some degree of order in the sport.

Traditional Test series were restored between major nations able to select their best players, and so far as the five-day game was concerned, business virtually went back to normal. Commercial opportunities might have been embraced, and player salaries rose, but the game looked the same.

However, it quickly became clear that World Series Cricket and its crazy band of marketing whizzkids had left an indelible mark on one-day cricket. They had transformed the product.

Packer appreciated the limited overs format, and from the outset regarded it as the ideal vehicle for his revolution. He challenged his commercial team to take one-day cricket and turn it into one of the most popular forms of entertainment in Australia. He demanded a vibe: something that appealed to young men and women, something that guaranteed fun, week after week, something that engaged emotions and drew huge audiences. He wanted events soaked in the spirit of what it meant to be an upbeat, winning Aussie.

The boss asked; and the boss received.

Creative people, often with little experience and less knowledge of cricket, looked at the game in a new light and put forward a list of proposals to revamp the one-day cricket experience.

'We've got to play at night,' said one. 'You can't stage entertainment events when everyone is at work. The games must start in the afternoon, and continue through to ten or eleven at night.'

So, many WSC matches were played at venues with floodlights, and Packer was delighted by the visual effect of established cricket grounds illuminated at night. The sun setting behind the old clock tower of the only surviving Victorian grandstand at the Sydney Cricket Ground would become one of the most beautiful sights in international sport. Suddenly, vast stadiums became theatres decked for drama.

'If we're playing under lights, we have to use a white ball,' ventured another, 'and you won't be able to see the ball if all the players are wearing white. We need coloured clothing.'

'Yes! In any case, white is so dull!'

So it was quickly resolved that each of the three teams in World Series Cricket would have its distinctive colour, and their clothing, pads, batting gloves and boots would be dyed accordingly. Decisions were taken: the Australians would play in wattle yellow, the Rest of the World in blue, and the West Indians in . . .

Clive Lloyd, Michael Holding, Viv Richards and the rest arrived in the dressing room, took one look at the specially designed playing kit hanging on the pegs, and expressed horror. This emphatically masculine group of sportsmen were being asked to play before millions of viewers in . . . coral pink. They protested passionately, and by the second WSC season the West Indians had changed into deep maroon.

'Floodlights and coloured clothing will make it look good,' declared another voice around the table, 'but our events must sound good as well. People like to dance, and we need music.'

The 40-minute interval between innings offered the most obvious gap in a match-day schedule for the introduction of music, and the WSC promoters literally drove a lorry through that gap. As soon as the players had left, a juggernaut containing a rock band was wheeled onto the field, and the concert began. Players and spectators were soon chewing their chicken salad to the booming beat of the music.

Yet more music was threaded into the event by the introduction of various jingles, to be played regularly over the public address system during the match. There would be tunes to celebrate the fall of wickets, a tune for boundaries, a tune for sixes, a rousing signature tune for each team, and more.

'C'mon Aussie, C'mon!' would become instantly recognised as the WSC mantra. Played incessantly when the Australian team was in action, the slogan instantly caught on, entered the Australian dictionary of common usage, and was cleverly extended into every element of the marketing campaign.

Channel Nine echoed to rousing, unashamedly patriotic television commercials that drew upon historical images to promote World Series Cricket as a part of daily life that made you proud to be an Australian, always concluding with a thunderous trademark rendition of 'C'mon Aussie, C'mon'.

After a pause, someone else asked: 'What about the drinks interval?'

'The what?'

'You know, the time when they bring drinks out for the fielders and the batsmen.'

'Well, the 12th man traditionally carries out the drinks.'

'Stuff that! Let's use a radio-controlled buggy. It will be fun.'

'Great idea, and we could also put a sponsor's logo on the side.'

So the 12th men were left to lounge in the dressing room while a red-and-white toy was used to take the orange squash out to the players; and yes, inevitably, the crowd were amused.

'And we must keep the spectators,' another voice suggested.

'How do you mean?'

'Well, we want to keep up the tempo. The pubic address announcer must act like a master of ceremonies, running competitions for spectators, giving prizes, constantly making announcements about milestones. People love milestones! Things like the fastest ball of the innings, the most catches held, the most runs scored: these make spectators believe they are watching something special. The game must always have the appearance of something important and historic.'

'We need a slogan for that.'

'How about . . . "Give your kids something to tell their kids about" . . . how does that sound?'

'Perfect!'

'Great!'

And so it was done.

Packer's people transformed the environment of one-day cricket, but World Series Cricket implemented only one change to the existing regulations of the game itself, the actual cricket.

It was Tony Greig who proposed to the WSC Governing Committee that two fielding circles be marked on the field, one at each end of the pitch, each drawn with a 30-yard radius from the stumps, and advocated rules that compelled the fielding captain to place only four fielders outside the ropes in the first 15 overs, and then to keep at least four men inside the two circles for the remainder of the innings.

The progressive former England captain had seen the circles work in South Africa, and believed it was an effective means of encouraging positive cricket. He concluded: 'It's no fun for anybody when, towards the end of the innings, the fielding captain places his entire team on the boundary.'

No fun? That was unthinkable. Greig's proposal was accepted. In time, the two circles would evolve into two semi-circles joined together by straight lines and, despite initial opposition among official bodies, by 1979 these regulations had become accepted practice in one-day cricket worldwide.

Indeed, the coral pink West Indian kit aside, most of Packer's innovations worked. Just as he had asked, one-day cricket did become one of Australia's favourite forms of entertainment. Traditionalists mocked the fun and scoffed at the gimmicks – John Woodcock, cricket correspondent of *The Times*, watched a WSC night match, and recoiled at 'the lust and passion of the bullring', concluding that the mood of the occasion was 'discordant and unattractive' – but thousands of paying Australians evidently loved every minute.

More than 24 000 spectators paid to watch the second-ever WSC floodlit match in Perth, and night cricket took its giant leap forward when Packer eventually secured permission to stage a match at the Sydney Cricket Ground. The WSC Australians were scheduled to play against the WSC West Indians under lights at the established venue on 27 November 1978, and even the most optimistic of Packer's organisers were hoping for a crowd in the region of 20 000; that would be regarded as a huge success in Sydney.

Two days earlier, only 2 000 people had paid to watch an 'authentic' one-day international between the ACB's Australia side and the official England touring team. 'The public are clearly tired of limited overs cricket,' declared an ACB official, bravely trying to explain the remarkably poor attendance.

He was soon proved wrong.

WSC officials began to get excited around noon: the free car parks seemed to fill more quickly than usual, and the concourses around the Sydney Cricket Ground looked busy. At a quarter past four the police chief gave instructions that the gates be closed because the ground was full. More than 44 000 people had flooded to see the home team take on the West Indians. For night cricket, this was lift-off.

Packer was thrilled and, eager not to disappoint his punters, personally intervened that evening to open the gates again and admit several thousand more spectators free of charge.

He had created an intoxicating atmosphere in the grounds, and in order to enhance the experience of the television viewers, Channel Nine commentators were instructed to be unequivocally upbeat and positive about the quality of cricket in general, and the Australian team in particular.

This was the essence of the WSC show, and the ultimate measure of its success is the fact that, once the establishment had made peace with Packer in April 1979, one-day cricket as played in Australia retained all the promotional gambits and gimmicks, all the bells and whistles, launched by WSC.

Indeed, aside from selling Channel Nine the rights to broadcast international cricket in their country, the Australian Cricket Board specifically agreed 'to consider favourably the introduction of 30-yard circles in limited overs matches, day-night matches, and to implement, on an experimental basis, the use of coloured clothing in the Benson and Hedges World Series one-day limited overs international matches.'

Furthermore, acknowledging the success of the WSC brand, the Board agreed that the World Series logo would continue to be worn by the Australian players during one-day internationals.

Game, set and match to Mr Packer.

The damaging schism in world cricket was ended, and WSC players were welcomed back into the official fold – instantly in the West Indies and Pakistan, but only after several months in England and Australia. Indeed, the latter two countries decided their WSC players would not be eligible for selection to play in the second World Cup, due to take place in June 1979.

And in 1979 the word 'World', as used in the name 'Cricket World Cup', happily represented much more of the globe than had been the case at the inaugural event four years earlier.

Where East Africa and Sri Lanka had simply been invited to join the six Test-playing countries in 1975, no fewer than 21 countries effectively competed for the 1979 World Cup. The six major sides automatically qualified again, but now the ICC had introduced a tournament, the ICC Trophy, to be played in England during May, at which its 15 associate members would compete for the other two places in the tournament proper.

These 15 nations were divided into three groups, with the three group-winners and the second-placed side with the best group record advancing to contest the semi-finals. Both semi-final winners would qualify for the World Cup, and then play a final for honour and the trophy later in the month. The plan was adjusted when Gibraltar withdrew at the eleventh hour, and Wales was admitted as a replacement, but only on a non-competitive basis because they were not associate members of the ICC.

Group A comprised Bermuda, East Africa, Papua-New Guinea, Singapore and Argentina; Group B was graced by Denmark, Canada, Bangladesh, Fiji and Malaysia; and Group C included Sri Lanka, the USA, Wales, Holland and Israel. All the matches were played on club grounds in the Midlands of England, producing such enticing sporting spectacles as the United States playing cricket against Israel at Blossomfield.

Unfortunately for the players and their enthusiastic groups of supporters, the fortnight was beset by persistent rain and little sunshine. No fewer than four matches were completely abandoned, but Bermuda, Denmark and Sri Lanka emerged as group winners, with Canada surviving as the best runners-up.

The increasingly competitive Sri Lankans beat Denmark by 208 runs in the first semi-final at the Butler's Ground in Birmingham, and a 24-year-old French teacher from Montreal, John Valentine, helped Canada to over-come Bermuda by four wickets in the other semi-final at Burton-on-Trent.

Valentine was enthusiastically hailed as a symbol of the ICC Trophy's success, and the opening bowler would sustain his form in the World Cup proper where he sensationally dismissed three Test openers – Majid Khan of Pakistan, Mike Brearley of England, and Rick Darling of Australia.

The Canadian's pure, amateur approach to the game stood in stark contrast to the naked commercialism and hard-nosed business approach of Packer's WSC, but international cricket had become an extremely broad church by the summer of 1979, and all its strands were pulled together for the second World Cup.

One-day cricket had advanced through a slow evolution from 1963 until 1977; now it was emerging from the fiery furnace of the Packer revolution stronger and more popular than ever.

It had become clear: limited overs, limitless potential.

Chapter Four

The Second World Cup

There was no dispute, and hardly any discussion.

The International Cricket Council decided that the 1979 Cricket World Cup would be staged in England, just as the inaugural event had been four years earlier. Scarcely anyone was asking, but officials nonetheless explained that there were not enough hours of daylight in any other cricketing country. 'We have to play 120 overs in a day,' they said, 'and that is only possible on a midsummer's day in England.'

A journalist wondered if games could be played under floodlights, but the ICC was not ready to consider something so new, and so plainly associated with Kerry Packer. This was *their* World Cup, and it would be played in natural light, with the players wearing traditional whites and using a red ball.

An Indian raised his hand towards the back of the room, wanting to mention that 60-overs matches were comfortably completed in Calcutta and Delhi, but nobody seemed to be paying attention.

In truth, hours of daylight aside, the game was not ready to cut the umbilical cord between the mother country and its toddler tournament. For now, the World Cup would cuddle close to Mum.

A substantial shadow – that of Mr Packer – darkened the days preceding the tournament as, one by one, countries ruled whether players returning from the disbanded WSC would be eligible to participate in the World Cup. Some said yes, others said no. Since the ICC lacked the authority to impose a firm, universal decision one way or the other, the tournament was distorted and unequal from the start.

England decided not to select the Packer players, leaving the likes of

Tony Greig and Allan Knott to watch the games on television; and the Australian Cricket Board reached the same verdict, overlooking Ian Chappell, Greg Chappell, Dennis Lillee, Doug Walters, Rodney Marsh and others, and relying upon the wholehearted and positive spirit of Kim Hughes to lead and inspire what amounted to a second team.

Taking a different view, officials in the Caribbean and Karachi decided to draw a line in the WSC sand and reunite without delay. The West Indies named ten WSC veterans in their 14-man squad, and Pakistan included eight players who had returned to the fold after taking the Packer dollar.

The format was unchanged from 1975, and when these two powerful full-strength teams were kept apart in the draw for the groups, many predicted they would eventually meet in the final.

These disparities aside, the international cricket community assembled in good heart. At least, the WSC upheaval was now in the past, and upbeat memories of the first World Cup raised expectations that the second tournament would prove equally successful. Prudential increased their sponsorship fee to £250 000, boosting total prize money to £25 900, and the game looked forward to an exciting fortnight.

England supporters, in particular, purred quietly in expectation because Mike Brearley's side appeared to be talented, streetwise and competitive. Gooch, Boycott and Gower headed a strong batting line-up; Willis and Hendrick led a disciplined bowling attack, and the infectious, jabbering presence of Derek Randall sustained the squad's enthusiasm and confidence. The mix somehow seemed right.

Drawn in the harder of the two groups, alongside Pakistan, Australia and Canada, England launched their campaign on 9 June, the opening day, with a match at Lord's against their oldest rivals.

As the names of the Australian players were slotted into place on the main grandstand scoreboard, home supporters could scarcely resist glancing down the list and feeling confident . . . Hilditch, Darling, Border, Hughes, Yallop, Cosier, Laughlin, Wright, Hogg, Hurst and Dymock. It wasn't a bad side, and they had defeated England in an 'official' one-day series five months earlier, but they looked beatable.

All aboard the emotional roller coaster. England was 'up' at the start, 'down' when Australia prospered to 91 for one, but 'up' when they seized eight wickets for 68 runs. Chasing a meagre 160 to win, they were 'down' when Boycott and Randall had gone with the score at five for two, 'up' when Brearley and Gooch stabilised the innings, and they remained 'up' as Gower and Botham took them to victory.

England's trials and tribulations had been exhausting, as usual, but the crowd gladly saluted an unlikely hero. Geoff Boycott was widely admired as a great opening batsman of impeccable technique, but his bowling talents as a purveyor of 'baby seamers' were not so often acknowledged. Yet, at a stage when the Australian batsmen seemed to have settled, Brearley had tossed the ball to the Yorkshireman.

Surprised MCC members in the Long Room sat bolt upright in their high chairs.

Reversing his blue England cap, Boycott trundled in, settled on a nagging line and length, and made a crucial breakthrough soon after lunch. A final analysis of two for 15 from six overs signalled his unanticipated emergence as an economical fifth bowler. Brearley had discovered a new option.

Boycott the bowler? It was something to talk about.

Canada had been heavily defeated by Pakistan on the same day, but this willing band of cricketers, most of whom seemed to be expatriate West Indians, were then soundly beaten by England at Old Trafford. Batting first, their total of 45 remains among the lowest ever scored in a World Cup match.

The Manchester rain pushed England's gentle jog to victory into a second day, but the win was secured in only the 14th over, albeit in miserable weather before a handful of diehard supporters.

Australia against Pakistan at Trent Bridge, Nottingham, now assumed the status of a virtual quarter-final, with the winner advancing to the semi-final and the loser facing early elimination.

Kim Hughes recognised the importance of victory. History had not dealt many trumps in this Australian captain's hand, but this engaging man would not give up without a fight. Born on Australia Day, he epitomised all the finest qualities of courage, skill and sportsmanship for which his country had become renowned around the world. Heart on his sleeve, or maybe in his mouth, he would give it a go.

The prospects were poor. When his strike bowler, Rodney Hogg, was injured and forced to withdraw, the captain considered his options and realised that, on this crucial day, his trio of back-up bowlers – Gary Cosier, Allan Border and Graham Yallop – would have to bowl 24 of the 60 overs. It was hardly ideal, but he spoke to each player, explained what was required, and urged them to believe in themselves.

With Hughes clap-clap-clapping at mid-off, the Australians effectively restricted Pakistan to only 125 for two in 35 overs, but it was then time for the part-timers to bowl. Majid Khan and Javed Miandad increased the tempo, and Asif Iqbal, Wasim Raja and Imran Khan thrashed 47 from the last five overs. Hughes could do very little as, in a blur, Pakistan raced to a commanding 286 for seven in 60 overs.

Australia's pursuit was interrupted by rain, but they never seemed likely to reach their target, eventually subsiding to 197 all out in the 58th over. An easy victory over hapless Canada in their last group match proved no consolation to Hughes and his players as they headed to Heathrow, and home.

England and Pakistan had already qualified for the second stage when they met in Leeds, but both teams were eager to win and most probably avoid the West Indies in the semi-finals.

Brearley sought a solid performance from his unpredictable team, but England was swiftly embroiled in a dogfight under overcast skies on a Headingley pitch that favoured the seamers. The conditions were typically English, but Brearley realised that this hardly amounted to an advantage because many of the top Pakistan players played in county cricket and, for at least half the year, called England home.

In fact, in all respects, home advantage was negligible. Quite apart from the fact that any local knowledge was shared because so many leading players spent so much time in England, the home supporters were often out-shouted in the stands by noisy expatriate Indians, Pakistanis and West Indians.

On this leaden day in Leeds, England was sent in to bat first. They lost Brearley and Randall with four on the board, and then slumped to a dismal 118 for eight. Taylor and Willis wagged the tail, adding 43 for the ninth wicket, but a total of 165 for nine in 60 overs hardly looked like the stuff of champions.

The home side needed early wickets to stay in the game, and Mike Hendrick of Derbyshire produced an outstanding spell of fast-medium bowling. He uprooted four of the top five Pakistan batsmen, and, with Botham also claiming a couple of wickets, Pakistan crumbled to 34 for six wickets.

Asif Iqbal and Wasim Raja tried to stage a revival, taking the score to 86; and even when they had both fallen in quick succession, hope remained with Imran Khan at the crease.

Brearley needed to squeeze the game, and once again he summoned Boycott to bowl at a crucial stage. The Headingley crowd applauded the reappearance of their favourite son, and the baby seamers began to buzz and whir on a nagging line and length. Wasim Bari was undone, Sikander

Bakht fell, and amid unbridled delight in the stands Boycott seized two for 15, and England won by 14 runs.

While the home side was leopard crawling like a commando unit to the top of Group A, the West Indians ruthlessly, imperiously blasted a path through the vegetation of Group B.

Clive Lloyd led a team of legends: stroke players Gordon Greenidge, Desmond Haynes, Viv Richards and Alvin Kallicharran; all-rounders Lloyd and Collis King, wicketkeeper Deryck Murray, and a four-man pace attack comprising veteran Andy Roberts, Joel Garner, Michael Holding and Colin Croft. More than just pre-tournament favourites, they were admired as perhaps the finest one-day side of all time.

India was first to face this cricketing combine harvester, at Edgbaston. Sunil Gavaskar hooked his first ball to the square leg boundary, and his brother-in-law, Gundappa Viswanath, struck a defiant 75, but the total of 190 all out in 53.1 overs was never likely to extend the West Indians.

Greenidge struck an unbeaten 106 and, to a calypso of clanking cans, India was crushed by nine wickets with 9.3 overs to spare. However, on 13, 14 and 15 June, the West Indies were beaten . . . by the weather. Their rain-affected match against Sri Lanka was abandoned as a draw, leaving Lloyd's team needing to win their last group fixture, versus New Zealand, to make certain of reaching the semi-finals.

Not for the first time, nor the last, New Zealand had arrived at a World Cup with a team that added up to more than the sum of its parts. Naturally competitive and cleverly led, they had already beaten Sri Lanka and India, on both occasions overhauling a target for the loss of one wicket. In form and with their semi-final place safely secured, the Kiwis were keen to give the West Indies a run for their money.

They won the toss, decided to bowl first, and set out to frustrate the illustrious batsmen. Their world-class fast bowler, Richard Hadlee, led the attack with distinction, and a clutch of military-medium-pacers dropped the ball just short of a length with no pace. Suddenly, batting didn't look so easy.

At one stage, the West Indians seemed unlikely to get past 200, but Lloyd managed to find some rhythm in the closing overs and his 73 in 80 balls dragged the score to 244 for seven. Confronted by clever tactics, the Caribbean team had kept their heads, worked hard and made a winning score.

In pursuit, New Zealand lost the gifted Bruce Edgar to an early run-out, and soon fell behind the required run rate. Hadlee struck 42 quick runs from 48 balls, but was eventually bowled by Roberts, and the underdogs ultimately subsided to 212 for nine in 60 overs, retaining honour in defeat.

Had their relentless seamers exposed a weakness in the West Indian armour? Or had the likes of Haynes, Greenidge and Richards suffered a rare off day? Pundits pontificated both ways, but the consensus desperately hoped that the World Cup would be a genuine race rather than a procession.

Two hours into the semi-final at the Oval, such sentiments appeared fanciful. In sweltering sunshine, the West Indian openers savaged the Pakistan attack. Greenidge and Haynes took the score to 132 without loss in 16 dazzling overs, and a record total seemed likely. Majid Khan and Asif Iqbal managed to dampen some of the late fireworks, but the West Indian total of 293 for six in 60 overs looked out of reach.

Phrases like 'men against boys' and 'lambs to the slaughter' bounced around the press box, and Pakistan seemed headed for a heavy defeat when Sadiq Mohammed did not last long. However, Majid and Zaheer Abbas were highly regarded as talented stroke players in their own right and, contrary to everyone's expectations, they started to enjoy the steady menu of fast bowlers on a true, flat pitch.

They added 50, then another 50, then another 50. Their partnership reached 166, and the semi-final was dramatically slipping away from the West Indians. The tapping typewriters changed their tune, now telling how the Pakistani batsmen had exposed a fatal lack of variety in the all-pace attack. Only 118 runs were required in 24 overs with nine wickets in hand, and the Oval crowd braced itself for a shock.

Lloyd paused for a moment, and recognised the need for a different angle of attack.

The captain summoned Vivian Richards to bowl his off-spinners, and although his first over cost 12 runs, the change of gear appeared to disturb the batsmen's rhythm. Croft was thundering in from the other end, and he exploited the moment of uncertainty by seizing three wickets in the space of 12 balls: Zaheer for 93, Majid for an anchor 81, and Javed Miandad for nothing. The tide was turning.

Richards, by now relishing every moment, dismissed Mudassar Nazar, Asif Iqbal and Imran Khan in quick succession, and in what seemed a few minutes Pakistan's thrilling march to victory had become a calamitous collapse. They had dared to threaten the established order, and been ruthlessly dismantled from 176 for one to 250 all out. Amid high-fives, the West Indies looked more impregnable than ever.

New Zealand had contained their batsmen for a while in the group match, and Pakistan briefly dominated their bowling in the semi-final, but Lloyd's team still prevailed. If one aspect of their game stuttered, they were more than powerful, confident and gifted enough to compensate in another.

On the opposite side of the draw, the England selectors were sufficiently convinced by Boycott's ability to get through his 12 overs and function as the fifth bowler that they included an extra specialist batsman, Wayne Larkins, for their semi-final against New Zealand at Old Trafford.

Sent in to bat under clear skies, the home side lost two early wickets but recovered when Brearley made a battling 53, and Graham Gooch, literally, left his mark on the occasion by advancing down the wicket to Brian McKechnie and driving a wonderful straight six into the Stretford End. 'The ball exploded into and through the sightscreen like a shell,' the batsman recalls, 'and it left a perfectly formed hole.'

The damage was not repaired, and for many seasons afterwards Gooch made a point of wandering over to inspect his handiwork every time he returned to play in Manchester.

He scored 71 in 84 balls, but received little support, and England's innings was only rescued from 145 for five by Randall's fighting unbeaten 42 in 50 balls. The tail contributed again, and 221 for eight in their 60 overs represented something like par on a pitch that encouraged the bowlers.

Wright and Edgar gave the New Zealand innings a steady start, but the pursuit stumbled when their top batsman, Geoff Howarth, fell LBW to a gentle full toss for only seven. This pivotal delivery was bowled around the wicket by the irrepressible Boycott, who once again emerged as his team's most economical bowler with the respectable analysis of one wicket for 24 runs in nine overs.

No England triumph would have seemed authentic without a few palpitations, and these were supplied by Warren Lees and Lance Cairns, each of whom struck a huge six towards the end of the innings, yet Brearley stayed calm, nurtured his bowlers, and led his side to a tense victory by nine runs.

Thus the 1979 Cricket World Cup secured what many considered its ideal final: England would play the West Indies at Lord's on Saturday 23 June. Everyone recognised Clive Lloyd's side as favourites, but Brearley led a team that knew most of the nooks and crannies in the one-day game.

The home players would fight hard to win their place in British sporting history, and their confidence was reflected in the decision to retain an extra batsman and persist with Boycott, supported by Gooch and Larkins, as the fifth bowler. The tactic had worked well throughout the tournament, and in the days preceding the final nobody stopped to suggest that it would not succeed once again.

On an overcast but dry day, Brearley won the toss and, following the mode of an era when everybody preferred to chase rather than set a target, asked his opponents to bat first.

Lord's was soon in tumult: Greenidge was run out by Randall, Haynes snicked a Chris Old outswinger to Hendrick at slip, Lloyd was caught and bowled by Old, and Kallicharran was bowled by Hendrick. Suddenly, the mighty West Indians were floundering in the mire at 99 for four wickets.

Brearley directed his fielders and rotated his bowlers while the effervescent Randall sparkled, fizzed and buzzed in the covers. Viv Richards was still at the crease, but he had been fortunate to survive a strong appeal for LBW on his second ball, and he generally looked out of form.

But the gifted Antiguan stuck to his task and guided his team to lunch at 125 for four after 34 overs. By anyone's measure, England had performed far beyond expectations.

Now Brearley faced an important choice: he could either attack, pushing his main bowlers through their overs and trying to dismiss the West Indies quickly; or he could defend the gains secured in the morning, use the fifth bowler and hopefully restrict the batsmen to a reasonably modest total.

The captain opted on the side of caution and ushered Boycott into action, but the World Cup final was to prove a match too far for the opener-turned-seamer. Boycott's first six overs cost 38 runs, and Brearley called upon first Gooch and then Larkins to turn their arms and fill in the gaps. In the end, the 12 overs bowled by England's composite, makeshift 'fifth' bowler yielded no fewer than 86 runs.

Many observers proved expert in the perfect science of hindsight, and subsequently criticised England for not including a fifth specialist bowler, but they had said nothing before the game.

It was Collis King who led the onslaught midway through the West Indian innings. Previously rejected as an overseas player by Glamorgan, the athletic all-rounder emerged from relative obscurity in a flurry of powerful straight drives and whipped hooks. He turned the final on its head, and struck 86 runs, comfortably outscoring Richards in a magnificent 77-minute partnership of 139 runs in 21 overs.

England might have hoped to regain some kind of control when King was eventually caught by Randall at square leg, but Richards chose this moment to launch his own assault.

Blissfully oblivious of the tail collapsing around him, Richards thrashed boundary after boundary and then completed the innings by stepping inside a textbook Hendrick yorker and calmly lifting the ball into the Mound Stand for a six that appeared emphatically, ruthlessly, to put England in their place. Gooch stood at mid-wicket and watched that final, sealing six in awe. 'Viv was imperious,' he reflects.

Richards finished with an unbeaten 138 from 156 balls, and his classic innings enabled the West Indies to post 286 for nine in 60 overs, the kind of awesome total that the home crowd feared.

Neither Brearley nor Boycott was willing to concede anything. Instead of searching for a towel to throw, the England opening batsmen reached for their calculators and planned the pursuit. Their strategy was to score at a reasonable three or four per over and, above all, to withstand the pace attack and retain wickets in hand for what, they hoped, would be a successful dash for glory in the closing overs.

They batted carefully and resourcefully, running well between the wickets and efficiently converting bad balls into boundaries, and they reached tea at 79 without loss from 25 overs.

'What do you think?' the Oxbridge captain asked the Yorkshireman over an egg sandwich.

'I think we're doing pretty well.'

'But do you think we're scoring fast enough?'

'We need to accelerate a bit, but let's not go mad.'

The openers returned to the crease and raised the tempo, adding 50 runs in the next 13 overs. Scoring at almost four an over against such a formidable attack was no mean achievement, and at 129 for no wicket after 38 overs, England seemed in a reasonable position to mount a challenge.

Michael Holding then removed both men in the space of six balls, Brearley for 64 and Boycott for 57. In an ideal world, one of them would have remained to anchor the innings, but both men had done their job. Now 158 runs were required in 22 overs. With eight wickets in hand, anything was possible, but the situation cried out for somebody to play the kind of innings that King had produced earlier in the day.

Gooch and Randall manfully tried to meet the challenge, and the pair added a further 48 runs in 43 balls, taking the total to 183 for two. The game was still alive. In the famous pavilion, in the members' stands, in the public stands, England supporters still believed their side could emerge in triumph. Even when Randall marched down the wicket to Croft and was clean-bowled, hope sprang eternal.

Then Lloyd recalled Joel Garner to bowl a second spell from the Nursery End. Standing 6'9" in his cricket boots, and delivering the ball from a height of almost eight feet, the giant widely known as 'Big Bird' prepared to produce one of the most devastating spells of bowling in World Cup history.

Gooch . . . bowled Garner 32.

Gower . . . bowled Garner 0.

Larkins . . . bowled Garner 0.

England had started the 48th over with genuine ambition at 183 for three, but in the space of six frenetic deliveries, Garner had reduced them to bemused disarray at 186 for six. Brearley noted later: 'Joel is the only man I know who effectively bowls out of the trees at the Nursery End. When he pitches the ball well, and fires the ball fast at the base of the stumps, he can become virtually unplayable.'

Botham went down blazing, caught on the boundary by his friend Richards for four, and hope fled. The end came quickly, with none of Old, Taylor and Hendrick troubling the scorers. In less than 20 minutes, England had collapsed from 183 for two wickets to 194 all out. Garner had twice taken two wickets in successive balls. The benignly beaming conqueror of all he surveyed, he finished with five for 38.

And still world champions!

The West Indies had won by 92 runs, and their supporters once again swarmed over Lord's, assembling beneath the pavilion to watch Clive Lloyd lift the Prudential Cup for a second time.

Richards was named as Man of the Match, and he and his team-mates celebrated with champagne. 'I just promised myself I would get into one hell of a state,' he recalls. 'It felt fantastic to be on top of the world once again. The sense of pride that the squad shared that evening was phenomenal.'

Nobody doubted their champion credentials. They had been extended by several opponents, but depth of talent set the West Indies apart from the rest. There were days when they clicked, and they overwhelmed their opposition. There were days when their batting or bowling faltered, but they still won. Lloyd's side had slumped to 55 for three in the 1975 final, and to 99 for four in 1979, but they won both matches.

The English press hailed the West Indies in victory but, seeking scapegoats for defeat, generally blamed the omission of a fifth bowler and the openers for having scored too slowly and put impossible pressure on the batsmen that followed. The former was hindsight; the latter seemed unjustified.

In reaching 129 without loss against one of the greatest bowling attacks in history, Boycott and Brearley had laid an outstanding foundation for what was always a daunting run chase. If more of their team-mates had showed similar resolve, England would not have suffered such a humbling collapse.

Reflecting on the tournament, Brearley tried to put the 1979 West Indian side in some kind of historical context. 'There have probably been better Test teams,' he noted, 'for this side lacks high-quality spinners. Yet I cannot imagine any team better equipped to dominate one-day cricket.'

The International Cricket Council met during the week following the final; and, having declared projected tournament profits of £350 000 to be distributed around the world, officials announced that the World Cup would be held every four years, and that the 1983 tournament would, again, be played in England.

Four years before the opening match, the West Indians were installed as favourites to secure a third successive world championship.

John Edrich opened the batting with Geoff Boycott in the first-ever One-Day International – which happened by accident on 5 January 1971 after a Test match between England and Australia in Melbourne was abandoned. Australia won by five wickets, but Edrich's knock of 82 earned him the first-ever ODI Man of the Match award.
(Getty Images/Touchline Photo)

Australia played England in the first semi-final of the 1975 Cricket World Cup. All-rounder Gary Gilmour was named Man of the Match. Not only did he open the bowling and achieve figures of six for 14 in 12 overs, he also scored 28 at a run a ball, effectively winning the game for Australia.
(Getty Images/Touchline Photo)

Australia faced the West Indies in the first Cricket World Cup final at Lord's in 1975. Captains Ian Chappell and Clive Lloyd are pictured together before the game. Thousands of spectators swarmed onto the field when the West Indies won by 17 runs to take the first World Cup trophy.
(Getty Images/Touchline Photo)

Still world champions! Clive Lloyd lifts the Prudential Cup for the second time after the West Indies beat England in the second World Cup in England in 1979.
(Getty Images/Touchline Photo)

Viv Richards. The great West Indian batsman was Man of the Match in the 1979 World Cup final after finishing with an unbeaten 138 from 156 balls.
(Getty Images/Touchline Photo)

Kerry Packer's World Series Cricket in the 1970s saw the introduction of the distinctive coloured one-day gear – Australia played in wattle yellow, the Rest of the World in blue. This picture shows two South Africans – Kepler Wessels, the fielder, playing for Australia, and batsman Barry Richards playing for the Rest of the World.
(Getty Images/Touchline Photo)

Winning captain Kapil Dev in action at the 1983 World Cup. The all-rounder, who proved early in his career that India could produce world-class fast bowlers, is remembered as much for his spirit as for his remarkable statistics.
(Getty Images/ Touchline Photo)

Beaming Indian captain Kapil Dev raises the trophy on the balcony at Lord's after his team defeated two-times world champions the West Indies in the 1983 final.
(Getty Images/Touchline Photo)

England captain Mike Gatting played
the reverse sweep against Australia
in the 1987 World Cup final in
Calcutta – with disastrous
consequences.
(Getty Images/Touchline Photo)

Victory in Calcutta: Allan Border is
carried high on the shoulders of
Jones and McDermott after
Australia's first World Cup triumph,
in 1987. They beat England by
seven runs in the final.
(Getty Images/ Touchline Photo)

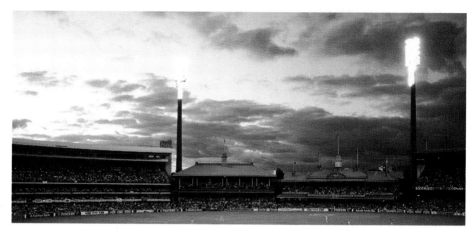

Sydney Cricket Ground on Wednesday 26 February 1992 – a memorable, emotional day in the history of South African sport. The newcomers beat the Australians by nine wickets in their opening match of the 1992 World Cup tournament.
(Getty Images/Touchline Photo)

Amid controversy, Martin Crowe led the New Zealand team in the 1992 World Cup in Australia and New Zealand. Crowe was vindicated when he was named Player of the Tournament.
(Getty Images/Touchline Photo)

Before a record crowd of more than 87 000 spectators at the Melbourne Cricket Ground, Pakistan captain Imran Khan scored 72 in partnership with Javed Miandad to build a winning platform in the World Cup final against England in 1992.
(Getty Images/Touchline Photo)

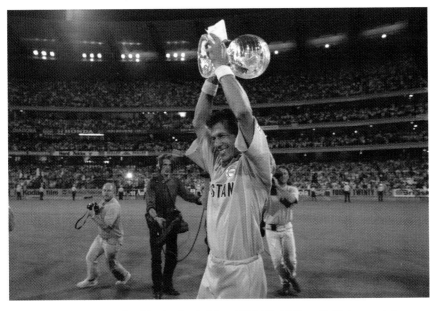

After beating England in the final of the 1992 World Cup, Pakistan captain Imran Khan triumphantly raises the game's greatest prize.
(Getty Images/Touchline Photo)

Kenyans celebrate after their surprise defeat of the West Indies in Pune in the 1996 World Cup. 'To us, this is like winning the World Cup,' said captain Maurice Odumbe. Left to right: Maurice Odumbe, Steve Tikolo and Hitesh Modi.
(Getty Images/Touchline Photo)

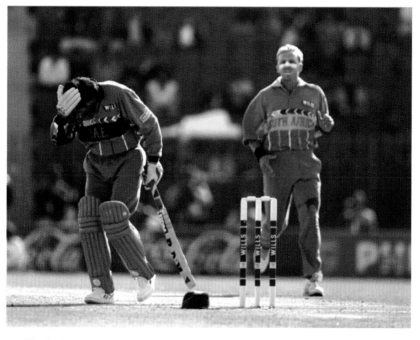

The United Arab Emirates brought a splash of colour and style to the 1996 World Cup tournament. However, their captain, the Sultan Zarawani, declined to wear a helmet when he faced South African fast bowler Allan Donald in his team's opening match – and was struck on the head first ball.
(Getty Images/Touchline Photo)

Viv Richards

The rumour was true, but he could never admit as much to his friends.

To Vivian Richards, son of the superintendent at the local prison in St John's on the island of Antigua, it seemed entirely reasonable: he loved batting, so he slept with his cricket bat in his arms.

'So do you or don't you?' they teased.

'Come on,' Viv grinned, changing the subject. 'I'll race you down to the beach.'

The cavorting group of friends arrived to find more than 30 boys already playing on the golden sand. It was always like this, and everyone always wanted to bat. Richards was content to wait his turn, fielding for an hour or so, eager to feel the bat in his hands, and hear the clunk of bat on ball.

Batting on the beach was not easy. With no limit to the number of players, a horde of youngsters would cluster around the bat, leaving the batsman with two options: either play the perfect defensive stroke, taking care not to give a catch, breaking the wrists at just the right time to ensure that the ball dropped dead; or hit out, trying to strike the ball as far as possible into the rolling, breaking surf.

Richards preferred the latter option, because he knew many of his friends could not swim. He would pull the ball 50 or 60 yards into the sea, and start jogging between the wickets.

'Come on, Viv, you can't do that!'

'Why not? I'm allowed to run. Fetch the ball!'

'Viv! It's not fair.'

And he would laugh ... throughout an illustrious career, he would always laugh. He also learned to stand his ground. When his parents decided they were emigrating to the United States, the resolute teenager said he wanted to remain in Antigua, and swiftly arranged to live with his grandmother.

Into his teens, Richards and his friends batted on. They played on roughly prepared grass wickets, where the unpredictable bounce forced them to develop sharp, fast reflexes; they wore pads cut from cardboard, and soon realised it was easier to attack and play their shots than to 'pad up' and defend.

Richards was blessed with a rare sporting talent – he played international soccer for Antigua at the age of 19, but the following year he travelled to England and focused on cricket. He befriended a youngster named Ian Botham in the Somerset under-25 team soon afterwards, and in April 1974, still only 22, the proud young man from Antigua made his county debut, striking a quick 81 against Glamorgan.

'He never wore a batting helmet,' Botham recalls. 'It was as if he was sending a message to the bowlers that he was not afraid of them, or anyone else. From those early days, he would play his strokes, whatever the situation in the match. Viv had the best eye of any cricketer I have ever seen.'

The master batsman was instrumental in Somerset's success during the 1970s and early 1980s but, with Botham and Joel Garner, he left the county in acrimonious circumstances during 1986.

It was, however, his performances through 16 years in the West Indies side that marked Richards as one of the most entertaining, most destructive batsmen ever to play the game.

From his Test debut against India in 1975, through two winning World Cup finals and regular series wins, through the day he inherited the captaincy from Clive Lloyd, through sweet drives and mighty pulls, to his final Test against England in 1991, he played each delivery on its length rather than its line. He batted with control, power and grace. He looked haughty, self-assured, every inch a cricketing Caesar.

'Viv was the only true genius of my time,' reflects Imran Khan. 'He never had the defence of Gavaskar or the poise of Barry Richards, but he had lightning reflexes that enabled him to get into position so quickly that bowlers never knew what length to bowl. He always seemed to have time.'

Richards loved nothing so much as launching an assault on the opposition's main strike bowler, coming in at No. 3 on the first morning of a Test match, waltzing down the wicket and driving him over the top, spreading the field, ruining reputations and shattering confidence. His onslaught against Bob Willis at Old Trafford in 1980 was unforgettably violent, a savage 60 that set the pattern of the Test.

A gifted off-spinner, a prowling, athletic, world-class fielder, a captain who led by example, he was driven by an almost indignant pride in being black and being West Indian; and he made no secret of relishing victories over England, his island's former colonial masters, more than anything in the game.

Awarded an honorary knighthood, Sir Vivian Richards was justly named in 2000, with Don Bradman, Jack Hobbs, Gary Sobers and Shane Warne, as one of the Five Cricketers of the Century.

He still lives in Antigua, coaching youngsters . . . some of whom most probably sleep with their bats.

Chapter Five

The Third World Cup

As the 1983 World Cup approached, many found it difficult to imagine any outcome other than the increasingly familiar scene of the bespectacled, slightly stooped figure of Clive Lloyd stepping forward on the balcony of the Lord's pavilion to raise the trophy, while joyful supporters clanked their cans below.

'So who will come second this time?' newspapers speculated valiantly.

The West Indies had played imperious cricket in winning the first two tournaments: the awesome battery of fast bowlers, the wonderful stroke play of their batsmen, the exceptional fielding, the desire to win and keep winning. And yet, their domination had become monotonous and predictable.

No matter how excellent the dish, nobody eats the same food every day. Into its third edition, the World Cup needed a new menu, something different, a shock result, a surprise hero.

Some hope.

Eight competing squads started to assemble in England during the first week of June, and a changing of the guard hardly seemed likely. Lloyd arrived with Gordon Greenidge, Desmond Haynes and Vivian Richards at the head of his batting order, and his quartet of fast bowling legends – Andy Roberts, Michael Holding, Malcolm Marshall and Joel Garner – primed to blast any upstart opposition into oblivion.

Most of the other teams seemed in disarray.

In trouncing Australia and India a few months earlier, Pakistan emerged as strong contenders but Imran Khan, their talisman and inspiration, seriously injured his foot. The first opinion was that he would have to miss the tournament, but it was later agreed that the all-rounder would play, but not bowl. Half an Imran was better than no Imran at all, but the deflated Pakistanis somehow looked half the team.

Australia suffered their own setback when their captain, Greg Chappell, picked up an injury on tour to Sri Lanka and decided to withdraw from the tournament. The selectors' decision to name Hughes to lead the team, rather than Rodney Marsh, prompted a division in the squad that proved fatal.

Captained by Bob Willis, England could call on match-winners like Gooch, Lamb, Gower and Botham, but seemed to lack the depth of quality that sets champions apart. New Zealand looked an ordinary side that relied too heavily on the thoroughbred Richard Hadlee, and India were in edgy transition, having appointed an eager young all-rounder named Kapil Dev to replace Gavaskar as captain. Sri Lanka, promoted to full membership of the ICC, qualified automatically but hardly threatened to rip up the floorboards.

So, where were the heirs apparent? Nowhere to be seen.

The West Indians were installed as odds-on favourites.

Ho-hum-drum.

A consequence of Sri Lanka's elevation to the elite had been the reduction of World Cup places to be won at the ICC Trophy tournament, from two at the 1979 event to just one. This was unfortunate. Although the ICC had aimed to enhance what was essentially a World Cup qualifying tournament by staging the event in its own space 12 months before the tournament proper, the message was confused.

On the one hand, the governing body declared it wanted to involve more of the world in what was, with licence, described as the 'World' Cup; on the other hand, they had effectively narrowed the gate through which the emerging cricket nations could reach the game's most prestigious stage.

'Sorry, lads,' officials had shrugged. 'What's the weather forecast?'

It wasn't good.

Committed, optimistic amateur teams from every corner of the planet deserved better than to arrive in the English Midlands and discover the wettest second fortnight of June since 1904. No fewer than three of the nine rounds were abandoned without a ball being bowled, and, worst affected of all, the bemused West Africans eventually returned home after completing only two of their seven matches.

When play was possible, newly independent Zimbabwe emerged as the strongest side in the field, fuelled by five players with first-class experience from when Rhodesia played in South Africa's Currie Cup, and a gifted off-spinner with a Test cap: John Traicos had played for the Springboks in 1970.

With Dave Houghton, Andrew Pycroft, Kevin Curran and Peter Rawson all in form, Zimbabwe were never dismissed during their smooth progress to the final at Grace Road, Leicester, where they defeated Bermuda by five wickets. Remarkably, a team drawn from no more than ten amateur cricket clubs in Harare and Bulawayo had earned the right to take their place as the eighth team in the 1983 World Cup.

The Africans arrived in England to find a tournament growing in all directions. Prudential Assurance had boosted their sponsorship fee to £1 million, a tenfold increase on their commitment to the inaugural event only eight years before; and the ICC had expanded the format, introducing a double round at the group stage, so teams in the two groups of four would play each other not once, but twice.

Announcing this decision, officials explained how, bearing in mind how bad weather had affected the ICC Trophy, they wanted to ensure that rain did not distort the World Cup. 'If there is one round of group games,' they said, 'a team could have two matches rained off and effectively be eliminated.'

This became the party line, and the formal press release made no mention of the fact that an increase in the number of matches, from 15 to 27, would prompt a substantial growth in gate receipts. However, the move was evidently motivated by the prospect of greater profits. An often impoverished sport had identified its World Cup as a cash cow, and it was simply seeking a more efficient means of milking.

The system worked. Blessed by generally fine weather (only three of the 27 matches were not completed in one day), the 1983 World Cup was watched by 233 081 paying spectators, compared to a total attendance of 132 076 four years earlier. Organisers were eventually able to proclaim a net profit in excess of £1,1 million, which was distributed to national associations throughout the cricketing world.

While such financial success was welcomed, and the benefits were far-reaching, it was widely recognised that the long-term health of the World Cup hinged on its success as a sporting spectacle. The event needed to be exciting and unpredictable, needed to engage emotions from Scarborough to Sydney.

Put bluntly, if the West Indians continued to obliterate all opposition, the ICC feared televisions would be switched off, the value of broadcast rights would fall, advertisers and sponsors would lose interest, and this still young and vulnerable event would rapidly start to struggle and fade. The concept may be hard to conceive, but in 1983 the tournament was far from an established entry on the calendar.

In an ideal world, the third World Cup would start with a shock. In reality, it seemed almost impossible to identify any match on the schedule as being likely to provide a surprise result.

The opening day of matches in Group B was a case in point.

At Old Trafford, the West Indians were preparing to demolish India, who had lost five of their six previous World Cup matches, and only ever beaten East Africa; and at Trent Bridge Australia looked forward to an easy start to their campaign against the unheralded country 'hicks' from Zimbabwe.

Everyone agreed: no chance of a shock either in Manchester or in Nottingham.

The start was delayed by drizzle at Old Trafford, but as India battled to 79 for three on a damp pitch the match appeared to be following the anticipated script. Then middle-order batsman Yashpal Sharma opened his shoulders and thumped a brisk 89, and India reached 262 for eight in 60 overs.

It wasn't a bad score. The news from Trent Bridge raised eyebrows as well.

Kim Hughes had won the toss and sent Zimbabwe in to bat. Wonderfully unfazed by the big occasion, the qualifiers made a careful start and then increased the tempo when Duncan Fletcher added 70 in 15 overs with Curran, and struck another 75 in 12 overs with Butchart. With the Australians managing to drop no fewer than five straightforward catches, Zimbabwe advanced to 239 for six in 60 overs.

That wasn't a bad score either.

It was becoming an intriguing day.

Back in Manchester, the West Indian openers launched their run chase efficiently, but Greenidge was run out in the 14th over and, unexpectedly, the Indian seamers began to contain and frustrate. The champions had tentatively reached 67 for two in 22 overs when rain forced an early close.

Sensationally, the Australians were being ambushed in Nottingham. The Zimbabweans fielded as though they had waited their whole lives for this opportunity. In many ways, they had; they bowled with vigour, held every catch, and showed no respect at all for their celebrated opponents.

Kepler Wessels made a defiant 76, but his team-mates meekly processed from pavilion to pitch and back to pavilion.

When Rodney Marsh prepared to face the first ball of the 60th and last over, Australia still needed 23 runs to win. The wicketkeeper clubbed that delivery for six, but there was to be no last gasp reprieve. Amid amazing scenes at Trent Bridge, the amateur outsiders beat the Australians by 13 runs.

Fletcher had enjoyed a fantastic day. A Lancashire League player, destined to be England's coach, he had followed an unbeaten 69 by taking four wickets for 42, and was named Man of the Match.

'We might have been complacent,' Hughes reflects, 'and we didn't know much about Zimbabwe, but the truth is we were outplayed on the day. It was a pretty humbling experience.'

Perhaps the Indian players took heart from watching highlights from Nottingham on television. Whatever the reason, Kapil Dev's team appeared irresistible when they resumed their match against the West Indies the next morning. They crucially dismissed Viv Richards early on, and never looked back.

All of a sudden, the World Cup was being turned upside down. The odds-on favourites were reduced to a staggering 157 for nine and, although Roberts and Garner added 71 for the last wicket, the surprise result was written into history when Garner strayed beyond his crease and was stumped by Kirmani.

India had defeated the West Indies by 34 runs.

'Please repeat,' asked the disbelieving copy typists in Fleet Street.

India had defeated the West Indies by 34 runs.

Correct.

The Group B standings showed India and Zimbabwe in the top two places, ahead of the West Indies and Australia. There was a long way to go, but people sat up and took notice. This was exactly what the World Cup needed, a shock to the system; and the tournament was up and running.

Clive Lloyd's team may also have benefited from the jolt, for they recovered from their opening defeat by winning their next five group matches and once again finished top, easing into the semi-finals. Overwhelming victory margins of 101 runs, eight wickets, 66 runs, seven wickets and ten wickets – including mighty centuries for Greenidge and Richards – ensured the odds-on favourites remained the odds-on favourites.

Zimbabwe, in contrast, lost their five remaining group matches, although their rugged, positive approach to the game and their outstanding fielding won applause around the country; and there were several moments when Houghton's eager team did threaten to injure professional pride once again.

They set the West Indies a target of 218 to win at Worcester, and quickly dismissed Haynes and Richards to leave the champions reeling at 23 for two. But Cinderella didn't get to the ball: Greenidge and Gomes added 196 for the third wicket, and calmly eased their side to victory by eight wickets.

Houghton's team also played their part in what unfolded as the most remarkable day of cricket in this, or perhaps in any, World Cup. The Zimbabwe versus India game may not have leapt out from the schedule, but a crowd of 6 000 at the small Tunbridge Wells ground were left blinking in amazement.

As the crowd gathered in marquees or eagerly hired red-and-white striped deck chairs, at just 50p for the day, Kapil Dev won the toss and decided to bat on what looked a reasonable pitch.

Forty-two frenetic minutes later the Indian captain returned to the middle, coming in to bat at No. 6 with his team standing at four wickets for nine runs during the tenth over. Rawson and Curran were moving the ball in both directions and wreaking havoc. After 12 overs, India were 17 for five.

Kapil leaned on his bat at the non-striker's end and drew breath. Back home, across India, many millions of radios were being shaken in anger. Was this possible? Seventeen for five?

The young captain calmly assessed the situation and proceeded to play the innings of his life. Cautiously at first, playing straight and true, he compiled partnerships with Roger Binny and Madan Lal that dragged India to a position of relative respectability at 140 for eight after 44 overs.

Dev then erupted. There is no other word. The batsman at the opposite end, Syed Kirmani, simply joined the crowd in marvelling at a single-handed destruction of the Zimbabwe attack. Driving and hooking with grace and awesome power, Dev pummelled 102 runs in a record ninth-wicket stand of 126.

India finished with 266 for eight from 60 overs, of which their captain had scored 175 not out, including no fewer than 16 boundaries and half a dozen sixes. Sunil Gavaskar, his predecessor as captain and supposed rival, met Kapil as he walked off the field, and handed him a glass of water. Yes, the match was played at the edge of the square. Yes, one boundary was invitingly short. Yes, it was an epic innings.

Dave Houghton was not giving up. 'OK, he played well,' the determined captain urged his team between innings, 'but there are runs in this pitch. We can win this. Let's get on with it.'

Zimbabwe prospered to 44 without loss, but their inexperience at this level caused two run-outs and, at 113 for six, their hopes were fading. Curran raised their hopes again with a stylish 73, but when he was tamely caught off the splice the courageous amateurs quickly slipped to 235 all out.

As soon as the last wicket fell, and a 31-run victory was secured, Kapil Dev fell to the ground and kissed the turf. Such antics were rare in Tunbridge Wells, but it had been that kind of day. The only regret for India's hero was that BBC cameramen had been on strike, and there was no TV record of his innings; however, Kapil found a supporter who had filmed the match on home video, and later bought the tape.

That evening at the hotel, the captain studied the situation in Group B and realised that his team still needed to win their last group match, against Australia in Chelmsford, to qualify for the semi-finals.

Kim Hughes was aware of the maths as well. His team was bitterly divided, disgruntled and disillusioned but, even with only two wins from five matches so far, it was still possible for them to beat India and, by virtue of a faster overall run rate, squeeze through to a place in the last four.

Recovering from their opening defeat against Zimbabwe and a subsequent thrashing by the West Indies, the Australians had dropped Dennis Lillee and promptly defeated India by 162 runs. The great fast bowler and his famous partner Jeff Thomson appeared shadows of their former selves, trundling in at not much more than medium pace and posing little threat. For both men, this was a tournament too far.

At the 1983 World Cup the infamous 'Lilian Thomson' was cast as a little old lady with no teeth. She had, nonetheless, not lost her tongue, and it wagged in dissent. The relationship between Lillee and Hughes harked back to an incident that occurred when they both played for Western Australia, and had deteriorated to a point at which the fast bowler spent one net session in England bowling bouncers at his captain.

Yet the Australians eked out a revenge victory over Zimbabwe, and an improved performance in losing to the West Indies at Lord's inspired the hope that they could defeat India and survive. They would have to do so, however, without Hughes, who had torn a hamstring at Lord's and withdrawn.

Vice-captain David Hookes, a middle-order batsman, led the team and started well, winning the toss and sending India in to bat. Not long into the innings, Australian 12th man Kepler Wessels jogged out to the pitch to relay a constructive tactical suggestion from Hughes, watching in the pavilion.

Rod Marsh, a staunch member of Lillee's faction, saw red. 'Tell bloody Hughes,' raged the wicketkeeper, 'that if he wants to run the bloody show, he should play in the bloody match.'

The Indians reached a middling 247 all out in 45.5 overs, with extras the second-highest score at 37, but such a battling team performance proved more than adequate. Australia made a decent start, but were undone by the seaming, swinging medium pace of Roger Binny. From 46 for one they collapsed to 78 for seven, finally being dismissed for 129 and shuffling shamefaced back to their London hotel.

Later that evening, several Australian players were sitting in the bar when they saw Hughes arrive in the foyer, dressed in his formal blazer. They asked if he was going to another function. No, he replied, I'm heading to the airport. Why, they asked. I'm flying home, the captain replied. The rest of the squad gradually returned to Australia in dribs and drabs, travelling as they had played, alienated from one another.

'It had been an unhappy tour,' Allan Border reflected, resolving to make amends in 1987.

England had hit the ground running in Group A, posting a winning score of 322 for six in an opening win against New Zealand, and producing another powerful batting performance against Sri Lanka in Taunton when David Gower scored a splendid 130. The blond left-hander struck a dozen boundaries and five sixes, including two sweet blows over the pavilion, batting with what the Olympic champion Harold Abrahams described in the Oscar-winning film *Chariots of Fire* as 'the effortless ease of gods'.

Willis's increasingly assured team then overcame Pakistan by eight wickets and looked forward to a fourth successive victory, versus New Zealand at Edgbaston, but the Kiwis would be no pushover, buoyed by a crucial win over Pakistan when Hadlee reduced the opposition to nought for three.

The English batting stalled on this overcast day in Birmingham. The selectors had experimented with Ian Botham at No. 3, but the out-of-form all-rounder made only 12, and Gower was left to produce another elegant, unbeaten 92 in coaxing the total to what seemed an adequate 234 all out.

Willis steamed in, removed Turner and Edgar with three on board, and appeared to have set his team on course to victory. However, Howarth's calm 60 built the foundation for Jeremy Coney and Hadlee to accelerate the run chase, and in the end Bracewell hit the winning runs off the penultimate ball.

Pakistan had been struggling to find their form, and this gifted, established side came perilously close to defeat against Sri Lanka. Only Imran Khan's century rescued their innings from 41 for four to a decent total of 235 all out in 60 overs. Then the improving 'Slankies' launched a confident pursuit: at one stage, they needed only 102 more runs from 20 overs with eight wickets in hand . . . it seemed easy.

Now Abdul Qadir stepped forward and leaped into the breach. The spinner took three wickets in the space of eight balls, and as the dominoes tumbled, seven wickets fell for 57 runs. A last-wicket stand between De Mel and John added a further 37 runs, but their achievement only emphasised Sri Lanka's missed opportunity. The Pakistanis, gratefully and fortunately, squeaked home to victory by seven runs.

All of a sudden, the group seemed wide open.

England kept their focus, recovered their form, reached Pakistan's target of 233 for the loss of only three wickets at Old Trafford, and confirmed their qualification for the semi-finals.

New Zealand lost their nerve in Derby on the same day. Reduced to 116 for nine by Sri Lanka, they were dismissed for 181 and beaten by five wickets with eight overs to spare. This careless defeat effectively granted the Pakistanis one last chance to find their form and seize a place in the last four.

It was all they needed.

Pakistan needed not only to beat New Zealand in their last group match, but also to score quickly enough to give them a better run rate than their rivals. Imran's team batted first, and an unbroken stand of 147 in 18 madcap overs between Zaheer Abbas and the captain helped them to reach 261 for three. Striking at the heart of their opponents' morale, they had pillaged 47 runs from Hadlee's last five overs.

The New Zealanders still reckoned the target was gettable, and even though they lost wickets regularly batsman after batsman arrived at the crease, chipped in, scampered singles, struck occasional boundaries, and kept the team in the hunt. Coney again led the charge: 85 were required off the last ten overs, 53 off the last five; finally, with one wicket standing, 13 runs were needed off the last over.

Trent Bridge was a hive of excitement, and the Pakistan fielding had become hysterical. Players shouted at one another, everybody was expressing opinions about everything; yet amid this turmoil Imran stood calm and aloof, imploring his team somehow to remain calm and focused.

Coney drove the first ball of the final over towards mid-on, where Javed Miandad swooped and hurled a wild throw way past his wicketkeeper. The batsmen turned to run the overthrow, but Imran had skipped to his left and, keeping his head while all about him were losing theirs, he retrieved the ball and calmly sent a throw to wicketkeeper Khan, who caught Coney fractionally short of his ground.

While Pakistan celebrated, the gallant New Zealander hung his head. In the end, his team had paid a heavy price for their unexpected defeat against Sri Lanka at Derby.

Imran Khan led his team to face the West Indies in the semi-final at the Oval, hoping his players would be spurred to make the most of their fortunate progress. In the event, Miandad was missing with flu and most of the other players turned up only in name. Mohsin Khan played through 57 of the 60 overs, and Zaheer hit a brisk 30, but a wretched batting effort was reflected in the total of 184 for eight.

Greenidge and Haynes launched the chase and, when both were dismissed, Richards and Gomes arrived to put Pakistan, and the disappointed crowd, quickly out of their misery. The West Indians cruised into a third successive World Cup final, winners by eight wickets with 11.2 overs to spare.

England prepared to face India in the other semi-final at Old Trafford, confident of reaching their second final in a row, and the home crowd was soon in good spirits. Sent in to bat, openers Chris Tavare and Graeme Fowler raced to 69 without loss in the 17th over, and seemed set for a big score.

Then, inexplicably, the innings became bogged down in the clawing quicksand of India's clever, persistent medium-pace attack. Roger Binny and Mohinder Amarnath settled into their monotonous rhythm, and the overs started to slip by. An hour passed without a boundary. Batting started to seem very hard. As the runs dried up, so the crowd became restless, brows furrowed, and the pressure increased.

Once the openers had fallen, Gower played a frustratingly airy shot, Lamb looked to have settled but was needlessly run out, Gatting was bowled through the gap, and amid extreme frustration England spluttered and scrapped to reach an unsatisfactory 213 in 60 overs. The batting guns that had fired so impressively during the group matches had simply failed to perform on the big semi-final occasion.

Willis realised that his bowlers had some work to do, and they dismissed Gavaskar and Srikkanth before India had reached 50, but Amarnath and Yashpal settled cautiously. Both batsmen survived confident LBW appeals, turned down by Englishmen Oslear and Evans in an age when the umpires needed only to be good rather than nominally 'neutral', and they began to grow in confidence, accelerating the chase.

The phlegmatic Amarnath had taken two for 46 with the ball, and now he began to frustrate England with the bat, stepping down the wicket and driving Allott for six. He was dismissed for 46, but the end was not far away. Yashpal and Patil promptly added 63 runs in only nine overs, and the England players had accepted their fate long before Yashpal hit the winning runs with five overs and two balls to spare.

Delighted Indian supporters flooded across Old Trafford, and the day ended with the intolerable spectacle of umpire Don Oslear brandishing a stump to defend himself from the hordes.

All was quiet in the England dressing room afterwards. A talented, confident team had failed to fulfil its potential, and had let themselves down. Willis was blamed for poor captaincy, and Botham was blamed for poor form, but the entire squad knew a golden opportunity had evaporated.

'India?' gasped one distressed supporter. 'How on earth could we lose to India?'

'And the final will be a walkover now,' said his friend.

'It will be hardly worth watching.'

Over London NW8, 25 June 1983 dawned blue and bright, and a capacity crowd of 24 609 packed into Lord's. The ideal stage was set for an ideal World Cup final . . . at least, it would have been ideal if England had won through to play the West Indies. Most spectators hoped the Indians would put up a decent fight, but very few expected to witness anything other than a Caribbean cakewalk.

Clive Lloyd won the toss and predictably sent the Indians in to bat. A murmur of disappointment rippled around Lord's because most of the crowd wanted the West Indies to bat first, thus extending the entertainment for as long as possible. Everybody knew that if India batted first and collapsed, Lloyd could have the Cup in his hands by mid-afternoon; and the match tickets had been too expensive for that.

There was no such pessimism back in India where, with the time ticking on towards five in the afternoon, excited crowds had begun to gather in the streets of vast cities and tiny villages alike. For hundreds of millions of ordinary people on the sub-continent, the only way to watch television was to huddle around a screen set up on a table outside a shop, or placed on a platform in a public space.

With amazing providence, long before anyone knew the Indian side would be involved, it had previously been arranged that the 1983 World Cup final would become the first complete day of cricket played overseas ever to be broadcast live on Indian television. The timing was faultless.

And so the nation stopped . . .

One particular group of firemen was called to deal with a blazing office building, and in the course of their duties they realised that their crane gave them not only a perch above the flames but also an unimpeded view of a television screen in an adjacent home. So the men extinguished the inferno, removed their protective clothing, and settled down to spend the rest of the day watching the cricket on television.

Kapil Dev stood in the middle of the Indian dressing room and told his players to believe in their ability to win the final. 'It doesn't matter what anyone else thinks,' he told them, wide eyes ablaze. The youthful captain reminded his team of what they had learned on tour to the West Indies prior to the World Cup, how they must not be afraid to go for their strokes against the fast bowlers, and how their seamers would seek to frustrate the flamboyant, stroke-playing batsmen by giving them no pace on the ball.

'We know these guys so well,' he concluded, smiling. 'We know how strong they are, and we also know we can beat them. Just remember what happened 16 days ago at Old Trafford.'

Silence. Kapil was right: beating them once proved they could do it again.

Sunil Gavaskar and Krishnamachari Srikkanth launched the innings circumspectly, but with only two runs on the board in the third over, Gavaskar was caught behind off Roberts. Srikkanth watched the legendary batsman head slowly towards the pavilion, and immediately decided he would throw all caution to the wind. This was a World Cup final, a one-off. Damn the consequences, he would play his strokes.

Roberts bowled . . . Srikkanth flat-batted him into the pavilion rails; then again . . . Srikkanth pulled him into the grandstand for six; and again . . . Srikkanth hooked immaculately for four.

The Lord's crowd loved every minute of this startling assault; and every time he dispatched the ball to the boundary, this rampant opening batsman would smile awkwardly and nod his head from side to side in the typical

Indian fashion. He hammered seven boundaries and one six, but this spectacular firework of an innings could not last and Srikkanth was eventually extinguished, LBW to Marshall for 38.

Amarnath and Yashpal took up the challenge, guiding the total to 90 for two in the 22nd over. Discernible relief spread around the ground: the final was unfolding as a contest. And in the feverish streets of New Delhi, the popular conviction that India would triumph grew stronger than ever.

Maybe, just maybe, against every prediction . . . er, no . . . maybe not.

Yashpal was caught off Gomes, Amarnath was bowled by Holding, Kapil crashed three superb boundaries but then drove Gomes tamely and was caught at long-on for 15, Azad survived three balls, Binny went for two, and in seven blurred overs, India had collapsed from 90 for two to 130 for seven.

MCC members sat back and tried to praise the West Indian bowling, but a pall of disappointment settled over the crowd: the final now seemed as predictably one-sided as everyone had feared. Patil anchored the wagging tail, with Madan Lal, Kirmani and Sandhu all pluckily reaching double figures, but the Indian total of 183 all out in 54.4 overs appeared totally inadequate, an easy target for the favourites.

Some West Indians were grinning as they walked off the field, clapping Andy Roberts off for taking three wickets. In their minds, maybe, the job was done. In fairness, everybody thought so. Between innings, queues formed beside the Lord's payphones as people made plans for the early evening.

Greenidge and Haynes looked cheerful as they emerged to launch the innings, and even when Greenidge was bowled for one, shouldering arms to Sandhu, the general response was not excitement that the final could yet be a genuine battle, but pleasure that Viv Richards would have more time to bat.

The hero of the 1979 World Cup final appeared to relish the grand stage once again, slipping quickly into his rhythm, accelerating the run rate. Twice he whipped decent deliveries from Kapil Dev sizzling to the square leg boundary. The Indian captain recalls: 'My line was just outside the off stump, and I was aiming to get Viv out with my outswinger. Both these balls looked pretty good, and each time I threw up my arms expecting an edge, only to turn and see the umpire waving his arm to signal another boundary.'

Richards dashed to 31 in as many balls, and the West Indians appeared to be cruising to victory at 50 for one when India's second- and third-string bowlers unexpectedly applied the brakes. Madan Lal and Roger Binny settled into a steady line and length and started to produce exceptional swing. Umpire 'Dickie' Bird remembers thinking to himself, if only India had made 240, they might have had a chance.

Kapil Dev also sensed the tide was beginning to turn, and as he waited to hand the ball to Lal at the start of another over from the Nursery End, the Indian captain casually approached the umpire.

'You know,' Kapil said, 'I think we will win this match after all.'

'I see,' Bird chirped.

'Yes, they think it's too easy.'

'Do they?'

'They'll get themselves out if we keep the ball up and bowl straight.'

With that, the captain passed the ball to Lal, clapped his hands, walked resolutely across to his place just wide of mid-on, and urged his players to keep their concentration.

'Come on, guys!'

The following 42 minutes of play stunned the sporting world.

Haynes drove carelessly, uppishly at Lal and was caught by Binny at cover; Clive Lloyd strode out to join Richards and promptly pulled his hamstring in setting off for his first single. After some discussion, Haynes was recalled as a runner for his captain. The final was assuming its own momentum.

Richards's instinctive response was to attack and regain control. He pulled Lal towards mid-wicket, but the ball skied off the top edge. Kapil took responsibility, sprinted backwards to get under the ball, and beneath the shadow of the Father Time wind vane took an outstanding catch. Richards angrily tucked his bat under his arm and departed the scene; he had struck seven boundaries in his innings of 33.

'Come on, guys,' implored Kapil, the wind at his back.

Gomes didn't last long, spooning Lal to Gavaskar, and minutes before tea a clearly uncomfortable Lloyd failed to get forward to Binny, and his timid drive was safely held by Kapil Dev. The cluster of Indian supporters in the Mound Stand, like many millions of their compatriots at home, hailed every wicket with a roar of delight, but the rest of the Lord's crowd seemed stunned, almost unable to take it all in.

The West Indies had crumbled from 50 for one to 66 for five.

Procession? What procession? This was now a dogfight.

Kapil prowled around the field, leading by example, contesting every run as though it was the last; and the West Indian batsmen, so haughty and self-assured in their pomp, now appeared nervous and exposed, as they staggered to tea at 75 for five. When play resumed, a single had been added when wicketkeeper Kirmani, diving athletically to his right, held a superb catch to dismiss Bacchus for eight.

At 76 for six, the 'impossible' now looked almost probable; yet the champions were not ready to concede their title. Jeff Dujon and Malcolm Marshall doggedly went back to basics, getting behind the line, pushing ones here, scampering a two there. They hit one boundary in an hour, but they occupied the crease and steadfastly edged closer to the target . . . into three figures, past 110, on and on and on.

Order was being restored. At 119 for six, with only 65 runs required from 18 overs and four wickets still standing, the West Indians appeared to have weathered the Indian storm.

Kapil needed a breakthrough, and he called 'Jimmy' Amarnath into the attack. This apparently innocuous seamer, a quiet man whose father, Lala, had scored India's first-ever Test century, marked out his run-up. His career had been threatened when his skull was fractured by a Hadlee bouncer in 1979, but he completed a full rehabilitation, recovered his nerve, and regained his place in the Indian side.

Now, at the business end of the 1983 World Cup final . . . this was his moment.

Amarnath bowled at Dujon, a drifting delivery just short of a length, deceiving the batsman into playing down the wrong line. As the bails rattled, the Indian fielders leaped with delight and, far away, a soulful roar of approval rumbled ecstatically through the streets and alleys of Calcutta.

In his next over, Amarnath ran in again, bowling to Marshall. This time the ball moved just a fraction off the seam, just enough to nick an audible edge, and Gavaskar held the fizzing catch at slip. Another roar of joy echoed around the sub-continent. It was happening. Kapil brought himself back to bowl; frantic to finish the job, the captain produced a ball that cut back and struck Roberts on the pad.

An impoverished nation screamed: 'Howzat!'

Umpire Barry Meyer raised his finger, and the scoreboard flapped on to 126 for nine.

Three overs later, his dark eyes glazed in recognition of the moment, Amarnath bowled again, a floating slow delivery that struck Michael Holding on the pad, square and adjacent.

'Howzat!' Amarnath enquired.

Umpire Bird raised his finger and, his sparkling Yorkshire eyes almost smiling, declared: 'That's out and, gentlemen, may I thank you for a wonderful game of cricket.'

The West Indies had been dismissed for 140, in 52 overs.

India had won by 43 runs.

World champions!

Amarnath seized a stump and, brandishing the prized souvenir of the greatest day of his life, ran for the sanctuary of the pavilion. For his battling 26 and his three for 12 at the death, the unsung all-rounder was declared Man of the Match, just as he had been after the semi-final against England. His successes reflected all the resourceful, courageous, intelligent qualities of India's champion team.

It was 7.28 on a warm summer evening in London, two minutes to midnight in India. At 1 am, within an hour of the last wicket falling, a government spokesman in New Delhi declared that the new day, Sunday 26 June 1983, would be a public holiday throughout India, set aside for national euphoria.

In the middle of the night, in sprawling cities and dusty settlements, in several hundred million hearts, this moment of triumph would stand alone in the history of Indian cricket. It was a triumph, plucked from the most outrageous of boyhood dreams, turned into reality at Lord's in London.

Kapil Dev stood at the apex of joy. He had taken only one wicket and scored just 15 runs in the final, but nobody doubted his central, inspiring role in India's victory. In the tournament overall he had averaged 60,60 with the bat and taken 12 wickets at an average of 20,41; as an improving captain, he had fired no more than a reasonably talented team with the guts to stand up and beat the world.

Beaming broadly, the fast bowler, big-hitting batsman and captain stepped forward on the balcony of the pavilion and received the Prudential Cup from Sir Anthony Tuke, MCC President.

For once, Clive Lloyd stood to one side and, ever the gentleman, applauded the Indians as they filed past to collect their medals. Lloyd subsequently announced his retirement as West Indies captain, but declined to seek excuses in defeat. 'Of course, we are very disappointed,' he told the world's media, 'but we didn't bat well today and India deserved their victory. We can have no complaints.'

India *did* deserve to win; they could have done no more. They might have been 66-1 outsiders before the tournament began, several thousand to one when they were 17 for five against Zimbabwe, and at least 100-1 between innings in the final; yet the fact remained that they had defeated Australia, the odds-on West Indians (twice), and the hosts, England.

Matthew Engel, writing in the *Guardian*, justifiably pointed out that 'people outside India will be less free with the title "world champions" than they have been during the West Indies' reign', but he astutely concluded his article with the statement that, for the game at large, 'the shock will do us all good.'

The Indian team returned home as heroes. Fêted up and down the country, the players were each given an apartment as reward for making their country so happy and so proud.

Whatever the future held – and, in fact, within six months, the Indian team was being roundly criticised for losing to the same West Indian side – Kapil Dev and his team-mates had become unassailable, forever cast as world champions, their glory preserved in history, their names revered in eternity.

Kapil Dev

The 15-year-old from the small village of Haryana outside Chandigarh was scraping the rice from his plate, eating the last grains one by one. He glumly complained that he was still hungry.

'Wasn't that enough food?' asked the coach at the youth cricket camp in Bombay.

'No,' replied young Kapildev Ramlal Nikhanj.

'You're just tired because you've spent the whole morning bowling in the nets.'

'I suppose so.'

'You shouldn't be so hard on yourself.'

'Why not?'

'Well, you must be realistic. India never produces decent fast bowlers.'

The teenager bristled, and stomped out of the dining room. The surge of angry indignation he felt at this precise moment would stay with him, and motivate him, for the next two decades.

Through gruelling days in the field, through arduous hours in the nets, through each pounding over after each pounding over, he drove himself to prove the youth coach in Bombay wrong.

Why not?

He knew Indian cricket was renowned for its skilful, wristy batsmen and its crafty, cunning spinners, but he could not understand why this vast, cricket-crazy country should not also be able to produce world-class fast bowlers. So the pitches were flat and dusty. So what? He would show them.

Tall and lean, Kapil Dev worked hard, making his way up the grades to the point when, aged only 19, he was selected to make his Test debut for India against Pakistan at Faisalabad in 1978.

Sadiq Mohammad took guard on the first morning, hardly noticing the rookie fast bowler marking out his run-up. The first ball was a bouncer, soaring, fast . . . the old pro rocked on his heels, blinked. The crowd gasped. Wicketkeeper Kirmani clapped his gloves and shouted for more. 'Shabhash! Aur ek!'

Sunil Gavaskar had heard about the youngster's potential, but this was extraordinary. As one of many bruised Indian Test batsmen who for so long had suffered a torrent of bouncers because their bowlers had no capacity to retaliate, this scene felt like something out of a dream.

Kapil Dev was now moving in again, smooth, swift, lithe, and he bowled . . . another short delivery, higher, faster. Sadiq ducked again, and the crowd roared. The opener had seen enough. Walking towards the pavilion, he removed his green cap and signalled for the 12th man to bring a helmet.

Gavaskar grinned. 'That single gesture transformed Indian cricket,' the captain recalls. 'As Sadiq called for his helmet, it felt to us as though he was telling the world that, at last, India had found a bowler capable of generating genuine speed. Our entire team grew in stature. It was remarkable.'

The second ball of Dev's fourth over struck Sadiq on the helmet, and two balls later the opener edged a stinging catch to Gavaskar at slip. Kapil had taken his first Test wicket, and embarked upon a record-breaking career that would establish him as one of the sport's greatest all-rounders.

Statistics expose only the bones of his legend: he played in 131 Tests and 225 one-day internationals for India between 1978 and 1994. His 434 wickets and 5 248 runs in Test cricket are unmatched. He led the team 108 times, and until his last year never missed a single match through injury. The World Cup triumph in 1983 and the series win in England three years later sparkle as jewels in his crown.

Yet Kapil Dev is remembered for his spirit as much as his stats: the spirit that shone in the Madras Test of 1978, when he matched the West Indian fast bowlers bumper for bumper; the spirit that shone one evening at Lord's in 1990 when, with India needing 16 runs to save the follow-on and one wicket standing, he resolved the crisis by crashing Eddie Hemmings for four boundaries in succession.

He was sometimes tangled in the political trauma of Indian cricket, being appointed, sacked, reappointed and sacked again as captain, but his exploits on the field and film-star looks secured a place in several hundred million hearts on the sub-continent. 'Kapil was the one guy who carried the Indian flag onto the field,' reflects Viv Richards. 'I admired him because he was a fighter and proud of his country.'

In 1999, towards the end of an unproductive spell as coach to the Indian team, this almost unblemished image was sullied when the icon was named in a match-fixing scandal. Nothing was proven, and in a harrowing television interview, with tears in his eyes, Kapil denied all charges. His reputation seemed to be restored when he was named, ahead of Gavaskar and Sachin Tendulkar, as India's cricketer of the century.

Certainly it is to be hoped, and trusted, that the image of Kapil Dev that long endures is not that of an angry, disillusioned hero withdrawing from any future involvement in the game, sobbing uncontrollably as he denied allegations of corruption . . . but that of the beaming captain raising the World Cup at Lord's.

The disgruntled 15-year-old, who dedicated the best years of his life to proving that India could, against the odds, produce a world-class fast bowler, surely deserves nothing less.

Chapter Six

Big Day Out

He loved his Grandad, and he loved cricket.

'But please,' Jason begged, 'can't we go to the one-day international instead?'

An uneasy silence descended on the family meal.

The old man had suggested that, as a Christmas present, he would take his 14-year-old grandson to the opening day of the fourth Test between Australia and Pakistan at the Melbourne Cricket Ground. Boxing Day at the MCG! Sport just didn't get any better than that. At least, he didn't think so.

'But, Grandad,' the boy protested, 'five-day cricket is so boring!'

'Jason,' his father intervened, 'just calm down.'

More silence. The old man recalled perfect days from his own youth. Huge crowds packing the MCG, men wearing suits and hats, excited boys being passed over shoulders to the front, Bradman, Ponsford and the rest, heroes in baggy green caps, real Test cricket: it didn't seem boring at the time.

'Grandad, please. The World Series is starting soon, and the opening match is Australia against the West Indies in a one-dayer at the MCG on 8 January. Let's go and watch that.'

'All right, all right.'

So the kindly grandfather bought two tickets in the south stand, and soon after breakfast on Wednesday 8 January 1984 the pair set off for the stadium. They arrived to find all the car parks full and the pavements packed with people making their way to the MCG. One-day cricket was booming in Australia, and officials were predicting a crowd of somewhere around 75 000 for the series opener.

Jason lapped up the vibe, and asked: 'Do you really not like this kind of cricket?'

'No, it's good,' said the old man, opting to suffer in silence rather than spoil the treat.

In truth, he found limited overs cricket just so . . . well, limited. Batsmen didn't build innings because they were limited to slogging; bowlers didn't try to take wickets because they were limited to saving runs; and even the best captains rarely tried anything new because the game was limited to a few formulae. For someone who had spent most of his life watching Tests, this predictable bash was hard to take.

It just wasn't the same. He realised times had changed, and he knew nothing can ever stay the same (even though, in quiet moments, he often wished it did). He did not share these views with his grandson, whose outlook seemed so far removed from his own.

The West Indians won the toss and reached an adequate 221 in their 50 overs, due largely to Clive Lloyd, who clouted an impressive 65. The veteran West Indian captain had dispatched one boundary to the rope right in front of where they were sitting, and to his grandfather's horror, Jason had jumped over the fence, collected the ball and waved at the television cameras before hurling it back to a fielder.

'What did you do that for?'

'Everyone does that, Grandad,' Jason replied, breathless and elated.

'Yes, but you shouldn't climb over the fence. Don't you remember what happened to Terry Alderman last season in Perth? That was caused by some overexcited idiot running onto the field.'

Jason sat still and sullen. He did recall how the Australian fast bowler had collided with a spectator in the outfield during the first Test against England at the WACA in November 1982, and how he had been carried off the field on a stretcher, and how the injured shoulder kept him out of action for months.

'Sorry, Grandad,' the boy mumbled, just as the innings ended.

'It's OK,' the old man said. 'I know you think I'm being old-fashioned, but there used to be a saying that if something wasn't cricket, then it wasn't right and proper. For me, the game has always been defined by decent manners and good behaviour, and I hope it will represent the same things to you.'

'What about Trevor Chappell?'

'Exactly! That's my point! You think one-day cricket is so wonderful, but one-day cricket has encouraged a lack of discipline in the stands and a decline in standards on the field.'

Jason had rarely seen his grandfather so disturbed.

'All right, Grandad, I'm sorry.'

The old man calmed down, and reluctantly found his mind drifting back to 1 February 1981, that fateful day when he had sat in the selfsame grandstand at the MCG and watched Trevor Chappell and his brother Greg bring shame on themselves, on their team, on their country and on their sport.

Australia had been playing New Zealand in the third match of the best-of-five World Series final, and with the Kiwis needing 15 runs to win, the Australian captain called his younger brother to bowl the last over. As the crowd grew progressively more excited, Hadlee hit the first ball for four, but fell LBW to the second; Ian Smith nicked the third ball for two, drove the fourth ball for two, and was bowled by the fifth.

As Brian McKechnie arrived, needing to hit the last ball for six to tie the match, the old man remembered seeing the Chappell brothers huddled in discussion. Trevor Chappell said something to Umpire Neser, who instantly relayed the message to the batsmen. Rodney Marsh was also within earshot, and the experienced wicketkeeper had seemed to turn away in disgust at what he heard.

What on earth was going on?

Chappell eventually ran in to bowl the last ball, but abruptly stopped at the crease and astoundingly rolled the ball underarm along the ground. McKechnie, clearly livid, could only play forward defensively and, amidst a cacophony of boos and whistles, Australia were declared the winners by six runs.

The ensuing row involved both governments, and even after Greg Chappell had apologised for giving the ruthless instruction to his brother, even after the rules of cricket had been altered to outlaw underarm bowling, New Zealanders continued to insist Australians suffered from an underarm problem.

'That Chappell saga was a disgrace,' the grandfather said, snapping back to the present day.

'I thought it was funny,' said Jason, casually.

'No,' barked the old man, once again aware of the blood rising in his neck. 'That incident said everything about the essentially superficial, ethically corrupt nature of one-day cricket.'

This Christmas treat seemed to be souring, but the grandfather successfully brightened the mood when he presented his grandson with an extra present for the day, a book of cricketing facts. Jason thanked him, and eagerly dipped his head into the chapter relating to one-day cricket.

'Well, Grandad,' he began, warily returning to the subject that divided them, 'there wouldn't be a World Cup if we didn't have one-day cricket, and the World Cup has been a good thing.'

'That's true.'

'And it says here,' said Jason, reading on with confidence, 'the first modern World Cup was played by women. Did you know that, Grandad? There was a women's World Cup in 1973.'

'Er, really?'

'Yes, look. It says here: *Seven national teams gathered in London and competed on a league basis. It was pure luck that the last fixture, England against Australia, turned out to be a de facto final. A PE teacher, Enid Blackwell, scored a century and England won.* Can you believe that?'

'What?'

'England won!'

'Won what?'

'Grandad, are you listening to me?'

'Yes, Jason,' the old man said, gazing at the sky. 'I'm just worried about those clouds over there. They don't look too good, and they said there was a 30 per cent chance of rain. I hope we get through the match. What do you reckon? Do you think the Aussies can get 222 runs to win?'

As the West Indian players made their way out to field, the boy appeared less interested in the answer to the pressing question of the day, and more engrossed in his new book.

'Don't worry about the weather, Grandad,' he chirped. 'It says here that *Since the advent of one-day cricket, players have been more prepared to play in imperfect conditions.*'

The old man was just starting to wonder if the cricket book had been such a good idea.

'Really?'

'Yes, let me read you this. It says here: *David Hughes, the Lancashire captain, came out to bat late in the day of a classic Gillette Cup semi-final against Gloucestershire at Old Trafford, and noticed the umpire was growing concerned about the fading light. "What do you see?" asked the umpire pointedly. "The moon," Hughes replied, adding, "Well, how much further do you want to see?"* Get it, Grandad?'

'Yes, yes. OK, put the book away. Let's watch the match.'

'Just one more . . .'

'The book . . . away!'

The Australians were soon struggling against the West Indian pace attack, and when Greg Matthews was caught behind off Wayne Daniel, the home side had slumped to 44 for four.

The old man sat back in his chair and, privately contemplating how the early loss of wickets meant that yet another one-day match would now peter out in a wholly predictable way, he relaxed and started to enjoy what had become a warm summer's afternoon down by the River Yarra. Allan Border and Rod Marsh bravely tried to rally the run chase, but they always seemed a step or two off the pace.

'Grandad?'

'Yes?'

'What do you think of the Australian team wearing yellow clothing?'

'Not much. I prefer whites.'

'Just another depressing sign of the times, then?'

'Exactly.'

'Well, it says here: *The players of Oxford and Cambridge Universities respectively wore dark blue and light blue shirts when they played during the 1880s.* So, it's hardly a new thing.'

'OK.'

The old man had by now decided the cricket book was definitely not a good idea, but he smiled peacefully at his young grandson. Looking around, he saw families and young people enjoying themselves at the cricket, and after many years of steadily dwindling crowds, this was encouraging. Whatever his reservations, one-day cricket had brought the people back to the MCG, and he was grateful for that.

It was fun. He understood that. And his grandson enjoyed it. He knew that too.

Towards the end of the Australian innings, Rodney Hogg hammered a few boundaries and revived hopes of a dramatic twist in the tail, but the wickets continued to fall and, with Border left unbeaten on 84, the home side was eventually dismissed for a disappointing 194, defeated by 27 runs.

Midway through what had turned out to be the last over of the match, a few sections of the crowd started rising to their feet while shouting and throwing their arms up in the air. Jason noticed the activity on the opposite side of the MCG and said they were trying to start a Mexican Wave. His grandfather groaned.

After several futile launches, the wave finally began to roll through and around the MCG stands, and quickly approached the area where they were sitting. Jason assumed a crouched position, eagerly preparing to participate in the fun.

'Come on, Grandad!'

'Oh, what the hell,' the old man murmured as, at the right moment, grinning broadly, he rose to his feet, threw both his arms up in the air, and gave out a blood-curling primeval roar.

Jason turned to look at his grandfather, eyes wide in surprise, and he beamed with pride.

'I love my Grandad,' he thought, 'and I love cricket.'

Chapter Seven

The Fourth World Cup

Did you hear the one about the match that was delayed because the playing kit went missing?

True story.

India and Australia were ready to play the third one-day international in a series of five to commemorate the golden jubilee of the Ranji Trophy in 1984 but, with a capacity crowd already in their seats at Jamshedpur, the game could not start because the truck carrying the players' clothing and equipment had got lost on the road from the airport to the ground. Play began three hours late.

'And the Indians reckon they can stage the World Cup?' guffawed one representative, as he shuffled his papers in preparation for the ICC meeting at Lord's in July 1984.

'They lost the kit?' smirked his colleague. 'You must be joking.'

'I know. It's hilarious.'

Mr N.K.P. Salve was sitting across the polished oak table. Delegate from the Board for Control of Cricket in India, Cabinet Minister of Steel and Mines in the Indian Government, veteran of the freedom struggle against British colonial rule, he could hear what was being said and he was not laughing.

Round-faced and bespectacled, this established man was no stranger to such condescending, disdainful attitudes. Only the previous year, when India had secured a place in the World Cup final, his request for match tickets on behalf of two eminent visitors from Delhi had been abruptly rejected. He had not complained, but he was weary of being treated like a second-class citizen in the cricketing community.

'We'll show them we can host the World Cup,' Salve murmured to the colleague at his side.

'You think so?'

'I know so.'

Salve believed in the mission. Ever since the week after the World Cup final in 1983, when the ICC had invited its member nations to bid for the right to stage the next World Cup, he had fervently lobbied on behalf of the sub-continent. England's cricket officials had campaigned to host a fourth World Cup in succession, but on this the day of the ICC decision, the Indian felt cautiously confident.

'We have,' he told the meeting firmly, 'addressed every issue.'

Detractors had suggested a joint bid was impossible because the historic antagonism between India and Pakistan meant that, in practice, the two countries would not be able to co-operate as hosts . . . yet Salve worked tirelessly to develop a strong, trusting relationship with his counterparts in Lahore.

Critics had then claimed that, following Prudential's decision to end their long association with the World Cup in 1983, the relatively impoverished sub-continent would be unable to attract a new title sponsor able and willing to spend the £1,3m required to fund the event . . . yet Salve had identified a company called Reliance, the Bombay-based petrochemical and textile giant, and early discussions were promising.

Even then, cynics thought the Indian government would be unwilling to underwrite the overall cost of the event and would fail to guarantee the provision of foreign exchange . . . yet Salve's political relations were sound, and Prime Minister Rajiv Gandhi supplied the necessary assurances in writing.

He countered the widespread perception of chaos and confusion in India and Pakistan by eulogising the most enthusiastic and fanatical cricket supporters in the world. Facing a barrage of fast, head-high questions, the Indian delegate stood tall, and calmly hooked every bouncer to the boundary.

'As I say,' Salve stated quietly, 'we have addressed every issue.'

He concluded his presentation with a volley of numbers: prize money would be increased by 50 per cent; every ICC country competing in the tournament would be paid a minimum £75 000 plus expenses; and, even though hosts England had seen fit to claim 40 per cent of net profits from the previous three World Cups, India and Pakistan would be content to divide the financial spoils equally with their fellow ICC members.

Nobody was laughing now.

A vote was taken and it was resolved, by a margin of 16 to 12, that the 1987 World Cup would be jointly hosted by India and Pakistan. Salve smiled, and said thank you. England graciously endorsed the decision: 'As much as we love to host the World Cup in England,' announced Colin Cowdrey, 'we recognise it is for the wider benefit of cricket that the venue should be allowed to circulate.'

Preparations began to gather momentum. It was agreed that the 1983 format – two groups of four playing a double round, with the top two teams in each section advancing to the semi-finals, and then the final – would remain unchanged, and no fewer than 21 grounds were accepted as World Cup venues. In addressing potential problems with bad light, it was decided that every match would start at nine o'clock in the morning, and that innings would be reduced from the usual 60 overs to 50 overs per side.

With Indians and Pakistanis working together as efficiently as ever before, and probably since, innovative proposals to assemble an international panel of neutral umpires and to use 30-yard fielding circles at the 1987 World Cup were approved by the ICC. Everything appeared to be going well until the South African issue raised its head and, for an unsettling period, jeopardised the entire tournament.

Since 1981, the South African Cricket Union had been recruiting unofficial touring teams to sustain their game in isolation. Top players from England, Sri Lanka and the West Indies were furtively lured to the republic, accepting generous cheques as compensation for the bans that followed. However, as time passed, the likes of John Emburey and Graham Gooch served their suspensions and became eligible again.

Conflict loomed.

India had always stood among the most determined supporters of the sporting boycott, and government spokesmen indicated that visas would not be granted to any players with South African connections. Fuming cricket officials in New Zealand, England and Australia responded by stating that they would not accept any interference in team selection and, if any took place, they would withdraw from the World Cup.

World cricket was threatened by a racial split down the middle, with the Asians and West Indians on one side of the dispute, and the three 'white' countries on the other.

Salve remained calm in the crisis, seeking common ground between his fellow cabinet ministers in Delhi and his colleagues at the ICC. Throughout this dispute, he was strengthened by the resolution of Reliance, who had not only signed a £1,3m deal to become the new World Cup sponsors, but also declared that their commitment to the tournament would remain strong if any countries decided not to take part.

In the end, a compromise was agreed. The Indian government said it would grant entry visas to players who publicly renounced apartheid; Gooch and Emburey were happy to oblige.

All faces saved, the cricket could begin, and eight teams gradually arrived in Asia, each carrying genuine hope to what seemed the most openly contested World Cup so far. Anyone could win.

The West Indies were talented and captained by Viv Richards, playing in his fourth World Cup, but their pace attack looked less intimidating than usual. India and Pakistan were both capable of beating anyone, but remained fantastically unpredictable in front of their exuberant supporters.

England were streetwise and competitive, but undermined by the absence of Botham and Gower. New Zealand, as usual, would be nobody's pushovers, and the Australians, led by Allan Border, didn't seem to have much to offer beyond their traditional qualities of guts and determination.

Sri Lanka were improving but off the pace; and the field was completed by Zimbabwe, who had qualified impressively, beating Holland in the final of the ICC Trophy in July 1986, but were weakened by the departure of prodigy Graeme Hick to Worcestershire and the retirement of Duncan Fletcher.

Who would win?

It was anyone's guess.

The scramble to advance from Group A was defined, and perhaps even determined, by an extraordinary opening match between India and Australia at the Chepauk Stadium in Madras. Urged on by a delirious crowd, and looking to pick up where they had left off at Lord's four years earlier, the home team was set 271 to win and seemed to have the match under control at 207 for two with 13 overs left.

Bonfires were being lit in the grandstands to hail an important victory, but Craig McDermott returned for a second spell, claimed four wickets and turned the game on its head. Amid manic excitement, India reached the 50th and last over, with one wicket standing and still needing six runs to win.

Steve Waugh took the ball, and held his nerve . . . dot, two, single, single. Then he bowled Maninder Singh with the fifth ball of the over, and

Australia won a great match by a single run.

Border's team had suddenly forged self-belief in the seething furnace of Madras, and after a tense wobble against Zimbabwe, when the captain dug them out of a hole at 20 for two, they travelled to Indore, where their match against New Zealand seemed likely to be abandoned because of heavy rain.

Amazingly, the waters cleared to allow a 30-over slog, and this match boiled down to another tight finish with New Zealand needing just seven runs to win from the last over. Yet again, Steve Waugh took the ball, and yet again, he held his nerve . . . he had Martin Crowe caught for 58 off his first delivery, dismissed Ian Smith with the second, and conceded just a single off each of the next four balls.

Out of nowhere, Australia had become contenders.

Unheralded at the outset, they had prevailed in two tense finishes and headed the group with three wins in three matches, apparently destined for the semi-finals at least. In a Cricket World Cup, the margins between triumph and disaster would often be infinitesimally small: for Australia in 1987, the difference between yielding a boundary in the last over of these crucial early games and winning by a run or two (as they did) represented the difference between a humiliating flight home and the real prospect of glory.

India recovered impressively from their initial setback, owing much to the form of their opening batsman Navjot Sidhu, who achieved the unprecedented feat of scoring a half-century in each of his first four innings in one-day international cricket. Emphatic victories over New Zealand and Zimbabwe enabled Kapil Dev to tell an expectant nation that his side would definitely reach the semi-finals.

Hundreds of millions of Indians wanted more than that; they believed their side needed to win Group A and thereby qualify for the semi-final in Bombay, rather than face an awkward trip to Pakistan.

To achieve this goal, Kapil's team first had to defeat Australia in Delhi, where N.K.P. Salve sat in the VIP section and relished every minute as India's trio of spinners defended a score of 289, and then to complete the group matches with a better run rate than the Australians. This had boiled down to reaching a target of 222 in only 42 overs and two balls to beat New Zealand by a wide enough margin.

Sunil Gavaskar rose to the occasion. He was reaching the end of his wonderful career, and the infamously guarded opener chose this moment to erupt in a blaze of strokeplay. Crashing Ewan Chatfield for two sixes and two boundaries in one over, the legend raced to reach his century in 85 balls, and India cantered to their target with more than ten overs to spare. 'It was like bowling in the television highlights,' groaned Willie Watson, one of several battered and bruised New Zealand bowlers, afterwards.

So, India won the group and headed to Bombay with Kapil Dev's dream of retaining the World Cup in the final at Eden Gardens, Calcutta, on 8 November, still very much alive.

This spectacle of an entire nation focused on the World Cup, desperate for success, was matched across the border in Pakistan, where the home team was making progress in Group B.

Imran Khan's team opened the tournament with a match against Sri Lanka in Hyderabad. Edgy officials feared their big occasion would be ruined by a dust storm blowing in from the Thar desert, but in the end the only turbulence was provided by Javed Miandad, whose superb century helped Pakistan reach 267 for seven, and the home side eventually ran out comfortable winners by 15 runs.

The match provoked questions in the National Assembly when an opposition member rose to enquire why the Prime Minister was watching cricket instead of taking part in a debate.

'That's a matter for him,' replied the Deputy Speaker, clinically closing the discussion, primarily because his boss, the Speaker, was also in Hyderabad, enjoying the home victory.

Pakistan's campaign was up and running, carried on a tide of popular enthusiasm. A consensus seemed to spread throughout the country that, whatever happened, Imran Khan and his team would ultimately emerge triumphant in what the captain had said would be his last major tournament.

'It is meant to be!' people exclaimed in the streets of Karachi.

Even when Miandad was amazed to be given out LBW on home soil, and the team had struggled to reach 239 for seven against England in Rawalpindi, spinner Abdul Qadir stepped up to claim two wickets in one over, prompting the English to lose six wickets for 15 runs, and Pakistan won again.

They would not be denied.

Chasing 217 to beat the West Indies in Lahore, they collapsed to 110 for five but still managed to find a path away from disaster. Imran started the recovery with wicketkeeper Salim Yousuf, but both fell to Courtney Walsh and, with 52 000 exhilarated spectators bellowing encouragement, the last-wicket pair, Abdul Qadir and Saleem Jaffer, came together needing to score 12 runs from the last over.

Walsh prepared to bowl ... Qadir nudged two off the first ball, completely missed the second, deflected the third for two and then heroically stepped down the wicket to strike a superb straight six. Amid pandemonium in the open stands, Pakistan now required only two runs from the last two balls.

The West Indian bowler moved in again, and stopped in his tracks. In a moment frozen in time, he stood holding the ball beside the stumps. Jaffer had backed up too far and was stranded outside his crease. If Walsh had chosen to dislodge the bails, the Pakistani would have been run out and the West Indians would have won the game, yet this noble cricketer preferred not to win any match in such a way.

Walsh simply smiled, and Jaffer gratefully returned to his crease.

Still two balls to go, still two runs needed. A sense of natural justice would have seen Walsh's exemplary sportsmanship rewarded; instead, Qadir prodded the fifth ball of the over through the off side and the batsmen scrambled the two runs that carried Pakistan to another remarkable triumph.

'It is meant to be,' declared spectators, hailing three wins out of three.

Straightforward victories over Sri Lanka in Faisalabad and England in Karachi soon made it five wins out of five, and Imran's side was safely on its way to a home semi-final in Lahore.

Pakistan's progress left England and the West Indies competing for the runners-up berth in Group B, and Mike Gatting's team seized an early advantage when they defeated their rivals in Guiranwala. With his team apparently out of contention at 153 for six, still needing 91 runs in the last ten overs, Allan Lamb rallied the tail and, fighting a severe bout of dehydration, bravely guided his team to victory with two balls to spare.

With Sri Lanka struggling to hold their own in the group (notably being destroyed by Vivian Richards who crashed a majestic 181 in only 125 balls in Karachi) and losing all their matches, the two-time world champions were left needing to beat England in Jaipur to maintain any hope of reaching the semi-finals.

Gooch responded to the pressure by anchoring the innings with an important 92; and, aided and abetted by careless West Indian bowlers who delivered no fewer than 22 wides, the opener guided England to a decent total of 269 for seven in 50 overs. Richards accepted the responsibility as well, and seemed to be taking charge when he dispatched successive deliveries from Eddie Hemmings for six over square leg.

However, undaunted, the spinner kept his nerve, and his line, and clean-bowled the West Indian captain for 51. In 1975 and 1979, even in 1983, others would have emerged to carry on the chase, but this Caribbean team lacked the same depth and character, and meekly subsided to 235 all out.

A parting victory over a Pakistan side already focused on the semi-final offered no consolation to the first West Indian team ever to be eliminated at the group stages of a World Cup.

Thus, the semi-finals were confirmed: India versus England in Bombay, and Pakistan against Australia in Lahore. The so-called 'dream' final was eagerly anticipated in both host countries, and yet tournament officials privately feared the consequences of a final between India and Pakistan.

Yes, the prospect of a World Cup final between two intense sporting rivals was thrilling, but any contest between these hostile neighbours would reach far beyond sport into the realm of religion. When Hindu clashed with Muslim, the police braced themselves for crowd violence and wider unrest.

'What's that?' one of the Australian players asked his captain in the foyer of their Lahore hotel.

'Just a press cutting,' Border replied.

'Can I see?'

'No problem.'

The Australian captain was on his way to the team room, where he intended to pin on the wall an article from a local newspaper in which Zaheer Abbas, the former Pakistan Test batsman, had described his country's semi-final opponents as being 'not much better than a bunch of club cricketers'.

Far from feeling insulted, Border was pleased by the remark. In fact, he found it hard to imagine a more effective way of motivating his side before their World Cup semi-final in the Gadaffi Stadium. He just sat back and watched the angry indignation simmer and boil among his players.

Imran Khan had dominated the pre-match headlines by pointing out that his decision to retire meant the semi-final would be his last one-day international on Pakistani soil, and, as match day dawned, the excitement, emotion and expectation in the streets of Lahore reached feverish proportions.

Border won the toss, decided to bat first, and steeled himself for the battle. 'Forget what's going on in the stands,' he told his players, wiping the oppressive heat from his brow. 'The crowd is going to get involved, but let's try and keep them quiet. We have to be professional and clinical out there.'

Openers Geoff Marsh and David Boon answered the call, launching the innings with a stand of 73 runs in 18 overs. The middle order built on this steady foundation and, with Mike Veletta scoring 48 and Steve Waugh adding an invaluable 32 off 26 balls at the end, Australia reached 267 for eight.

Border was satisfied.

'Well done, guys,' he said between innings. 'Not bad for club cricketers.'

Pakistan had been riding a swell of fanatical public support throughout the tournament, but now this huge emotional wave seemed to overwhelm them. Batting under enormous pressure, playing what seemed the most important match of their lives, the home batsmen became hesitant and tentative.

Craig McDermott kept the ball in the channel of uncertainty outside the off stump, and the wickets began to fall. After 11 overs, Pakistan were sliding to an unthinkable defeat at 38 for three.

Javed Miandad and Imran Khan, maybe the greatest Pakistani players of their generation, came together in crisis, and played like heroes. Carefully at first, then more fluently, they added 112 runs in 26 overs, hauling their side right back into the match, inspiring the crowd back into full voice.

Border knew he had to break the partnership, and characteristically backed himself to do the job. In the pivotal moment of the match, the Australian captain's tender off-spin confounded the Pakistan captain, and to the crowd's horror Imran was gone, caught behind off Border for 58.

Not long afterwards Miandad was bowled by Bruce Reid for 70, and Pakistan's absolute conviction that, somehow, they would prevail began to die a slow, agonising death. The tail wagged gamely but in vain, and the home team was eventually dismissed for 249, beaten by 18 runs.

McDermott finished with five wickets and was named Man of the Match, although most of the home team would not have heard this news because only three of the distraught Pakistan players dragged themselves to the post-game presentation ceremony; and Imran was left to contemplate whether, after all, he would not fight off retirement for four more years and have one more crack at winning the World Cup.

The following day, all eyes turned to Bombay.

Kapil Dev won the toss and, having closely inspected a worn pitch, surprised many observers by sending England in to bat. Graham Gooch heard the news with equanimity, and almost broke into a smile as he reached for his pads. Amid the heat and the haze, the in-form opener was a man with a plan.

He had decided, literally, to sweep away the threat posed by India's spin attack. The previous afternoon, the strongly motivated Gooch had arranged for several local spinners to bowl at him in the nets, giving him the opportunity to hone and polish three distinctive brands of sweep shot.

The first was a delicate, paddled sweep guided down to fine leg for one or maybe two; the second was a conventional sweep, firmly directed to deep square leg for one; and the third was almost a pull, a full-blooded slog-sweep for four or possibly six. He practised and practised, until he was happy.

On match day, the plan worked.

'At one stage, I was sweeping five balls out of every six,' Gooch recalls. He eased past 50, successfully coaxing left-arm spinners Ravi Shastri and Maninder Singh into the leg side, and by the time he was caught on the boundary for a superb 115, he had directed a formidable England innings.

Lamb, all guts and energy, muscled a brisk 32 from 39 balls towards the end, and Gatting appeared cautiously content when his team finished with 254 for seven from their 50 overs.

India looked to the veteran Gavaskar to provide a steady start, but he was bowled by Phil de Freitas for four. Mohammed Azharuddin played himself in and brought some class and rhythm to the run chase, but every time the home side appeared to be taking control, they would lose another wicket. As the blazing heat dripped out of an orange sun, the World Cup semi-final hung precariously in the balance.

Cue: firecrackers in the stands. Enter: Kapil Dev, wheeling his bat.

Urged on by a capacity crowd desperate for their team to succeed where Pakistan had failed the previous day, urged on by hundreds of millions huddled around black-and-white televisions in the streets, spurred by his own sense of pride and destiny, Kapil strode out to win the semi-final.

The national icon rose to the occasion, striking one boundary, then another, and another. As Kapil rushed to 30, inside and outside the stadium thrilled Indians started to believe.

Hemmings was facing the brunt of the assault, and once again Kapil pulled the England spinner high and handsome towards the mid-wicket boundary; but this time, towards Gatting as well. England's captain took the catch, Kapil was out for 30, and Bombay's boiling cauldron fell as still as a pond.

Azharuddin remained for a while but his dismissal, LBW to the vindicated Hemmings for 64, triggered a catastrophic collapse. India lost their last five wickets for 15 runs, and relinquished the title of world champions. Ultimately dismissed for 219 with five overs to spare, they had lost by 35 runs.

Kapil praised England as 'a thoroughly professional side' afterwards, but some of his compatriots proved less gracious in defeat. More than 80 people were injured in riots across the country.

After two magnificent, draining, tumultuous days of cricket, the 1987 World Cup was left with a final that nobody had predicted: England would play Australia at Eden Gardens, Calcutta.

'Do you think we'll get a decent crowd?' asked an anxious English official.

'In Calcutta?' replied a local organiser.

'Yes, now that India are out, do you think people will still turn up to watch the final?'

The Indian smiled, but only said: 'Wait and see.'

Unbeknown to this particular Englishman, the citizens of Calcutta had developed a worldwide reputation for their ludicrously fanatical approach to sport. Several years earlier, when news leaked out that Pele would be spending two hours in transit at the airport, more than 200 000 people crowded around the terminal in hope of glimpsing the Brazilian legend . . . and that was at two o'clock in the morning.

These were certainly not the kind of people to disregard a World Cup final on their doorstep just because their team was not taking part, and the vast concrete bowl known as Eden Gardens was packed to capacity on Sunday 8 November 1987 when Border and Gatting emerged for the toss.

'Heads please, AB,' called the stout, feisty England captain.

The stout, feisty Australian tossed, looked down and said: 'It's tails, Gatt. We'll have a bat.'

Border trusted his batsmen to impose their authority on the final, and he was well served by his openers, David Boon and Geoff Marsh, who advanced to 75 without loss. England's opening bowlers may have provided more loose balls than they would have wanted, but the Australian batsmen ran well between the wickets, kept wickets in hand for the closing onslaught, and produced a rock-solid team performance.

Boon earthed the innings with 75, Marsh made 24, Dean Jones contributed 33, and Border scored 31 in as many balls. They each hustled and bustled with purpose, and when Mike Veletta had led the closing onslaught, thrashing 45 runs in 31 balls, Australia were content at 253 for five in 50 overs.

'It's gettable, lads,' chirped Gatting, back in the dressing room. 'It's gettable.'

Judging by the persistent buzz of chatter and enthusiasm within Eden Gardens, the 90 000 Indians in the ground seemed to be enjoying the close-fought contest. Some had anticipated the local supporters would back Australia, or indeed anyone, against their former colonial masters, but in the event, the Calcutta crowd simply wanted to enjoy their big day out, and applauded good cricket on both sides.

Even the formidable Gooch, India's nemesis in the semi-final, was cheered when he stepped into sight to launch the run chase. The Indians knew a great batsman when they saw one.

Evidently relishing the occasion, the England opener began scoring freely, and for almost an hour looked capable of winning the final on his own. However, when he had reached 35 he misread the flight of a ball from Simon O'Donnell and, amid ecstatic Australian fielders, was deemed LBW.

Gatting joined Bill Athey in the middle, and having steadied the innings for a couple of overs, they began to accelerate, carefully, busily and professionally. At 135 for two, England appeared on course for victory. Once again, in difficulty, the Australian captain took responsibility, and the ball.

He had turned the semi-final by dismissing his opposite number, Imran Khan; now Border measured out his short run-up as the pumped-up England captain settled into his stance 22 yards away.

The first delivery pitched just outside leg-stump. Gatting reached forward and played the reverse sweep, attempting to guide the ball down towards third man; instead, the ball fizzed off his bat, unfortunately clipped his shoulder, and looped into the air. Wicketkeeper Greg Dyer took the catch, and the fielders were celebrating again. Border gasped; Gatting was gone for 41; Australia were back in the game.

Had the England captain played an irresponsible stroke?

Had he thrown away his team's golden chance of winning the World Cup?

Across England, where millions were struggling to keep warm as they watched the final on television over breakfast on a cold winter's morning, Gatting was swiftly condemned. People just didn't like the reverse sweep; they saw it as an expression of cocky overconfidence, an intolerable indulgence when England only needed the disciplined application of those strokes that did appear in the MCC batting manual.

In time, the captain would vigorously defend himself. He would explain how the stroke was well suited to slow Indian pitches, and how it disrupted a bowler's rhythm; and he would recall that nobody complained when he scored freely with the reverse sweep in the semi-final against India; and he would point out that it was the first time the stroke had cost him his wicket; and he would say he was just unlucky.

And he would, in all fairness, probably be right.

But it had not looked good.

Athey ran himself out for 58, going for a third run that never was, but England were not done yet, and Allan Lamb carried the fight back to the Australians. Keeping pace with the required run rate of just over seven runs per over, the plucky South African-born batsman scurried 45 runs in even time and hurried the World Cup final towards a heart-stopping conclusion. It could have gone either way.

It came down to this: Australia apparently in control with England at 220 for seven, still needing 34 runs from the last three overs. Neil Foster pushes a single, giving Phil de Freitas the strike. Dot ball. Boundary. The Lancashire all-rounder blows out his cheeks. Another boundary. The crowd are on their feet. Border is anxiously checking his field placings. De Freitas swings hard again. It's a maximum! Six.

England players are clapping their hands above their heads. It's on again. They require 19 runs from the last two overs. Border calls Steve Waugh to bowl. The young New South Wales all-rounder, dubbed 'Iceman' by his team-mates after his focused bowling at the death earlier in the tournament, does the job again, having De Freitas caught by Reid, and conceding no more than two runs in the over.

Now, the advantage has swung back to Australia. England need 17 runs from the last over. And it proves too much. They get ones and twos. Flares are being lit in the stands. Now Border claps his hands, imploring his players to keep concentrating right to the end. The captain glances across at the vast scoreboard and sees that 10 runs are needed from the last ball. He allows himself a smile.

Foster swings, and scuttles two. It's all over. Australia win by seven runs. The new world champions rush into one another's arms, a jubilant, triumphant burst of yellow in Eden Gardens.

Border led his team on an exhilarated victory lap around the ground, at one stage being carried high on the shoulders of McDermott and Jones. He had guided his team through lean times and criticism, kept working hard, and now he had emerged on the other side, clasping the Reliance

World Cup.

Later that night, indeed much later, at the Oberoi Grand Hotel in Calcutta, the Australian captain was to be found sitting on the floor, legs crossed, still holding the remarkably ornate trophy, sipping on a beer, daring to wonder if this World Cup success might just be the start of something big . . .

'It was no more than a hunch,' Border reflects, 'but we were a young side that had won nothing in the previous year. We were either going to fall apart and fade away, or mature and dominate. That seven-run win put us on the high road and, with hindsight, I think you can trace our Ashes wins in 1989 and 1993, and even the series win over the West Indies in 1995, back to that final in Calcutta.'

The big picture may have been exciting, but Border was not the type of man to ignore his more pressing responsibilities, which included safe-guarding the diamond-studded Reliance World Cup during his team's trip home. So he carried it aboard the plane, kept it belted into a business-class seat beside him during the flight, and emerged at Brisbane airport, beaming with pride, still carrying the trophy.

In all the important ways, nobody would ever take that World Cup away from him.

Gatting responded to the narrow defeat in typical fashion, praising his team for getting as far as the final in the absence of Botham and Gower, and eagerly looking forward to the tour of Pakistan that was scheduled to follow the World Cup. In the event, this whole-hearted leader moved from the frying pan of his much-criticised reverse sweep into the fire of his finger-wagging dispute with Umpire Shakoor Rana.

This damaging rumpus was doubly unfortunate: it yet again reflected badly on cricket in Asia, and it also too quickly obscured the positive messages of the 1987 Cricket World Cup . . . that India and Pakistan had hosted 27 days of constantly exciting cricket without any significant problem, that the players had endured an onerous travel programme and, with few exceptions, relished the sub-continent's inimitable buzz.

N.K.P. Salve had been vindicated.

He had said Asia could host a successful World Cup, and Asia had hosted a successful World Cup.

Allan Border

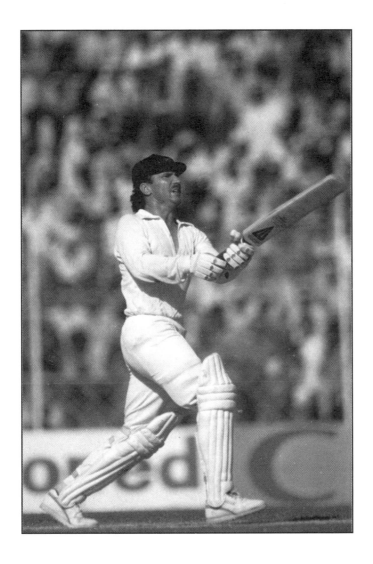

As the boy produced yet another immaculate cover drive and moved on to 92, John Border agonised over what he should do. Should he stay and watch his ten-year-old son complete his first-ever century, or should he dash through the Sydney traffic, collect his wife from the shop where she was working, and hope they would get back to the cricket oval in time to see young Allan reach this special milestone?

OK, he thought, I'll try . . . he gambled, and he won, fretfully getting back to the ground to find his son had reached 97; and his wife Sheila's face lit up when a perfect pull brought up the ton.

The Borders were just another young, decent, optimistic Australian family. Settled in the quiet suburb of Mosman, 15 minutes' drive from the Sydney Harbour Bridge, Mum, Dad and their four sons lived in a typical red-brick, grey-slate-roofed house across the road from the local cricket oval.

Sport dominated the boys' lives. Mark, Allan, John and Brett played in the yard, played at school, played hard, played to win, played honest and fair, played with humour and guts.

It was not in the least surprising that such a quintessentially Australian environment should produce one of the most popular, quintessentially Australian sportsmen of the 20th century.

Allan Border, record-breaking left-handed batsman and occasional left-arm slow bowler, endeared himself to his compatriots because, in 15 seasons at the top, he reflected the best in them. Through 156 Tests and 273 one-day internationals, he never appeared anything less than 'pure Aussie'.

As Dean Jones, the Test batsman, memorably put it: 'AB is totally competitive. He loves a fight. If dogs played cricket, he would be the short-haired Highland Terrier, forever biting at the Doberman's feet and giving it a hard time. He always seemed to be the pedigree pretending to be a mongrel.'

From his run-hungry youth at the Mosman Oval, Border advanced smoothly through age-group ranks, on to the New South Wales side until, at the age of 23 in 1978, he was chosen to play for Australia in the second Test against England in Melbourne. The rookie was relegated to 12th man for the fifth Test of that losing series, but amazingly Border did not miss another Test until his retirement in 1994.

His record of 153 consecutive Test appearances for his country remains unmatched.

He never claimed to be the most stylish batsman to play the game, but few have been as effective in the art of accumulating runs. Nudging the ball here, pushing the ball there, concentrating, making no mistakes, giving nothing away, relishing every cut and pull, he kept the scoreboard ticking.

His greatest innings were not extravagant exhibitions of strokeplay. They were typically hewn from crisis, played when his team was in trouble. 'His performance against the West Indies at Port of Spain in 1984 stands out,' recalls Richie Benaud, the former captain. 'Allan almost single-handedly resisted a great West Indian fast bowling attack on a lethal pitch, and heroically salvaged a draw. He scored an unbeaten 98 out of a total of 255 in the first innings, and then 100 not out in the second innings 299 for nine.'

And the scoreboards of the cricketing world ticked on ... until 26 February 1993. Batting in the first Test against New Zealand, he passed Sunil Gavaskar's record and became, at the time, the leading run scorer in the history of Test cricket. Typically, he shied away from accolades, referring to his feat as a millstone rather than a milestone, and retired 14 months later, having scored 11 174 runs at an average of 50,56.

More than a great batsman, Border also became a great captain.

He inherited a disheartened Australian team in January 1985, instilled discipline, and earned the nickname 'Captain Cranky' for his periodic out-bursts. 'AB never gave up on a situation,' recalls one of his opponents, Ian Botham, 'and he demanded the same level of commitment from everyone around him.'

The strategy did not yield instant results. Australia won only three of his first 25 Tests in charge, painfully losing two series to England in the process, and the captain was coming under pressure when, against all odds, he led his team to victory in the 1987 World Cup. Self-belief flooded through the ranks.

Within two months he finally led Australia to a series victory, over New Zealand at home. And within two years his team had regained the Ashes, winning by four Tests to nil in England and triumphantly arriving home to a ticker-tape parade in Sydney. Border was awarded the Order of Australia.

Success followed success. Australia was generally acknowledged as the strongest team in the world, and Border was widely recognised as the dominant figure in the game. Emphatic Ashes victories, by 3-0 at home in 1990/91 and 4-1 in England in 1993, instilled an aura of invincibility. The captain wanted to exit at the top and did so in 1994, after drawing home and away Test series against readmitted South Africa.

Allan Border remains involved in the game today, as a coach and selector. His reputation, launched in Mosman and enhanced around the world, will shine as long as Australians play the game.

Chapter Eight

The Fifth World Cup

In 1975, the first World Cup final was watched by 23 377 spectators in the ground, and played by teams using a red ball and wearing whites; and the match finished as dusk fell on a long summer's day.

Just over 16 years passed.

In 1992, the fifth World Cup final was watched by 87 182 spectators, in a stadium so large that the south stand alone held more than twice as many people as most Test grounds around the world. One team appeared in royal blue clothing, and the other in a kitschy shade of electric pea green. They used two white balls, one at each end, and the match reached its conclusion late at night, under floodlights.

Was this progress?

Some people said so.

Most of them were Australian.

They loved the multicoloured kit, sang along to all the jingles, basked under the floodlights, enjoyed the on-message television presentation when they were at home, and understood when to 'ooh' and 'aaah' on cue at the contrived drama when they were in the ground. In their view, the razzmatazz had taken the sport into a new era, enhanced the vibe, attracted younger audiences, increased revenue, and turned the old game of the British Empire into a booming, profitable form of mass entertainment.

Others disagreed.

For them, the 1992 World Cup was the occasion when the ICC crossed the Rubicon by allowing business, marketing and other commercial considerations to take precedence over the pure sport. They believed that, in terms of its size, policy and tone, the tournament was irreversibly spoiled.

It was entirely predictable that the World Cup should become larger and larger, and it was obvious to all that this continuing expansion had nothing to do with the game and everything to do with the reality that more matches meant more television income, more gate receipts and more money.

If the welfare of cricket and cricketers had been paramount, the tournament would have needed only to be short enough to sustain public interest and long enough to produce authentic one-day world champions. It was widely accepted that, against these pure criteria, the World Cups of 1975 and 1979 had proved perfectly adequate: each event comprised only 15 games, and fizzed through a riveting fortnight.

The format was enlarged to include 27 matches in 1983, and this remained unchanged in 1987, but these dimensions were still manageable. In both tournaments, the all-important sense of momentum was maintained by a consistent flow of keenly contested and meaningful fixtures.

If money had whispered in the organisers' ear then, now it was beginning to shout.

The Australian organisers of the 1992 World Cup listened well.

And they acted accordingly.

First, they postponed the tournament. The World Cup was supposed to be staged every four years, which meant it was due in 1991, but the organisers ignored such details. They would not forgo the profits from their money-spinning annual World Series event, and insisted upon staging the three-way contest between the West Indies, India and the home team in the latter part of their 1991/92 season.

So money budged the Cricket World Cup into 1992 and out of its quadrennial step. It is hard to imagine the Olympic Games or football World Cup being scheduled with such untidy disdain.

Second, the organisers identified the sale of television rights as a prime source of income, and took every step to maximise income from this source, irrespective of any impact on the actual game.

They needed more television hours to sell, so the schedule was expanded to 39 matches, including 25 in Australia and a further 14 in New Zealand. Never mind if the players had to endure exhausting travel schedules as they were moved back and forth across the Antipodes – the poor Sri Lankans were handed an itinerary that took them on a ridiculous 15 000-mile marathon. Never mind if supporters began to lose interest as the 33-day event dragged on and on, and too many games seemed less than crucial.

In their quest for money, the organisers then took a decision to sell their broadcast rights to the highest bidder, and began doing business with elite subscription satellite channels.

This jam-today policy appeared in stark contrast to the strategy pursued by the International Olympic Committee and FIFA, who insisted that their events were shown on terrestrial free television, because they believed mass viewership was more important than a premium rights fee. In their view, a global audience was essential to secure the enduring benefits of being recognised as a genuinely global event.

In 1992 the Cricket World Cup made a dash for the cash, flogging the broadcast rights to elite channels such as Sky in Britain and M-Net Supersport in South Africa, with the result that, in terms of public awareness across the globe, this still embryonic tournament began to contract.

Where long-term vision was required, the officials demonstrated only short-sighted greed.

Taking this into account, it seems scarcely surprising that many cricket followers watched the 1992 World Cup unfold and concluded that, in their wisdom, the organisers had inherited a neat, successful, growing event, stripped away its dignity and integrity, and produced a brash, vulgar shambles.

'Nobody cares about a few fuddy-duddy Poms,' the Australians might have responded.

And, of course, they were right.

Hardly anyone did care.

The traditionalists had long since lost the battle for cricket's soul, and the process of 'modernisation' – of pumping up the volume, tricking up the match action and increasing revenue regardless of the broader effects on the game – was not going to be reversed. Like toothpaste squeezed out of the tube, this relentless battery of innovations and policies was never going back from whence it came.

By 1992 the hard-nosed businessmen had raised the money, won the argument and taken control. The philosophical sons of Kerry Packer, and many of the tycoon's former employees, had longed to get their hands on cricket's precious showpiece tournament. Now, at last, it was all theirs.

Ironically, it was a New Zealander who first promoted the idea of taking the World Cup down under. Bob Vance, chairman of the New Zealand Cricket Council, launched the campaign after watching Australia and New Zealand successfully combine to host the Rugby World Cup in 1987, and the triumph of Allan Border's team at Eden Gardens later that year served to spark Australian enthusiasm for the bid.

A formal proposal was submitted to the ICC in 1988, and, following the approved principle that the World Cup would circulate among member countries, the bid was duly accepted.

There was no option.

The Australian organisers announced a new format. The eight competing countries would form one group, in which everyone played everyone else, and the leading four sides on the complete league table would then advance to the semi-finals, from which the winners would contest the final.

It was further resolved that matches would remain restricted to 50, rather than 60, overs per side, even though the fading light problems that necessitated this reduction in Asia four years earlier had been alleviated by the decision that floodlights would be used for the first time in a World Cup.

Only four months before the tournament was due to start, political developments on the opposite side of the Indian Ocean provided the organisers with more spice for their marketing mix.

Following the release of Nelson Mandela and the repeal of every apartheid law in 1990, South Africa was restored as a full member of the ICC. They celebrated their return to the official fold by travelling to play three hastily arranged, wonderfully successful one-day internationals in India during November 1991, prompting the suggestion that they be given a last-minute wild card to play in the World Cup.

ICC president Colin Cowdrey seemed to hesitate, but the South Africans were bursting to compete at the highest level, and the opportunistic tournament organisers salivated at the prospect of promoting the 'prodigal sons' of international cricket as the surprise guests at their extravaganza.

Discussions involving Australian Prime Minister Bob Hawke, British Prime Minister John Major, and even Mandela himself, led to a special ICC meeting at Sharjah in late November, where the proposal that the South Africans be invited to participate in the 1992 World Cup was historically approved.

The fixture list was quickly reorganised, and when the players of the nine competing squads gathered for an opening photograph on the deck of *HMS Canberra*, all seemed well. As ACB president Malcolm Gray said at the gala banquet that night, 'It was inspiring to watch what was the greatest gathering of cricket talent in the history of the game, with the exception of whenever Sir Donald Bradman dines alone.'

A fundamental element of the organisers' perfect scenario was that their Australian side would thrash all opposition and successfully defend the title they had won four years earlier. Border's team certainly began their campaign as firm favourites, with pundits citing their record of having won an unequalled 76 per cent of their one-day internationals since 1987. Everybody automatically assumed they would cruise to victory in their opening game against an apparently hapless and hopeless team in disarray, New Zealand.

However, on 22 February 1992, at Eden Park, Auckland, cricket struck back.

In all its unpredictable, unfathomable glory, the game managed to produce a saga so far-fetched that it revived and invigorated an otherwise shallow and contrived landscape. The story of New Zealand's campaign at the 1992 World Cup unfolded like the synopsis of an outrageous fantasy film.

Scene One: Twenty-four hours after announcing their World Cup squad, the national selectors ask Martin Crowe to resign as captain and play purely as a batsman. He refuses. A complex, emotional character, he says he is not prepared to throw away 18 months of planning and preparation. He acknowledges his side's form has been poor, losing a home series to England, but he believes they can raise the nation's spirits, depressed since the All Blacks' defeat against the Australians in the Rugby World Cup. So, he stays.

Scene Two: Crowe and coach Wally Lees are deep in discussion, finalising their strategy. Playing all their group matches at home, on the slow pitches they know so well, they focus on three areas: make their bowling light and feathery; back up the 'dibbly-dobbly' attack with demon fielding; and, in matches scheduled at rugby grounds, take special measures to protect the short square boundaries.

'Wally, I think Dipak Patel should open the bowling,' says Crowe.

'Why not? We'll need something different to beat the Aussies,' the open-minded coach replies.

It's agreed. They have nothing to lose. New Zealand's unheralded right-arm off-spinner will take the new ball in their opening match of the tournament, against Australia in Auckland.

Scene Three: Through the closing lines of the national anthem, the captain struggles to hold his emotions in check. 'Make her praises heard afar,' he sings, 'God defend New Zealand.' This is it. Eden Park resounds to the deafening noise of 30 000 cheap party hooters, imported from China and distributed free to people as they enter the ground. Kiwis unite in hope. Crowe wins the toss, and decides to bat first.

As he settles into his stance, he mutters to himself: 'Courage and skill, courage and skill.' It has become a mantra. 'Soft hands,' he mumbles, 'watch the ball.' The routine works. Crowe emerges from an awkward period in his public and personal life to score an unbeaten century. The captain had wanted to 'show a bit of guts out there', and he guides his side to 248 for six in 50 overs.

Scene Four: What's happening? People are aghast when Patel opens the bowling, but they smile when his seven overs yield only 19 runs. The batsmen are unsettled. Crowe is enthused and excited, and he has another plan. Named after a former Otago selector, it's known as the Hunt Shuffle and involves incessantly rotating the bowlers to keep the batsmen on the hop, to deny them any kind of rhythm.

Crowe conducts the orchestra of slower-than-slow-medium-pacers: it's Chris Harris for just two overs at one end, Rod Latham for a couple from the other, Willie Watson for one, Gavin Larsen for two. And the captain is loving every minute, and the Australians are becoming frustrated, falling behind the run rate, losing wickets, losing the game. Eden Park is a buzzing hive of joy. New Zealand win by 37 runs.

Scene Five: At a team meeting the next morning, Crowe takes care to ground his side again, keeping the players looking forward to the next challenge. He tries to dehumanise the opposition by referring to rival teams as colours, so Australia are known as 'yellow', Zimbabwe as 'red', England as 'blue', etc. He is resolved that his team will approach every match in the tournament with the same intensity.

Scene Six: After defeating Sri Lanka by six wickets in Hamilton, Crowe leads his side against South Africa in Auckland and watches Mark Greatbatch erupt in a blaze of strokeplay. Drafted in to replace the injured John Wright, he has scored only 30 runs in his previous five international innings but he smashes 68 runs in 60 balls and inspires New Zealand to a third win on the trot. The team is humming.

Scene Seven: Crowe ignites a rain-reduced match against Zimbabwe in Napier, scoring the fastest 50 in World Cup history in 31 balls. He finishes with an unbeaten 74 in his team's commanding total of 162 in almost 21 overs. Zimbabwe never threaten to reach the target, and the Kiwis smile again.

Scene Eight: The astonishing now seems normal: Patel opens the bowling against the West Indians, and concedes just 19 runs in 10 overs against Haynes and Lara; 'Paddy' Greatbatch leads the pursuit of 204 to win, driving

Marshall out of the ground and reaching 50 in 16 scoring strokes ... 4444616161411412. Crowe strokes a wonderful 81 runs in only 81 balls, and ends the match with a straight drive for four.

The captain's form is irrepressible. He has won three Man-of-the-Match awards in five matches, scoring a total of 263 runs and being out only once. A captivated country is starting to believe.

Scene Nine: The weather might be cold in Dunedin, but Greatbatch is still red-hot. Chasing 231 to defeat India, he launches another blistering assault in the first 15 overs, pounding 73 runs in 76 balls. Andrew Jones's unbeaten 67 secures another win. Mocked in January, the team looks unbeatable in March.

Scene Ten: Play it again, Dipak. The off-spinner opens the bowling and claims two for 26 against England in Wellington. Who will get the 201 needed to win? Obvious. Greatbatch smashes 35 in 37 balls: Jones anchors with another steady 78; and captain Crowe takes his side home with an unbeaten 73. Seven wins in seven matches have secured the team's place in the semi-finals. The dream is taking flight.

From rank outsiders to serious contenders in ten scenes, New Zealand's success went down like a ton of bricks across the Tasman Sea. 'The Aussies always said the host nation would win this World Cup,' crowed one Kiwi supporter, 'and they were right. They just got the wrong host nation!'

While Crowe's team was flying, Border's side had struggled.

Rattled by a wave of unorthodox tactics in Auckland, the Australians flew back to Sydney and were swept aside by the wave of emotion surrounding South Africa's debut appearance at the World Cup. Their batting was modest, their bowling was poor, and their fielding was deplorable. All of a sudden, the raging hot favourites had lost their first two matches; and, fleeting glimpses of form aside, they never recovered.

They were fortunate to survive an exciting match against India in Brisbane, when Javagal Srinath needed to score four runs from the last ball of the 50th over. Tom Moody bowled, Srinath swung. Border's first reaction was that the ball was going for six, but Steve Waugh sprinted from wide mid-on and seemed in position to take the catch. He dropped the chance. The batsmen were now running frantically.

Waugh hurled the ball to wicketkeeper David Boon, who narrowly ran out Venkatapathy Raju. Thus, amid great excitement at the Gabba, Australia won by one run and not more than three inches.

Was this the start of a gutsy comeback and a dramatic revival?

'No,' was Ian Botham's reply, delivered with vigour, at the Sydney Cricket

Ground.

The belligerent all-rounder dominated the match between England and Australia. He started by declaring how he wanted to win the World Cup in front of '100 000 convicts'; he then seized four for 32 in dismissing the home team for 171. After thrashing 53 in 79 balls as England cruised to an eight-wicket victory, he finished the day with a jibe at Australian republicans. 'I hope the Queen was watching,' he grinned.

Nerves were starting to fray. Having beaten Sri Lanka, Border's side became embroiled in an ill-tempered dogfight with Pakistan. Mike Whitney clashed angrily with Moin Khan and, chasing 221 to win, the home team's batting collapsed again: only Marsh, Jones, Steve Waugh and Extras reached double figures, and the fallen idols were 172 all out, beaten by 48 runs. With two wins in six, the curtain was falling.

An emphatic win against Zimbabwe produced a slim glimmer of hope going into the last round of group matches, but they were relying on other results to fall their way and, even though they did belatedly rediscover their best form to beat the West Indies in Melbourne, their efforts proved in vain. To everybody's surprise, and to the horror of the organisers, the Australians were eliminated at the group stage.

Border accepted the enormous disappointment with grace, but the pain was obvious. 'We wanted to win too much,' Boon reflected. 'Perhaps we forgot that, in order to succeed, you have to enjoy what you're doing. As we lost one match after another, the squad became so intense and serious. We seemed to lose that edge of humour which tends to pervade Australian teams when they are performing well.'

Maybe the burden of expectation had been too great.

The South Africans faced no similar difficulties, simply because most people had no idea what to expect from a side that arrived at the World Cup like new boys on the first day of term. Only a few were recognised by the most dedicated followers of the game: captain Kepler Wessels had averaged 42.95 in 24 Tests for Australia before returning to the land of his birth, Peter Kirsten had thrived with Derbyshire, and fast bowler Allan Donald enjoyed a growing reputation. Coach Mike Procter had been revered at Gloucestershire in his playing days, but he now applied himself to the task of guiding a largely unproven group of players.

It was not an easy job. The squad was forged out of controversy when the selectors omitted heroes Clive Rice, Jimmy Cook and Kirsten. A prolonged and unprecedented burst of public outrage resulted in Kirsten being recalled into the final group, but the panel's general view prevailed:

they said South Africa's best chance at the World Cup was to pick a young, physically fit side bonded by Wessels's iron discipline.

'None of you can imagine the size of the task that lies ahead of us,' the captain, firm and clear-sighted, told his callow team. A keen amateur boxer, a steely-eyed leader, Wessels led from the front. 'It will be tough for everyone,' he said, 'but, if we can stick together, we have a reasonable chance.'

Their campaign started not with a gentle match against minor opposition at some rural ground, but with a mighty challenge against Australia at the Sydney Cricket Ground. Wednesday 26 February unfolded as one of the most emotional, memorable days in the history of South African sport.

They didn't stroll out to field first; they sprinted, a dark green line zig-zagging onto the world stage. And Donald took the ball, and ran in, and bowled a quick, rising delivery outside the off-stump. Geoff Marsh fended at the ball, clearly nicked it. Dave Richardson took the catch. What a start!

No. Umpire Brian Aldridge stood still. Maybe the only man in the SCG not to hear the edge, he shook his head. Donald looked incredulous, bemused as he headed back to his mark.

It didn't matter. The tone was struck. Australia battled to reach 171 for nine. Wessels led the run chase, scoring an unbeaten 81, and his team coasted to a remarkably easy nine-wicket victory.

Steve Tshwete, the African National Congress spokesman on sport, the architect of unity in South African cricket, had watched from the pavilion and he made his way to the visitors' dressing room. The former Robben Island prisoner found Wessels amid the throng, and embraced him. Photographs of the hug flashed around the globe, and became the enduring image of South Africa's arrival at the World Cup.

After the joy, the harsh reality. The team travelled to New Zealand and their inexperience was ruthlessly exposed on the slow, crusty pitches. Defeat against the home team was followed by a mediocre display against Sri Lanka. Suddenly, a record of played three, lost two left the debutants facing what Wessels described as 'the nightmare scenario'. Maybe they were, as some had suggested, out of their depth.

'We must win four of the last five to survive,' declared the captain, drawing on every ounce of resolve to withstand the reams of vitriol arriving by fax from critics in South Africa.

Meyrick Pringle, a gangling fast bowler, stepped out of obscurity into the team to play the West Indies at Christchurch, and set the campaign back on the rails. Famously, he once asked an umpire during an over, 'How many balls?' and, being told three, then enquired, 'Is that three gone or three to go?' But Pringle demonstrated that you don't need a Master's degree to exhilarate your country and roll over the West Indians.

Bowling to defend 200, he had Lara caught by Jonty Rhodes at point, Richardson adjudged LBW, Hooper and then Arthurton caught at slip by Wessels. In form, in raptures, Pringle took four wickets in the space of 11 balls, reducing the Caribbean heroes to 19 for four and, eventually, 136 all out.

Even as the last West Indian wicket fell, the South Africans revealed their inexperience. Andrew Hudson, the talented opener, sought a souvenir and seized one of the stumps as he ran towards the pavilion. It was not until he reached the boundary that he realised he had taken the stump that houses the mini television camera and that, to his embarrassment, he was trailing ten metres of cable behind him.

Eagerly returning to the faster pitches in Australia, Wessels's side scored a decent 211 against Pakistan in Brisbane but seemed to be heading for another defeat when Imran Khan and Inzamam-ul-Haq mounted a charge towards a rain-reduced target. Someone needed to do something special.

At this moment, in a boyish blur, Rhodes arrived on the world stage.

The exuberant 22-year-old from Natal might easily have been included in the South African hockey team for the 1992 Olympic Games in Barcelona, but he had focused all his remarkable energies into cricket and, with only one first-class century to his name, had been a surprise selection for the World Cup.

Rhodes's batting was resourceful and never less than gutsy, but it was his fielding that quickly caught the imagination of the cricketing world. Invariably positioned at cover point, he was the image of perpetual motion, running in as the bowler bowled, then sprinting 20 yards back to his place, encouraging, clapping hands, diving to save boundaries, catching bullets, chatting, grinning, obviously loving every moment.

This infectious presence complemented the captain's natural reticence. 'Jonty was a positive influence on the team,' Wessels recalls. 'He fielded on one side of the wicket and Hansie Cronje on the other, and they kept everyone on their toes. That enabled me to concentrate on the strategy.'

Inzamam had reached 48 in only 45 balls when he pushed the ball towards point. He called for the single, but Imran sent him back. Rhodes collected the ball and assessed the situation. He didn't have to risk a throw; he would back his speed off the mark and race the Pakistani to the crease. Inzamam stretched, Rhodes dived forward and, flying horizontal to the turf, spectacularly clattered the ball into the stumps.

Out! The Gabba gasped.

When Pakistan eventually finished 20 runs short, South Africa had secured another two points and moved up to third on the table, and cricket had discovered a brand new icon. Rhodes soon became as popular in Delhi as in Durban, the smiling epitome of everything good in the game.

Victory over Zimbabwe took the South Africans another step closer to the semi-finals, but a close-fought defeat against England in Melbourne left them needing to win their last group match, against India in Adelaide, to reach the knockout stages. Rain reduced the game to a frenetic 30-overs per side thrash for glory, and the Indians seemed well placed when Azharuddin's 77 helped them to reach 180.

Kirsten rose magnificently to the occasion.

This competitive, feisty man had played through almost two decades of international isolation, captaining his country in rebel series, scoring many thousands of runs, maintaining high standards. Now, after the drama of political reform and a bitter selection controversy, the top-class 38-year-old batsman suddenly found himself granted the chance for which he had waited so long, officially to represent his country.

The veteran eagerly seized the opportunity, time and again holding his side's batting together, emerging as the leading run scorer in the group stages, amassing 410 runs at an average of 68.33. In six innings before the decisive match against India, he had made 49 not out, 90, 47, 56, 62 not out and 11; now, on an overcast day in Adelaide, he settled into the groove again and scored 84 runs in only 86 balls.

Others sustained the momentum, and when Hansie Cronje hit the winning runs from the first ball of the 30th over, the South Africans had secured a semi-final place. The rookies had endured a rollercoaster ride and, with courage compensating for inexperience, had achieved their goal.

Azharuddin, the Muslim captain of a predominantly Hindu team, was dismayed in defeat. Citing bad luck with the weather as one reason for India's elimination, he also conceded that his squad had looked weary after four months on the road. A full tour of Australia prior to the World Cup had taken its toll.

Their campaign had started with such promise when the selectors named an 18-year-old prodigy, Sachin Tendulkar, in their squad. The young hero was selected alongside Vinod Kambli, with whom he had compiled a world record partnership of 664 in an age-group match, but the side suffered two narrow, unfortunate defeats, against England and then against

Australia, in their first three matches.

Under pressure, Azharuddin took his side to Sydney for a match against Pakistan. The first-ever meeting in a World Cup between these two intense rivals generated huge interest back home in the sub-continent, and fears that conflict was inevitable seemed to be borne out when Javed Miandad pulled away before the ball was bowled, complaining that wicketkeeper Kiran More was talking too much.

David Shepherd, the umpire at the bowler's end, made a sign to suggest Miandad should 'zip' his mouth shut, a gesture that prompted More to laugh out loud. The Pakistani was not amused. More furious words were exchanged, but the umpires decided not to mention the incident in their report. 'We could not have done that,' Shepherd recalls, 'because we had absolutely no idea what was being said.'

Tendulkar chose this frenzied stage to confirm his talent to the world, stroking 54 runs in 62 balls in the Indian total of 217 for six, and then taking three for 37 as Pakistan fell 43 runs short. The Indians enjoyed a historic and gleefully celebrated triumph, but their challenge soon faded away.

The West Indians were also battling. Several stalwarts, including Viv Richards, had retired after the 1991 tour to England, and Richie Richardson was asked to captain a squad in which inter-island rivalries had started to resurface. They could not have started more impressively, annihilating Pakistan by ten wickets in Melbourne, but various factions started to emerge, sadly undermining team spirit.

Brian Lara, the entertaining 22-year-old left-hander, left his mark on the tournament, scoring four fine half-centuries, but defeats against South Africa and New Zealand left the West Indies needing to win their last group match, against Australia at the MCG, to reach the knockout stages.

Richardson was the image of optimism approaching the game, but, chasing 217 to win, his team crumbled to 159 all out and the captain was left mumbling about how the West Indies remained the spiritual home of the World Cup trophy. In fact, the prize had not been taken back to the Caribbean for 12 years.

By contrast, England appeared motivated and professional. Efficiently led by Graham Gooch, they slipped into form when Robin Smith led the charge against India. Gooch then took the sword to the West Indians, only rain denied them victory after dismissing Pakistan for 74, and Botham savaged Australia.

Victory over Sri Lanka by 106 runs secured England's progress to the knockout stages two weeks before the semi-finals were to be played. The strategy of packing the side with five genuine all-rounders – Botham, De Freitas, Chris Lewis, Derek Pringle and Dermot Reeve – was paying dividends.

Two group matches remained and, with nothing concrete at stake, England lost both. The setbacks did not appear significant at the time, although precious momentum was lost when Crowe led a comfortable chase for New Zealand in Wellington; and, infamously, dignity was lost at Albury.

Since winning their first-ever World Cup match, versus Australia at Southampton in 1983, Zimbabwe had suffered no fewer than 18 consecutive defeats in the tournament. Nobody predicted anything other than a 19th loss when Dave Houghton's side arrived to play England in this rural Victorian town.

They had qualified for the tournament by winning the ICC Trophy competition played almost 20 months before in June 1990, an event played on matting wickets in the Netherlands. The Zimbabweans had prevailed by beating Bangladesh in the semi-final and overcoming the host country in the final.

Desperate for another win at the World Cup, they had been on course for victory over Sri Lanka in their first match of the 1992 event. Opener Andy Flower scored an unbeaten 115 in an excellent total of 312 for 4 in 50 overs, but, to African dismay, Arjuna Ranatunga inspired a striking and successful chase.

Six more defeats followed, and, sent in to bat by Gooch in Albury, the Zimbabweans were bowled out for 134 on a lively wicket. They were staring a 'played eight, lost eight' record in the face, a potentially disastrous showing in view of their plans to apply for ICC full membership five months later.

Houghton was animated in the team changing room: 'We've let ourselves down in this tournament and we've let the country down because we haven't helped our chances of getting Test status,' the captain told his players before they set out to defend what seemed to be an undefendable total. 'Now, we have one last chance to put things right. It's all we've got. Let's get out there and show what we can do.'

Eddo Brandes, a chicken farmer, listened carefully, figuratively beat his breast, opened the bowling, ran in and dramatically pinned Gooch LBW with the very first ball of the innings.

With Alec Stewart batting at No. 7, England should still have cantered to victory but Brandes was bowling with real passion. He tilted Robin

Smith's off-stump, induced Allan Lamb to mistime a pull to mid-on, and then, to his unbridled delight, produced the perfect yorker that clean bowled his old friend from Prince Edward School in Harare, and his dinner companion from the previous night, Graeme Hick.

Botham fell soon afterwards, and despite some plucky resistance from Stewart and Fairbrother, England were dismissed for 125. Zimbabwe won by eight runs before 5 645 mouths gaping in wonder. Brandes finished with analysis of four for 21 in 10 overs, and a dinner story to last a lifetime.

'It's been a long time since we played Australia in 1983,' Houghton said, eyes misting at the post-match press conference. 'I didn't remember how good it felt to win a World Cup match. Eddo bowled brilliantly. If you want to get the best out of him, you just put Graeme Hick in the other side.'

This remarkable upset enabled the Zimbabweans to return home with pride intact, and added substance to their ultimately successful presentation at the ICC meeting in July. As full members, the Zimbabweans would start playing Test cricket and qualify automatically for World Cups to come.

The smiling Sri Lankans had been similarly promoted a decade earlier, and they maintained a steady rate of progress at the 1992 tournament, even if their encouraging start – two victories and one rain-ruined draw in their first three matches – eventually fizzled out with five successive defeats.

While their fielding was greatly improved, the team's weakness remained an over-reliance on the batting talents of Aravinda de Silva and Arjuna Ranatunga. The team only seemed to post a decent total when either of these stalwarts thrived, as Ranatunga did against both Zimbabwe and South Africa. Four years on, at the 1996 World Cup, greater batting depth would spectacularly improve their results.

The Pakistanis were once again cast as the enigma.

On any given day . . . able to beat the best and lose to the worst.

They arrived in Australia with a blend of youth and experience, but once again their preparations for the tournament veered from crisis to drama and back again. First Javed Miandad was going to miss the tournament with a sore back, but he recovered and took his place. Then Waqar Younis was set to open the attack but broke down with stress fractures and was booked on the next flight home.

Imran Khan stood apart. Having abandoned his declared intention to retire after the 1987 World Cup, the 39-year-old announced that he was motivated to play in one more tournament by the hope that winning the trophy would help raise money for his project to build a cancer hospital in Lahore.

When his team had played five matches, he appeared to be wasting his time.

Pakistan were apparently on their way home.

The captain had withdrawn from the first game with a painful shoulder, and he watched with dismay while his side suffered a humbling 10-wicket defeat against the West Indies. They did recover to defeat Zimbabwe, with Aamir Sohail scoring 144 and Miandad hitting a wonderful 89 in 94 balls, but then, playing England in Adelaide, they were bowled out for 74. Only 74! Such humiliation was hard to bear. Pakistan had been 42 for seven, and the English openers had walked out to launch their innings well before lunch.

Imran's team looked in disarray, a dry desert of indiscipline and infighting.

Then, the rain arrived.

England's innings was stopped by the downpour and, at 24 for one, the match was abandoned as a draw. With luck, Pakistan escaped from this disastrous day with one crucial point.

It surely couldn't get worse. It could. It is hard to exaggerate the pain suffered by millions of Pakistanis on 4 March 1992, when their team was overcome by India under floodlights in Sydney. The anguish reached far beyond cricket. Effigies of the players were being torched in the streets.

When they lost to South Africa in Brisbane, newspaper columnists began urging the government to bring the side home and thereby avoid any further national shame and disgrace. Imran glanced at the table: his side had played five, lost three, won one and drawn the other. 'We can still qualify for the semi-final,' he said, 'but now we must play like cornered tigers. We have nowhere to go. We must fight.'

Despite the captain's resolutely optimistic approach, Pakistan seemed to be playing only for pride when they found some form and defeated Australia in Perth. However, they beat Sri Lanka at the same WACA ground four days later, and all of a sudden, with other results falling their way, the mood began to change. The round-robin format was working in their favour, and their World Cup hopes were still alive.

It boiled down to this: on the last day of group matches, Imran's side needed to overcome New Zealand in Christchurch and then hope Australia could defeat the West Indies in Melbourne. This combination of results would enable them to finish fourth on the table, and miraculously advance.

There was even better news for Pakistan. New Zealand was unbeaten and already sure of their place in the semi-finals. Now the closely contested state of the competition put the Kiwis in the following dilemma: if Martin Crowe's team lost to Pakistan, they would certainly play their semi-final in Auckland and the Australians would be eliminated. On the other hand, if they were careless enough to win the match, it seemed very likely that they would earn the backhanded reward of a semi-final against Australia at the Sydney Cricket Ground.

Kiwi pride demanded that the team tried their best, but the fact was they were bowled out for 166, and Ramiz Raja's century helped Pakistan ease to a seven-wicket win. 'We have won once, now we must win again,' said Imran, as he sat down to watch Australia play the West Indies on television.

It was ten minutes to midnight in Christchurch when the last West Indian wicket fell at the MCG, and the jubilant Pakistanis knew for certain that they had qualified for the semi-finals.

From the confusing myriad of possibilities, out of group stages that had often seemed interminable, the two semi-finals were confirmed: New Zealand would play Pakistan in Auckland, and England would meet South Africa at the Sydney Cricket Ground in a floodlit match the following day.

Confounding every prediction, the three former World Cup-winning countries – the West Indies, India and Australia – had all been eliminated. The trophy was up for grabs.

The buzz of excitement was nowhere greater than across New Zealand, where a small country obsessed with rugby was being exhilarated by the success of its cricket team. Players who would not have been recognised on the streets three weeks earlier were suddenly being mobbed and cheered.

Eden Park, scene of the All Black triumph in the 1987 Rugby World Cup final, was packed and roaring for the semi-final. The national anthem echoed through the stands, and tears rolled down the cheeks of the team's burly big-hitter, Mark Greatbatch. To this team, on this day, this meant so much.

Crowe won the toss and instinctively wanted to field first. Yet the weather forecast was unsettled, and so many teams batting second had fallen foul of the tournament's notorious rain rule that he decided to bat. Then, in typical fashion, the Kiwi captain backed up his decision with a magnificent innings. He drove and hooked his team into a commanding position until, when he had reached 81, the day turned.

Setting off for a single, he severely pulled the hamstring in his left leg. A runner was summoned from the pavilion and, although Crowe still managed to hook Imran for six and advance his own score to 91, it very soon became obvious that he would be unable to take his place in the field.

Maybe it didn't matter. New Zealand posted an outstanding score of 261 for seven in their 50 overs, and even with their captain's leg in a brace they seemed firmly on course for the final.

John Wright, the vice-captain, took charge of the team in the field and all seemed well. Like many others before them in the tournament, the Pakistani batsmen struggled to score against the 'dibbly-dobbly' bowling on the crusty, dusty pitch, and at 140 for four in 36 overs, their run chase seemed hopeless. The Eden Park crowd was growing excited, sensing the inevitability of a famous New Zealand sporting triumph.

Imran Khan took a different view. This legendary cricketer had sometimes been criticised as arrogant, but the flip side of his nature was an unflinching self-confidence that refused to concede defeat. He was still batting with 23-year-old Inzamam ul-Haq, and together they set about the daunting required run rate of 8.2 per over, taking care not to lose further wickets, stealing singles, hitting boundaries now and then.

Ball by ball, they chipped away at the target.

Run by run, they inexorably transferred the pressure to the bowlers and fielders.

The spectators grew perceptibly quieter and, watching from his seat in the pavilion, Crowe was beginning to feel anxious. He needed to do something, needed to communicate with his team. He was missing them and, as the tension rose, they were missing him. Throughout the tournament, it was the captain who planned every bowling change and field placing. It was he who directed the unconventional campaign. It was in his direction that every player had been told to glance after each ball to check what would happen next.

And now, he wasn't there.

Wright was struggling to control the constant bowling changes, and he sent word to Crowe asking for an indication of how the bowlers should be rotated for the remainder of the innings. The injured captain obliged by scribbling out a note, which the 12th man carried straight out to Wright. Everything was now happening so fast. Imran and Inzamam were raising the tempo, and Wright struggled to read the message.

Maybe some bowlers were kept on too long: Inzamam erupted, advancing his score from 10 to 50 in only 21 balls. Perhaps the short boundaries were not efficiently protected: Inzamam made 60 in 37 balls. Moin Khan cracked 20 in 11 balls, and Javed Miandad arrived to drive the surge for victory in the closing overs, moving the ball around and guiding Pakistan to what had seemed an impossible goal.

When he hit the winning runs, Javed fell to his knees and kissed the Auckland turf in jubilation.

Crowe sat on the edge of his seat in the pavilion, and wept.

In the depths of disappointment, amid tears and gut-wrenching despair, the New Zealand team roused themselves for a final lap of honour, and Eden Park's reception indicated that, although Crowe's side may not have won the World Cup, they had won the hearts of their compatriots.

For Pakistan, everything remained possible. Yes, they would have been knocked out *if* rain had not saved them against England, or *if* Australia had not defeated the West Indies, but the '*ifs*' didn't matter any more. This young team had faithfully followed their inspirational captain, ridden their luck, grabbed their chances, and now, all of a sudden, they found themselves in form and preparing for the World Cup final.

The following day in Sydney, England and South Africa produced a semi-final that matched the wonderful drama and emotion in Auckland, and added a substantial dose of controversy.

Kepler Wessels and his side were up for the occasion. In fact, the South Africans had been 'up' ever since they arrived in Australia, propelled by adrenalin on an emotional voyage through historic first-ever matches with Sri Lanka, the West Indies and Pakistan, through moments of crisis and moments of triumph. The captain had looked forward to a quieter period in the week between the last group match and the semi-final, but his hopes were confounded by events unfolding back home in South Africa.

The turbulent process of political reform had reached a stage at which State President F.W. de Klerk felt he needed a new mandate to take the country forward, so he called a national referendum, challenging the White, Coloured and Asian voters either to endorse or reject his policies. This crucial poll was to be held on 18 March 1992, only three days after Wessels's team had qualified for the semi-final.

Unavoidably, in fact willingly, the cricketers found themselves drawn into the debate.

Players publicly supported the 'Yes' campaign, pointing out that their very participation in the tournament was a consequence of reform. Geoff Dakin, President of the United Cricket Board of South Africa, further raised the stakes when he announced that, if the country did vote 'No', the UCBSA would instantly withdraw the team from the World Cup. Such action initially looked improbable, but when South African newspapers began saying the result was 'on a knife-edge', anxiety spread through the team hotel in Sydney.

Relief arrived with breakfast on the morning of 19 March. News of a 68.7 per cent 'Yes' vote enabled a drained De Klerk to appear on the steps of his official residence in Cape Town, Tuynhuis, and declare 'the closing of the book on apartheid' . . . and it finally allowed the cricketers to focus on the cricket again.

'That was great news,' Wessels recalls. 'Everything seemed to be going our way.'

So it seemed, and the South Africans were brimming with confidence and enthusiasm when they arrived at the SCG before the semi-final, almost unrecognisable from the self-conscious, nervous newcomers who had walked into the same stadium before their first match against Australia almost a month earlier.

England remained professional and streetwise, and had been justifiably installed as the new favourites to win the World Cup, but nobody was discounting the wild card, least of all the vast majority of Australians in the stands who instinctively rallied to support any team playing against the 'Poms'.

Wessels won the toss and opted to field first, a decision that was looking good when England slumped to 39 for two with Gooch and Botham back in the pavilion. Hick might easily have joined them, but he survived a confident LBW appeal off his first ball, and was then caught at slip off a no-ball. Making the most of his fortune, the former Zimbabwean prospered to score an outstanding 83 in 90 balls.

Reeve and Lewis effectively eased on the accelerator in the closing stages, the former clobbering Donald for 15 runs in one over, and England seemed on course for a total of 300 when the umpires called a halt to the innings after only 45 of the scheduled 50 overs. People wondered what was going on.

Pandering to the demands of television, the organisers had tried to ensure that the match would fit precisely into the broadcast schedule by allocating a fixed time period for each innings. Using this regulation, Wessels had deliberately slowed down the pace of the game in order to stem the flow of England's runs. So, when time was called on the innings, England were left stranded on 252 for six after 45 overs.

It was a decent score, but it would have been even larger if the innings had been completed. Once again, an official decision made to satisfy the needs of the people paying the US dollars rather than the people playing the game had seriously backfired, prompting commercial distortion of the semi-final.

Worse was to come.

South Africa lost stalwarts Wessels and Kirsten with 61 on the board, but Hudson moved smoothly to his fourth consecutive half-century and anchored a valiant chase. Adrian Kuiper seemed to be assuming control of the situation when he struck Gladstone Small for three successive boundaries, but this potential match-winner fell for 36. Cronje then struck a brisk 26, and Rhodes improvised a swift 43.

It was approaching mid-morning in South Africa, but hardly anyone had started work. People had stayed home, or were gathering around televisions in schools and offices, cheering every run. Never quite in control of the pursuit, yet never quite out of contention, the underdogs were hanging tough.

Dave Richardson and Brian McMillan came together with work to do and 44 runs still needed from the last five overs, but their sensible and resourceful batting gradually diminished the target to the point where 22 runs were required from the last 13 balls of what had become a nerve-tingling contest.

Suddenly the evening air turned cold, and a steady drizzle became visible in the glare of the floodlights. The umpires asked Gooch if he wanted to continue; the England captain replied by asking if they believed conditions were fit for play. They said no, and Gooch left the field.

Alan Jordaan, the South African team manager, was sitting beside his captain in the row of seats in front of the visiting team's dressing room. He turned to Wessels and said: 'We're stuffed.'

Of all its many imperfections, the 1992 Cricket World Cup is remembered for the ridiculous rain rule that significantly affected six group matches and now ruined the semi-final in Sydney.

In essence, with the best intentions and motivated by no less an authority than Richie Benaud, the World Cup Committee had adopted a scheme whereby, if the second innings was interrupted by rain, the reduction in the target would be commensurate with the lowest-scoring overs of the side that batted first. The rule might have seemed reasonable on paper, but it proved disastrous in practice.

On this dramatic overcast evening in Sydney, this particular shower lasted 12 minutes, which meant the South African innings would be reduced by two overs. The two lowest-scoring overs in the English innings were both maidens. Thus, South Africa's target was reduced from 22 runs off

13 balls to 22 runs from 1 ball.

This news was confirmed on the electronic scoreboard, prompting a chorus of boos around the SCG and expressions of angry indignation among the South Africans. Yet the rule was clear. When the players returned to bowl the last ball, McMillan blocked it grimly; and England had won by 21 runs.

Instead of an electrifying finish, there was anti-climax and dismay. The English were denied any glory in victory, and, as they took the crowd's applause on a lap of honour, the South Africans were left with a sense of injustice in defeat. 'We weren't cheated,' Wessels said later, 'but it was unsatisfactory.'

The captain and his young team had performed beyond all expectations, and they flew home to be hailed as heroes by hundreds of thousands at the airport and on the streets of Johannesburg.

Incidentally, there was no further rain in Sydney that evening. A normal cricket match played for its own sake, alone, would have been agreeably completed, and won without controversy or rancour. Miserably, it had become clear that the World Cup semi-final was not a normal cricket match. It was a fiasco.

England shrugged and moved on. Semi-finalists in 1975, finalists in 1979, semi-finalists in 1983, finalists in 1987: for them, at last, approaching a third final, there was a World Cup to be won.

'I thought it was one of the best one-day sides England has ever put together,' Gooch remembers. 'We started the tournament as a tight-knit unit and played really well. The victory over Australia in Sydney gave us plenty of self-belief and, although we had lost a couple of games, we felt confident.'

And yet, as an Australian record crowd of 87 182 spectators packed into the Melbourne Cricket Ground, the Pakistanis were planning their own bid for glory. 'We watched their semi-final closely,' Imran recalls, 'and we realised that Pringle and De Freitas used the ball well when it had seam and shine on it. I decided to bat at number three to see off that shine and protect our big hitters down the order.'

The captain was certainly not hiding in the shadow of the awe-inspiring Great South Stand, specially built for the tournament. Unfazed by the greatest stage in the game, unconcerned by a television audience in excess of one billon viewers in 29 countries, Imran put himself in the front line and set to work.

He won the toss and, aware that no team had ever won a World Cup final chasing runs, he decided to bat first. When his side started slowly, stuttering at 24 for two after nine overs, he assumed responsibility and took control of the innings, setting the tone and pace, consolidating with caution. On nine he survived a half-chance when Gooch spilled a swirling catch; then he steadied and prospered.

Imran was eventually dismissed for 72. In partnership with the pugnacious Miandad he had constructed a platform on which less experienced batsmen could perform in the closing stages of the innings. Inzamam, Wasim Akram and others swung with relish, and 153 runs were reaped from the last 20 overs.

Pakistan's total of 249 for seven in 50 overs equated to something like level par. Halfway through a finely balanced contest, both teams sensed they had moved halfway towards triumph.

Botham and Gooch opened the England innings and battle was joined. Akram moved in, all grace and speed, power and rhythm, left-arm over the wicket. Botham groped, but made no contact. Moin Khan took the ball, and appealed. To English horror, umpire Brian Aldridge raised his finger.

'Heh, Both,' chirped Aamir Sohail, rubbing in the agony as he brushed past the departing batsman, 'why don't you send your mother-in-law out now? She couldn't do any worse.'

The reference to the all-rounder's light-hearted comment almost six years earlier, that he would not even send his mother-in-law to Pakistan, hinted at the intensity of the contest.

England were wobbling. Stewart was caught behind, Hick fell LBW to a Mushtaq Ahmed googly, and, in a state of frustration, Gooch swept and was wonderfully caught by Aaqib Javed at square leg. At 69 for four, with their team in crisis, Neil Fairbrother and Allan Lamb launched the fightback. The pair added 72 in 14 overs and brought the final back into the balance. Just 109 runs were needed from the last 15 overs.

Imran summoned Akram for a second spell, and the quick bowler produced two magnificent fast, dipping in-swingers, shattering the stumps of Lamb and Chris Lewis in successive deliveries. The MCG rose to acclaim a decisive burst of bowling, later hailed by Gooch, graciously, as 'quite brilliant'.

The English tail continued to rage against the dying of their hopes but, with the target drifting further and further away on this breezy autumn evening in Melbourne, Imran returned to the attack. Illingworth drove hard and high, and Ramiz Raja took the catch at mid-off. Pakistan had won by 22 runs.

Imran raised his arms in triumph. After winning only one of their first five matches of the tournament, his side had won five in succession and emerged as world champions.

Back home in Pakistan, it was just after a quarter past five in the evening on the 18th day of Ramadan, and millions of people poured onto the streets of major cities and isolated villages alike. As the *iftari* (the breaking of the fast at sunset) approached, the national celebrations began. In all its sports history, through great days in hockey and squash, this small country had never known a triumph such as this.

Colin Cowdrey, a former England captain and the current ICC chairman, stepped forward to present the Benson and Hedges World Cup, a glittering Waterford crystal globe, and Imran Khan responded with a speech that, overlooking his team and country, seemed to celebrate a personal triumph.

Gooch and his players stood in a disconsolate huddle and endured the gloating. The losing captain looked and felt gutted. 'The better side won,' he reflected later. 'We might have bowled them out for 74 in the group match, but they came through when it really mattered. Perhaps we were tired after so long on tour, but we did come off the boil. It was hard. Some of us had played in three World Cup finals, and lost all three.'

Imran simply beamed, and confirmed his retirement at the pinnacle of the game in precisely the manner he had planned all along . . . clutching the game's greatest prize, hailed and admired.

Imran Khan

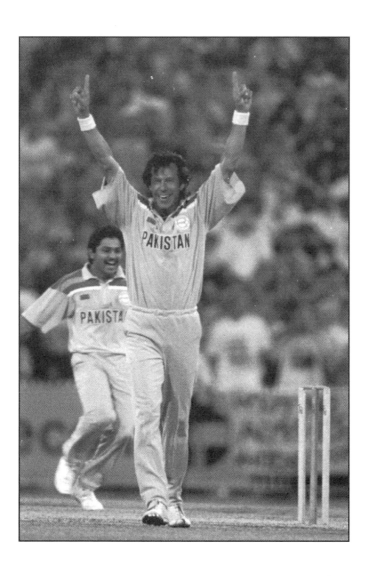

Born into an aristocratic cricketing family, educated at the eminent Aitchison College in Lahore, coached at the elite Gymkhana Club, he calmly decided that, one day, he would play for Pakistan.

There was no argument and, at only 11 years old, Imran Ahmed Khan Niazi used to ask his sisters and the family servants to bowl at him, relentlessly, outdoors and indoors, often past midnight. Two servants left to seek work in another house, but this privileged, talented young man made progress.

Two of his cousins had shown the way: he had watched from the stands when Javed Burki scored a great 138 against the 1961/62 English tourists in Lahore, and then basked in reflected glory when Burki made 101 at Lord's a few months later. And he had always idolised Majid Khan, six years his senior, a majestic stroke player who made a first-class century aged 15, and launched a fine Test career three years later.

'Cricketing excellence was in my blood,' Imran would later reflect, in characteristic fashion, 'so who was I to argue with the fates that had so liberally sprinkled me with stardust?'

He underscored this arrogant sense of destiny with sweat and toil. At the sweltering height of summer in Lahore, when his family retreated to the hills, the young cricketer opted to stay in town and play for Gymkhana in the Wazir Ali league. Matches were played in two sessions, from seven in the morning until eleven, and then from four in the afternoon until stumps, enabling the players to escape the midday sun.

Imran was emerging as a prolific batsman, and, as he grew taller, he realised he could generate speed off the uniformly slow pitches, even making the opposition jump around the crease. Into his late teens, he became known as a genuine all-rounder, both a top-class batsman and a top-class fast bowler.

In May 1971, still four months short of his 19th birthday, he was selected to make his Test debut, playing for Pakistan against England at Edgbaston in Birmingham. His legend was born.

Through the next two decades, until his last Test, against Sri Lanka at Faisalabad in 1992, he appeared in 88 Tests for Pakistan, scoring 3 807 runs and taking 362 wickets. He was selected to play in his country's first-ever limited overs match, against England in 1974, and remained maybe the central pillar in the team through 175 one-day internationals to the crowning triumph in his last game, the 1992 World Cup final.

At stages, he came over as amazingly self-important, sneering at opponents as if they didn't deserve to be playing on the same field, and yet he showed care and sensitivity in his captaincy, quietly encouraging his players whenever possible, using more carrot than stick, always leading by example.

A thoroughbred athlete, charismatic and dashing, intelligent and brave, noble and handsome, he seemed to have been incredibly blessed, and he remained vastly popular throughout Pakistan and among the supporters of his adopted teams, Sussex in England and New South Wales in Australia.

These legions of admirers recognised first and foremost a genuinely fine cricketer who rarely allowed his standards to drop below world class. He could bat with iron discipline to save a Test, or with bludgeoning power to accelerate a run chase. He bowled with both raw aggression and shrewd intelligence.

And they also appreciated his rare ability to galvanise those playing around him. No team with Imran in its ranks was ever beaten until the last run was scored against them or the last wicket taken. Perhaps because he had been able always to play the game just for pleasure, he began to personify an almost Corinthian degree of freedom and gusto. A clever professional in his commercial affairs, he seemed an amateur at heart.

Imran captained Pakistan by sheer force of character, instilling discipline in all matters, and transforming an otherwise temperamental and easily dispirited group into, as he put it, 'cornered tigers'.

'He appeared to carry a natural authority,' Geoffrey Boycott recalls, 'and this enabled him to pull each of the strings together. Under his benevolent dictatorship, Pakistan became a major power in world cricket, even if there were some who only fully appreciated his contribution when he had gone.'

His status as a respected statesman of the game was tested in the mid-1990s, when he became involved in a courtroom duel against two old opponents, Botham and Lamb. They sued him for calling the England team 'racist' in his autobiography, and both sides muttered accusations of ball tampering. The judge found in Imran's favour but, all said and done, cricket was the loser and the lawyers were the winners.

Imran moved on and worked hard to raise funds to build a cancer hospital in Lahore. This project came to fruition with the opening of the Shaukat-Khanum Memorial Hospital in December 1994.

The next phase of his life, he decided, would be politics. True to form, Imran opted to found and develop his own party and, ever willing to speak his mind, he raised eyebrows by publicly criticising both the army and intelligence agencies, two bodies often regarded as the political kingmakers in Pakistan.

Despite some crushing electoral defeats, he remains a major figure in public affairs. 'Can Imran become Pakistan's next Prime Minister?' asked a newspaper in 2002.

Stranger things have happened.

Chapter Nine

Night of a Thousand Stars

On 5 January 1996 the world's outstanding players did not assemble at a glittering gala awards banquet to celebrate the 25th anniversary of one-day international cricket, but if they had . . .

Tony Greig, master of ceremonies, steps forward. Tall, smooth, shiny, resplendent in a sweetcorn-yellow blazer, the ex-England captain has been promoted to major in the Channel Nine army, and appears to personify the colourful, vibrant, brash and occasionally superficial culture of one-day cricket.

'Good evening, ladies and gentlemen,' he declares, staring into a television camera identified as 'live' by a red light on top. The dinner guests, like the crowd at a match, are treated like scenery. 'Welcome to the first Benson and Hedges Silver Jubilee One-Day Cricket Awards Gala, brought to you in conjunction with our friends at Channel Nine, Emirates, McDonald's, Super Snappy Snacks and Fancy Fashions.

'It is, of course, an enormous pleasure and privilege for us all to be here in Sharjah.'

The banquet is being hosted in the United Arab Emirates because this oasis in the desert is famous as the venue of an annual one-day international tournament and has now become synonymous with the proliferation of limited overs cricket, and also because Abdul Rahman Bukhatir, a local mover and sheikh, dedicated creator of the Sharjah event, is paying the bills. This noble pioneer smiles at the main table.

Greig continues: 'One-day international cricket has advanced from its accidental origins in Melbourne 25 years ago to a point where hardly a day seems to pass when there is not a one-day international being played somewhere in the world. Tonight, we celebrate the achievements of this golden era.'

The four World Cup-winning captains – Clive Lloyd, Kapil Dev, Allan Border and Imran Khan – are seated at the same table. Lara, Rhodes and Tendulkar chatter happily. All the stars are out.

'And now, ladies and gentlemen,' Greig smiles, 'may I invite perhaps the greatest all-rounder of all time on stage to present the batting awards. He played one solitary one-day international at the end of his eminent career, and he was bowled for a duck, but he remains the great Sir Gary Sobers.'

Applause surges through the hall as the West Indian makes his way between the tables, into a hug from Greig and, finally, to the podium, where he announces winners in the following categories:

Most Runs Scored in One Over: and the winner is . . . Sanath Jayasuriya, of Sri Lanka, who embarked on a blazing hitting spree against Aamir Sohail at Singapore, hammering the Pakistani bowler for no fewer than 29 runs in one over. In six balls, he crashed 6,4,6,6,6 and finished with a single.

Highest Team Score: and the winner is . . . Sri Lanka, who thrilled their home crowd at Kandy by scoring an astounding 398 for five in their allotted 50 overs against Kenya late in 1995.

Lowest Team Score: and the winner is . . . Pakistan, who totalled 43 against the West Indies at Newlands, Cape Town, in February 1993. The innings lasted only 19 overs and five balls.

Most Dramatic Surge to Victory: and the winner is . . . Wasim Akram, who struck two consecutive sixes to secure victory for Pakistan against Bangladesh at Sharjah in 1995.

Most Exciting Last-ball Victory: and the winner is . . . Ian Botham, who needed to hit the last ball of the match for four to help England beat Pakistan at Sahiwal in 1977, and did so.

Most Hours of Practice: and the winner is . . . Sachin Tendulkar, star of India, who practised his batting endlessly through his early teens. Day after day, he would get in the nets from seven till nine in the morning, play a match from 09:30 until 16:30, and be back in the nets from five until seven in the evening.

Most Centuries: and the winner is . . . once again, and not by coincidence, Sachin Tendulkar, who has so far made 19 centuries in one-day internationals and averages a century every six innings.

Fastest Century: and the winner is . . . Shahid Afridi of Pakistan, who blasted his way to three figures in 37 balls when playing against Sri Lanka in Nairobi. At the age of only 16 years and 217 days, Afridi hammered no fewer than 11 sixes and six boundaries in his remarkable onslaught.

Oldest Player to Score a Century: and the winner is . . . Geoffrey Boycott, who, at the age of 39 years and 51 days, scored a fluent 105 for England against Australia at Sydney in 1979.

First Man to Carry Bat Through an Innings: and the winner is . . . Grant Flower, who first achieved the feat by scoring 84 not out for Zimbabwe against England at Sydney in 1994.

Most Consecutive Ducks: and the winner is . . . Gus Logie, of the West Indies, who was dismissed for 0 in four consecutive one-day internationals during the course of 1986.

Ushering Sir Gary off stage, Greig expertly oils the cogs of the evening and invites Dennis Lillee forward to present the bowling awards. 'Don't worry, this won't take long,' the Australian declares bluntly. 'As you all know, one-day cricket is all about batsmen these days. People only want to see runs, so we bowlers must run in on dead-flat pitches, with defensive fields, and simply serve the ball.

'Even so, we've got some things right,' he adds, before presenting the following awards.

Most Wickets Taken In a Match: and the winner is . . . Aqib Javed, of Pakistan, who seized seven Indian wickets at a cost of only 37 runs during a match at Sharjah in 1992.

Most Telephone Calls Received by a Bowler during a Match: and the winner is . . . Ian Botham, the England all rounder who asked umpire Harold Bird to look after his mobile telephone during a match against Pakistan at Edgbaston in 1987. There were three calls: the first was from Botham's business manager, then his wife, and finally a friend trying to confirm the details of a weekend angling trip.

Most Deceptive Delivery: and the winner is . . . Fanie de Villiers, the South African opening bowler, who started the 42nd over of the one-day international against Zimbabwe at Harare in October 1995 by bowling not a cricket ball but a paper cup at the flabbergasted batsman, Henry Olonga.

Conceding Most Extras in an Innings: and the winner is . . . the West Indies, who gave away 59 extras in a match against Pakistan at Brisbane in 1988. This gift comprised eight byes, ten leg byes, four no-balls and a remarkably generous 37 wides. It was also decisive: Pakistan won by 55 runs.

'And finally,' Greig announces, 'I realise it's getting late, and I can see some of the younger players here tonight are anxious to finish their isotonic energy drinks and get to bed, but please stay right where you are for this last part of the evening, the presentation of the Miscellaneous Awards.

'And to present these prizes, I give you the legend who came up with the idea to stage that first one-day international in Melbourne all those 25 years ago tonight . . . Sir Donald Bradman.'

The Don makes his way through a rousing standing ovation and reaches the microphone where, playing an admirably straight bat to some off-beat bowling, he announces the following winners:

Most Catches in an Innings: and the winner is . . . Jonty Rhodes, of South Africa, who leaped, swooped and jumped to seize five catches against the West Indies during the Hero Cup at Bombay.

Most International Venues in a Country: and the winner is . . . India, who have staged more one-day internationals (192) at more grounds (34) and in more cities (30) than anyone else.

Most Unlucky Victim of a Third Umpire: and the winner is . . . South Africa's Dave Richardson, who was given out by the third umpire, Atiq Khan, when he had made his ground against Pakistan at Karachi in

1994. Mr Khan later apologised, admitting he had pressed the wrong button on his machine.

Longest Name: and the winner is . . . the Sri Lankan bowler who made his international debut on 15 February 1994 and is known as Warnakulasuriya Patabendige Ushantha Chaminda Joseph Vaas.

Most Embarrassing Pitch Inspection by a TV Presenter: and the winner is . . . our MC for the evening, Tony Greig who, while inspecting the pitch before a match between South Africa and Australia at the WACA in Perth on 16 January 1994, somehow managed to drop a hotel key into one of the lateral cracks. He could not retrieve it, and the key remained embedded in the pitch for the duration of the game.

Amid peals of laughter, Bradman hands the last statuette to the bashful, embarrassed and utterly thrilled Greig, who slickly and smoothly ends the night with a closing vote of thanks.

'On behalf of everyone in the game, thank you to all the players who provide such consistently wonderful entertainment, and who travel around the globe to play one-day internationals in the famous old grounds as well as the newer venues like Nairobi, Toronto, Singapore and, of course, Sharjah.

'And thank you to our sponsors. Without money, none of this would have been possible.'

Greig grins . . . and Bradman returns to his seat, smiling thinly.

Chapter Ten

The Sixth World Cup

In 1993, one year after the first primarily commercial cricket World Cup, the ICC came to a crossroads: either they would sustain the principle of rotation and take the next tournament back to its roots in England, or they would single-mindedly pursue profit and award the event to the highest bidder.

The Council didn't hesitate.

Dollars prevailed over logic, expediency over principle, and greed over tradition.

The English delegation, still believing in old values, had ambled into the meeting and cheerfully put their case to stage the World Cup in 1996. After Asia in 1987 and Australia in 1992, they argued, it was time for the tournament to come back to the old country. They had expected unanimous approval and a decent lunch, but instead a strong rival bid from India ambushed their ambitions.

Carrying Pakistan and Sri Lanka as co-hosts in their bid, the carefully prepared, confident Indians flexed their commercial muscles: they projected a huge increase in sponsorship revenue; they proposed an expanded 12-nation tournament, with two round-robin groups of six, advancing to knockout quarter-finals; and they deftly swayed votes by creating three places in the draw for the associate members.

'And,' the smiling Asians concluded, 'we will increase the total prize money by 22 per cent.'

Traditionalists slumped ever deeper into their leather seats.

What started as a hazy impression now had to be accepted as a simple

134

fact. Cricket could generate more money in the Indian sub-continent than anywhere else in the world. By virtue of their game's vast popularity in sprawling cities and countless villages, the Indians could sell their game to multinational sponsors as a perfect vehicle to carry brands into the vast, largely untapped markets of southern Asia.

The Englishmen looked at one another and shrugged. Plainly unable to match these financial projections, and sensing the ICC would certainly vote for the prospect of larger profits rather than the principle of rotation, they reluctantly decided to sue for peace in the face of humiliating defeat.

'Mr Chairman,' the TCCB delegate began. 'In view of the obvious impasse that has developed today, we would like to propose that India, Pakistan and Sri Lanka co-host the next tournament and that we, irrevocably, confirm here and now that the 1999 World Cup will be staged in England.'

All hands raised, and the compromise motion was agreed. Amid uneasy handshakes and grinding of teeth, one of the most antagonistic, unpleasant ICC meetings came to a close. Once upon a time, the administration of cricket had been oiled by lifelong friendships and a few gin and tonics.

No longer.

In the mid-1990s, the game's governing body appeared doubly divided.

First, there was a racial split between the 'white' establishment (as represented by England, Australia and New Zealand) and the increasingly firm 'non-white' nations (India, Pakistan, Sri Lanka and the West Indies). A delicate balance of power between the two factions had been disturbed by the arrival at the table of the South Africans, and they increasingly found themselves left with a casting vote.

Secondly, the Council was divided between the purists who believed the interests of the game should be paramount at all times, and the modernists who took a brutal commercial view, reckoning nothing was sacred and everything was justified in the drive to make as much money as possible.

At the ICC meeting in 1993, it was the 'non-white' modernists who wore the widest smiles.

The game's showpiece event was heading back to the sub-continent, but it soon began to take shape as a dramatically different tournament from the World Cup in 1987. Then, the Asian organisers had wanted to prove they could stage a top-class event; now they wanted to make money.

In preparations for the 1996 World Cup, the local organising committee, Pilcom, seemed less concerned about the welfare of the players than with finding an official chewing gum supplier.

They created a cricketing theme park but, when the squads began to arrive, newspaper headlines were being dominated by the security situation in Sri Lanka. A terrorist bomb attack had killed 73 people in Colombo a fortnight earlier, prompting Australian and West Indian officials to declare that they would not put their players at risk by playing scheduled matches against Sri Lanka in the capital city.

The Australians were particularly anxious. Several of their leading players were vilified in Asia for making allegations of attempts to bribe them during their last visit to the sub-continent in 1994. Shane Warne said he was receiving death threats, and unknown sources had warned the ACB that their squad would be met by a suicide bomber when they arrived in the baggage claim area at Colombo airport.

'Nothing is more important than the safety of our players,' the ACB announced.

The organisers worked hard to resolve the situation. Desperate to complete their entire match schedule, and so maintain the integrity of the tournament, they suggested the players could assemble at a port in India early on the morning of the game and be flown by helicopter gunship directly to the Premadasa cricket stadium in Colombo. They would play and be whisked back to India straight after the game.

'No, thanks,' the Australians replied. 'We'll forfeit the match.'

The West Indians followed suit.

Pilcom was enraged. Officials called a press conference, and effectively launched the tournament in bitter acrimony by accusing Australia and the West Indies of pursuing some kind of vendetta against the Third World by trying to disrupt the event. Sir Clyde Walcott, the ICC chairman, skilfully sapped the venom by pointing out that the Caribbean Islands were, by general consent, part of the Third World.

The decisions not to play in Colombo were motivated by genuine concern, but they were encouraged by a flawed format. With four teams qualifying from each group of six, both the Australians and West Indies worked out that they could each sacrifice one game and still comfortably advance to the quarter-finals.

And they were right.

The group stages proved astonishingly dull. Three weeks of exhausting travel, and too often meaningless cricket, produced the completely predictable outcome that Zimbabwe and the three associate member debutant teams – Holland, UAE and Kenya – were the teams eliminated and sent home before the quarter-finals.

When sports events are structured for sport's sake, every match counts and high levels of excitement are maintained, but the 1996 World Cup was designed for sponsors, maximising their exposure during the bloated group phase and almost ensuring the top sides would advance to the knock-out stages.

The event could have buzzed if only two teams progressed from each group straight into the semi-finals, but the financial bonanza of four quarter-finals, with all the attendant gate receipts and television exposure, proved too much for the organisers to resist. Yet again, they made a dash for the cash.

Incredibly, the first 30 matches served no cricketing purpose other than to eliminate four also-ran teams, and, although the Indian supporters turned up in large numbers, crowds in Pakistan were small.

The showpiece had been reduced to a shambles.

A lavish opening ceremony in Calcutta flopped when the wind played havoc with a laser show, balloons were released but refused to take flight, and the public address announcer introduced the Zimbabweans as the UAE, and the Pakistanis as South Africans. The highly paid Italian director of the muddled extravaganza fled.

He may have considered himself lucky to escape. Players, media and supporters were left to endure the logistical chaos of travelling to and fro between venues spread across three countries, and the strain began to take its toll on the players, already irritated by having to play in sub-standard kit.

It seemed somehow fitting (sic) that the abiding image of a tournament that reduced the World Cup to a marketing wheeze should be the spectacle of the game's superstars being made to look like schoolboys, forced to perform in trousers that stopped two or three inches above the ankles.

Group A seemed to be following the official script. India was sustained by the brilliant Sachin Tendulkar, Brian Lara scored enough runs to keep the West Indians on track, and the Waugh twins inspired an increasingly powerful Australian challenge. Sri Lanka benefited from two walkovers and gained confidence, Zimbabwe again lacked the consistency needed to make a real impact, and Kenya managed to compete without threatening to win ... at least until they arrived in the town of Pune, where they would play the West Indies.

It was 29 February, an extraordinary kind of day for an extraordinary kind of occasion.

The East Africans were sent in to bat, and, once star batsman Steve

Tikolo was caught behind for 29 (he had scored 65 against India), they collapsed to 81 for six. However, 17-year-old Thomas Odoyo then struck 24 in a wagging tail, and the underdogs scrambled to 166 all out in 49.3 overs.

Maurice Odumbe, the Kenyan captain, had feared for his team's prospects when he lost the toss, and now prepared himself for apparently inevitable defeat. 'Just do your best,' he told his players, resplendent in bright pea-green kit, as they took the field to defend what seemed an undefendable total.

Rajab Ali resolutely tried his best. The seamer ran in and uprooted Richie Richardson's leg stump, Martin Suji clean-bowled Sherwin Campbell, and when Rajab found the edge of Lara's princely bat, the portly, genial wicketkeeper Tariq Ali managed to hold the priceless catch. The Kenyans were leaping with excitement. When Keith Arthurton was run out for nought, the West Indians stood at 35 for four.

Even then, sages in the press box assumed that one of the batsmen would eventually get his head down and rescue the two-time champions. It didn't happen. Only Shivnarine Chanderpaul and Roger Harper reached double figures, and the West Indies were dismissed for 93.

Odumbe stood at the apex of perhaps the greatest shock result in cricket World Cup history, and rubbed his eyes. 'To us, this is like winning the World Cup,' said the Kenyan captain, eyes ablaze with delight. 'When the last wicket fell, everybody was very excited. We have made history here. I can't believe it. I think the size of what we have done will only hit me when I wake up in the morning.'

In a taut and tightly structured tournament, such humiliation would have sent the West Indians heading for home, and yet, at the 1996 World Cup, there would still be one more chance for this team that had forfeited one match in Colombo on grounds of security and had now lost to Kenya.

Incredibly – some said ridiculously – Richardson's side could still reach the quarter-finals if they managed to win their last group match, against Australia in Jaipur; and they did, with the defiant captain scoring 93 and Lara making 60 in a successful, reputation-restoring pursuit of 230 to win.

This round of matches in Group A also produced another major step forward in the evolution of 'the way to play one-day cricket', the core strategy followed throughout the cricket community.

Ever since Ted Dexter had blazed a pioneering path during the early years of the Gillette Cup in England, it had been accepted that one-day innings should be launched by opening batsmen playing cautiously, aiming to score around three runs per over, keeping wickets in hand for the late onslaught. This was considered 'par', and any team standing at 50 without loss after 15 overs was content.

This standard changed dramatically in 1996.

Ripping up the consensus, the Sri Lankans looked objectively at the first 15 overs of an innings, when the rules compelled the fielding captain to place most of his men inside the 30-metre circles, and suddenly saw this period as a golden opportunity to attack, play strokes and hit over the infield.

Sanath Jayasuriya and Romesh Kaluwitharana, Sri Lanka's opening batsmen, cast caution aside and, in a blaze of strokeplay, translated the idea into reality, launching their team's innings so effectively that their team's score generally reached 90 or maybe 100 for the loss of one or two after 15 overs. Rival captains watched in wonder and admiration, and immediately started to imitate.

Thus, the game changed and Sri Lanka advanced without losing a match in Group A.

The organisers had situated Group B in Pakistan, with only a few matches being played in India, and the predictable progress to the quarter-finals of Pakistan, England, New Zealand and South Africa, with Holland and the United Arab Emirates being eliminated, duly came to pass.

South Africa won the group. Intelligently coached by Bob Woolmer, strongly captained by Hansie Cronje, the dark horses emerged as favourites, winning five out of five group matches with aggressive batting, steady bowling and exceptional fielding. The team practised their fielding drills for three hours before the match with Holland, and such intense dedication yielded a sequence of dazzling run-outs.

Woolmer described the overall team performance against New Zealand as 'close to awesome', but Gary Kirsten won individual acclaim for his outstanding innings of 188 against the UAE.

Pakistan did not start their matches until after the Muslim fasting month of Ramadan, and aside from one setback against South Africa, they safely claimed second place in the group. With Javed Miandad sustaining his record of having played in every World Cup, they launched the defence of their title with skilful resolve and, at one stage, some confusion. Against New Zealand in Lahore, Saeed Anwar and Inzamam ul-Haq both appeared in shirts marked 'Younis' across the shoulders. In 1996, anything went.

The New Zealanders competed effectively once again, with Nathan

Astle's century versus England getting them off to a sound start and Roger Twose's strong form ensuring solid progress.

England arrived at the tournament in poor form, and seemed to lurch from one problem to another. After losing to New Zealand, they travelled to play the UAE in Peshawar, a fiercely Islamic city where all women were covered from head to toe and where, it soon became clear, the only alcoholic refreshments were dusty bottles of weak lager on sale at the bar of the Pearl Hotel. This beverage was only sold to people willing to sign a form, giving their personal details and acknowledging their status as alcoholics.

The entire England team, their management and the attendant press corps and photographers all confessed to being alcoholics, and the evidence remains at the Pearl Hotel, Peshawar.

Mike Atherton's team recovered to beat the UAE and virtually ensure their progress by defeating Holland, but they were in difficulty again when the lucid Lancastrian captain lost patience during a crass question at the press conference after losing to South Africa and called a Pakistani journalist a 'buffoon'. As outrage broke out among his easily offended hosts, and the casual remark was blown into an international incident echoing back to the colonial era, a bemused Atherton agreed to apologise the following day.

Holland performed respectably throughout, but were bitterly disappointed to lose their 'mini-final' against the UAE and eventually return home with five defeats in five matches.

For their part, the Emirates had brought a splash of colour and style to the tournament. Crowned as ICC Trophy champions, they were captained by the Sultan Zarawani, a millionaire of whom it was said that his leg spin was significantly less impressive than his gleaming red Lamborghini.

At any rate, in his team's opening match against South Africa, chasing a huge 322, the Sultan declined to wear a helmet when he faced Allan Donald and was promptly struck on the head, first ball. Caught for 0 in the following over, he spent the rest of the evening having check-ups in hospital.

Zarawani's squad included two players born in the Emirates, of whom he was one. Of the 12 others, one was born in the USA, two in Sri Lanka, one in India and eight in Pakistan. In fact, Saleem Raza was able to hit the winning runs in the pride match against Holland in his home town, Lahore.

The World Cup officially started on 14 February but, after all the huffing and puffing, and travelling, the competition effectively began 23 days later, on 9 March, when Sri Lanka faced England in the first quarter-final at Faisalabad. Now, at last, the game mattered. The losers would go home.

Atherton won the toss and batted first, aiming for 300. In the event, only Phil de Freitas remotely rose to the challenge – he made 67 in 64 balls – and England was indebted to a 62-run stand between Dermot Reeve and Darren Gough for taking them past 200 to a mediocre total of 235 for eight.

Enter the Sri Lankan openers, primed to attack.

Kaluwitharana clouted his first two balls to the boundary but was then bowled by Richard Illingworth, a spinner opening the bowling. English success was short-lived because Jayasuriya erupted. The talented opener scored the fastest 50 in the history of the tournament, from only 29 balls, and was finally caught behind for 82 in 44 balls, an extraordinary innings that included three sixes and 14 fours.

He was dismissed in the 13th over of the innings, leaving his side at 113 for two, almost halfway to their target. The contest was over, and Arjuna Ranatunga gently eased his team into the semi-final.

England was left to reflect upon the first time they had failed to reach the last four of a World Cup. The team manager, Raymond Illingworth, subsequently told how he had been approached by a bookmaker before the game but, as Gough sardonically remarked, 'I couldn't imagine anyone paying money for us to play badly because in this World Cup, we were perfectly capable of doing that by ourselves.'

Meanwhile, under floodlights in Bangalore, India and Pakistan contested a quarter-final that many of their compatriots seemed to regard as an acceptable substitute for the constantly threatened war between the two neighbours and co-hosts. In the event, the teams produced a thriller that swung first one way, then the other, back and forth, concluding with ecstasy on one side and scandal on the other.

India chose to bat first and, though Navjot Sidhu made 93, they appeared to be scoring too slowly until Ajay Jadeja sparked a late onslaught. As he hammered 45 in 25 balls, the home team plundered 51 runs from the last three overs and reached an impressive 287 for eight in 50 overs.

To their credit, the Pakistanis picked up the gauntlet. Following the Sri Lankan fashion, Saeed Anwar and Aamir Sohail launched the chase in a blur, racing to 113 for two in 15 overs. Salim Malik then made 38, Rashid Latif hit two sixes in his 26, but Pakistan kept losing wickets and, when the defiant Miandad was run out for 38 with the score at 239 for eight, the Indian crowd could start to celebrate.

The defending champions ended 39 runs short, and a nation wept. A hysterical supporter shot one bullet into his television set and another into his chest. Effigies of Wasim Akram were burned on the streets. This seemed a trifle harsh. The captain had withdrawn from the game with pulled muscles in his side; but, in the search for a scapegoat, with no evidence, he was accused of being involved in a plot to throw the match.

'I do not deserve this,' Akram declared, after he had received death threats and seen his house pelted with stones, eggs and tomatoes. 'I have always played my best for Pakistan. I am prepared to swear over the holy Koran that I have never been involved in betting and that I am clean.'

Two days later in Karachi, South Africa approached their quarter-final against the West Indians with such confidence that they rested their most feared bowler. In search of a new world record 11th successive one-day international victory, they decided to omit Donald and play an extra spinner.

The fast bowler recalls: 'Hansie (Cronje) came to my room on the evening before the game, looking serious, and I said, "forget it, don't tell me". There had been negative vibes. When I was on my own, I cried my eyes out. Bob Woolmer came to see me later and said he didn't know I felt so strongly. He said they planned for two spinners on a slow pitch to frustrate the batsmen. I understood that, but it still hurt like hell.'

In the event, there was no planning for Lara. The genius arrived at the crease with his side at 42 for one, scored an outstanding 111 in only 94 balls, and enabled the previously unimpressive West Indians to find form when it really mattered and post a very respectable 264 for eight in 50 overs.

The grimly positive South Africans seemed on course for victory when Andrew Hudson and Daryll Cullinan took the score to 118 for one, but both fell to the slow left-arm spin of Jimmy Adams. Suddenly under pressure for the first time in the tournament, the newly installed favourites wilted. Rhodes was caught on the mid-wicket boundary, and Cronje fought bravely before falling to Adams for a hard-hitting 40.

Defeat by 19 runs left South Africa stunned. 'I can't believe what has happened,' Cronje said afterwards, disappointed that his side would not emulate their rugby counterparts and become world champions. 'Till this point of the tournament, we have been playing the best cricket and everything has gone 100 per cent to plan. Now we have one poor match and we are gone. I feel sorry for Bob Woolmer. It isn't his fault.'

For Richardson and his team, the humbling defeat against Kenya suddenly seemed a long time ago. They had defeated the in-form side and, fearing nobody, stood just two wins from glory.

On the same day in Madras, the indomitable Waugh twins propelled

Australia through a testing semi-final against New Zealand. The Kiwis had batted first and, with Chris Harris striking 130 from 124 balls, managed to post 286 for nine, their highest score in 63 one-day games against their neighbours.

Undaunted, Mark Waugh led the reply with purpose, soon found his rhythm, and stroked 110 in 112 balls, in the process becoming the first player to score three centuries in a World Cup. Brother Steve then took over and his unbeaten 59 ensured victory with two overs to spare.

Oddly, each of the quarter-finals had been won by the team from Group A, condemning the qualifiers from Group B (by coincidence, the four semi-finalists in 1992) to pack their bags and go home.

Like an Olympic cycling race, the tournament had started slowly and uneventfully, wandering through lap after lap, but now it was hurtling towards a frenzied, exciting conclusion.

More than 106 000 people descended upon Eden Gardens, Calcutta, desperate to see India overcome Sri Lanka in the first semi-final, and this vast, seething crowd roared with delight when both Sri Lanka's celebrated opening batsmen were dismissed in the very first over of the day. First Kaluwitharana then Jayasuriya slashed flamboyantly at Javagal Srinath, and both were gleefully caught at third man.

From the shock of two wickets for one run, Aravinda de Silva and Roshan Mahanama bravely maintained their aggressive strategy, playing their strokes, scoring 66 and 58 respectively. With sterling support down the order, the Sri Lankans were ultimately relieved to post a decent 251 for eight in 50 overs.

'That target shouldn't be a problem,' murmured 106 000 excited Indians in unison.

Sachin Tendulkar and Sanjay Manjrekar confirmed the mood of optimism, advancing from the early loss of Sidhu to set the home team apparently on course for a comfortable victory. Calcutta was preparing to party, but India's World Cup ambitions were then shattered by a freakish collapse.

Tendulkar was stumped off Jayasuriya for 65, Azharuddin prodded a return catch to Dharmasena without scoring, and the wickets began to tumble. As they watched their side crumble from 98 for one to 120 for seven, the mood of the vast, seething crowd changed from silent shock to raging fury.

Spectators had started throwing bottles of water and other forms of debris at the Sri Lankan fielders, and when De Silva held a running catch to dismiss Kapoor, reducing India to 120 for eight, the unrest in the stands turned for the worse. Clive Lloyd, the match referee, had seen enough. The former West Indian captain walked out to the middle and decisively ordered the players to return to the pavilion.

In his view, the players were in danger and, after consulting both umpires, he abandoned the match and awarded the semi-final to Sri Lanka by default. The Indians made no complaint.

Amidst unbearable heat and humidity, Eden Gardens had become a frenzied cauldron of rage, confusion, disappointment and blazing bonfires but, remarkably, the crowd dispersed without further incident. It looked as if, having made their protest, the fanatical people of Calcutta were content to go home.

'It is impossible to be Indian today and not be ashamed,' declared an editorial column on the front page of the *Indian Express* the following morning, and various official apologies were tendered to Arjuna Ranatunga and his side. They did not mind. Once the whipping boys of World Cup cricket, the 'Slankies' had electrified the tournament with their aggressive batting and secured a place in the final.

Australia and the West Indies produced an equally dramatic semi-final the following day in Mohali, but in this remarkable game the action was mercifully confined to the field of play.

After only 40 minutes the match seemed dead as a contest. Curtly Ambrose and Ian Bishop had rumbled in, removing Mark Taylor, Ricky Ponting and both Waugh brothers for a combined total of four runs. Stuart Law and Michael Bevan led the fightback, adding 138 in 32 overs, but even the most optimistic Australian could see that a total of 207 for eight in 50 overs seemed inadequate on a decent pitch.

Lara established the pace of the chase with 45 off as many balls, then Chanderpaul and Richardson took control, easing their side to within touching distance of victory at 165 for two. The West Indies only needed to score 43 runs from the last nine overs with eight wickets in hand: it was a doddle.

At least, it should have been a doddle.

Chanderpaul looked well set, but he started to suffer cramp as he neared his century and, with his score on 80, was caught off McGrath. The Australians sensed a chance. Roger Harper and Otis Gibson were promoted in the order to hit hard and hasten the end, but both swung and both missed.

The innings was on the skids. Richardson held firm at one end, but

Warne produced one of his trademark spells of unplayable bowling, claiming three wickets for six runs in two overs. Jimmy Adams went for two, Keith Arthurton didn't trouble the scorers, and, with the crowd spellbound by the drama, the West Indies battled their way to the start of the last over still needing 10 runs to win, with two wickets left.

Richardson took guard as Fleming moved in. The first ball was a fraction too full, and the batsman sent it purring to the boundary. Back home, hundreds of thousands of Caribbean faces pressed to thousands of radios dared to smile. Next ball, inexplicably, the captain called Ambrose for a quick single. The tall, gangly tail-ender galloped to make his ground but, after a television replay, was adjudged run out.

Courtney Walsh arrived at the crease with six runs required from four balls. He opened his shoulders and heaved for glory, missed the ball completely, and was bowled. Australia had won.

Richardson had declared his intention to resign after the World Cup. The captain was left stranded at the non-striker's end, left unbeaten on 49, and left to wonder how his team had panicked so close to victory and thrown away a place in the final. He had hoped to leave the international stage on the shoulders of his triumphant team-mates; instead, he trudged to the pavilion, alone.

'The West Indians won 95 per cent of this match,' Taylor, the Australian captain, conceded afterwards, 'but we didn't stop trying and managed to win the 5 per cent that really mattered.'

It was late on a Thursday night when the Australians got to bed after the day/night semi-final. They flew to Lahore on the Friday, trained lightly on the Saturday, and were thrust into the World Cup final at lunch time on the Sunday. In a tournament that seemed to have dragged on for several months, it seemed ridiculous that less than 60 hours recovery time had been scheduled between the second semi-final and the final.

Inevitably, when the big day dawned, the Australians looked flat.

In any event, the tournament had produced a neat conclusion. Australia had declined to play Sri Lanka in Colombo at the beginning of the competition, but now they were meeting this same opposition in the final. The state of relations between the two teams appeared to be, at best, poor.

Considerably more spectators than the official capacity of 23 826 packed into Lahore's Gaddafi Stadium for what was the first day/night match played in Pakistan, and cricket historians among them may have feared for the Sri Lankans when Ranatunga won the toss and decided to field first. Not one of the five previous cricket World Cup finals had been won by the team batting second.

'I felt we were happier chasing a target,' the captain recalls, although he may have doubted his decision when Taylor and Ponting settled and prospered to 137 for one after 27 overs. They had laid the foundations for an impressive Australian score, but Muttiah Muralitharan and the other Sri Lankan spinners found some rhythm and consistency, and artfully bowled their team back into contention.

De Silva's thoughtful off-spin dismissed Taylor for 74 and Ponting for 45, and the Australian middle order was becalmed by the four-man spin attack. Unable to hit a single boundary between the 24th and the 49th over, the batsmen appeared strangely lethargic, and most observers judged their eventual total of 241 for seven in their 50 overs to be, perhaps, 30 or 40 runs short of a cup-winning performance.

The early wickets of Jayasuriya and Kaluwitharana suggested that the match could yet be a close contest, but Aravinda de Silva and Asanka Gurusinha thrived into the cool evening. Taylor implored his players to raise their game one more time, but the Australians were running on empty. Their bowlers presented too many balls to be hit, and, most fatally, four catches, including one sitter, went to ground.

The fielders' task was not made any easier by the settling dew, but as first De Silva and then Gurusinha passed 50, the final became a procession. Even Warne appeared powerless to halt Sri Lanka's charge for glory, and in one over the great spin bowler was unceremoniously clobbered for 6, 4, 2, 1, 4 and 4.

'Aravinda accumulates runs so quickly,' Ian Healy, the Australian wicketkeeper, said. 'You think you are containing him, but you look at the scoreboard and see he's got 40 off 45 balls without doing much; and, when he releases the dynamite, he does some damage. That's what happened in Lahore.'

Gurusinha was eventually bowled for an excellent 65, but his departure brought Ranatunga out to join De Silva in the middle. It seemed entirely fitting that this small, resolute country should be steered to the greatest triumph in its history by its two most talented and celebrated cricketers.

Victory was secured by seven wickets with almost five overs to spare. De Silva finished unbeaten with an outstanding, aggressive 107, and Ranatunga stroked his way to a confident 47 not out. Eyes wide with delight, both men had evidently enjoyed every minute of their golden day in Lahore.

'The most important factor in our success was the way the team came together as a family,' Ranatunga recalls. 'One night before the final, a panel of television experts was picking a Player of the Tournament, and it came down to a choice between Tendulkar and Jayasuriya. When they voted unanimously for our opener, I wanted to congratulate Sanath, so I went to his room in the hotel. I pushed open the door and discovered that the rest of the guys had got there before me. That was typical of our family spirit.'

The tournament that was launched with a bungled opening ceremony predictably reached its conclusion with a bungled closing ceremony. Once Ian Chappell and an army of officials had squeezed onto a small, fragile podium, the former Australian captain had to reach across Benazir Bhutto, a bemused Pakistan prime minister, to conduct a series of ungainly interviews with the Man of the Match and captains.

However, amid a comical bout of blazered elbowing and jockeying for position, the Wills World Cup was placed in Ranatunga's hands and, with the broadest of smiles, he held the trophy aloft.

There was more: inadequate crowd control denied the jubilant Sri Lankans an opportunity to undertake a lap of honour, and in the ensuing melee the £30 000 winners' cheque was stolen.

Such turmoil aside, Ranatunga's team emerged as popular champions. They had played consistently bold and attractive cricket; their bowling had been disciplined, and their fielding was outstanding, yet their triumph in 1996 will forever be associated with the aggressive strokeplay of their batsmen.

Jayasuriya, Kaluwitharana, De Silva, Ranatunga and the rest had changed the way international one-day cricket was played. Their high-scoring assault in the first 15 overs was much more than a risky slog. It was an audacious, technically correct, open-shouldered, thoughtful assault; and it worked.

Sri Lanka had dared to be different, and the title of 'world champions' was their reward.

Aravinda de Silva

Soon after Pinnaduwage Aravinda de Silva was born on 17 October 1965, his father put a small cricket bat in his crib. This was not just the gesture of an eccentric fan; this was a religious act.

Among Buddhist families in Sri Lanka, it was considered auspicious to mark the birth of a child by placing special objects of devotion in and around the home and the local temple. In the De Silva household, there were no more significant, cherished objects of devotion than a cricket bat and ball.

'My father always wanted me to be a cricketer,' De Silva recalls. 'For him, cricket represented moral and social standards, good conduct, civility and fraternity. He appreciated its rites and regulations, its practices and precepts, and its ethic of individuality within a team framework. I can remember him often telling me the game would make me a better person, and he loved to quote Lord Harris saying the act of playing cricket keenly and honourably, and with genuine self-sacrifice, was a moral lesson in itself.'

It soon became clear that young Aravinda possessed exceptional talent, and, nurtured by endless hours of facing balls thrown by his father, he eventually grew into a formidable cricketer. He was wisely coached by Abu Fuard, a famous off-spinner during the 1960s; and, by happy coincidence, Fuard was serving as the Sri Lankan national team manager when De Silva made his Test debut at Lord's in 1984.

Only 5'3" tall, stocky and strong, the stylish young batsman soon earned a reputation for tearing into the bowlers from the start of every innings. 'Each time I reach the crease,' he explained, 'I have one aim in mind, and that is to get on top of the opposition from the first ball. In my youth, I took this to extremes and, after an exciting tour to India in 1986, people were starting to call me Mad Max.'

While he was fortunate to emerge in a period when Sri Lanka was granted Test status, and her cricketers enjoyed unimagined opportunities, De Silva made certain he seized his chance.

Experience gradually honed his forceful instincts, and after a successful season of English county cricket with Kent in 1995, Aravinda embarked upon a run of exceptional form that propelled him onto a higher plane, where he was commonly ranked alongside the finest batsmen in the world.

Wide eyes blazing, fiercely competitive, bullish, gifted: he cut an impressive figure.

His reputation soared after his exploits at the 1996 World Cup, when he earned Man of the Match awards in four games, including both the semi-final against India and the final against Australia, and he followed these heroics with nine Test centuries between April 1997 and August 1998.

Invitations to play in various World XI matches began to roll through his fax machine, and his standing in Sri Lanka remained, in the words of his long-time team-mate, Arjuna Ranatunga (the captain who once resigned in protest when Aravinda was omitted from the team), 'huge.'

By the end of the decade, the national selectors were using the same adjective to describe the size of his body, and he was dropped from the Test team. Whether concerns over his physical fitness were authentic or, as he maintains, he fell victim to political wrangling, De Silva wasted 18 months in the wilderness.

His status fell further in 2000 when his name was mentioned in an Indian Central Bureau of Investigation (CBI) report into corruption and match fixing, but he was later cleared by the Board of Control for Cricket in Sri Lanka (BCCSL) inquiry into specific allegations by a bookmaker. 'As long as I know that I am clean, and that I have always been clean,' he states, 'it does not matter what someone else says.'

Many suspected the portly old warhorse was finished.

They were wrong. Michael Tissera was appointed chairman of a fresh selection panel in January 2002, and the legend was recalled to tour England. Eleven kilograms lighter, more resolute than ever, he contributed with bat and ball, scoring runs in the middle order and delivering useful off-spinners.

In October 2002, on his own terms, De Silva decided to retire from Test cricket but, only two weeks short of his 37th birthday, said he would continue to be available for Sri Lanka's one-day side.

When he does finally slip away from the cricketing limelight, he will do so with more than 15 000 runs in international cricket to his name, and the enduring affection of his compatriots.

While he has not ruled out future involvement in the game, perhaps as national coach, it seems probable that he will often be found in his back garden, tirelessly throwing balls at his young son.

There is, as he knows, a noble precedent.

The 1996 World Cup final: Australia versus Sri Lanka in Lahore. Aravinda de Silva finished unbeaten on an aggressive 107.
(Getty Images/ Touchline Photo)

Victors in 1996. Sri Lankan captain Arjuna Ranatunga holds aloft the silver trophy.
(Getty Images/Touchline Photo)

Player of the Tournament in the 1996 World Cup, Sanath Jayasuriya scored the fastest 50 (29 balls) in the history of the tournament, against England in Faisalabad. *(Getty Images/ Touchline Photo)*

Where there was Klusener, there was always hope. South African Lance Klusener, Player of the Tournament in the 1999 World Cup in England, always appeared the personification of calm and focused resolve. *(Duif du Toit/ Touchline Photo)*

The peerless Australian fast bowler Glenn McGrath in action at the 1999 World Cup in England.
(Getty Images/Touchline Photo)

Steve Waugh in action at the World Cup in England in 1999. As captain of the Australian one-day side from December 1997 to February 2002, he will be remembered as one of the toughest, sharpest cricketers of all time.
(Getty Images/Touchline Photo)

Australian captain Steve Waugh on the pavilion balcony at Lord's after his team's victory against Pakistan in the 1999 World Cup final. Once again, the Australian team had proved their amazing mental toughness under pressure.
(Getty Images/Touchline Photo)

The stunning Newlands cricket stadium in Cape Town hosted the opening match of the 2003 World Cup in the shadow of Table Mountain, the day after a bright and entertaining opening ceremony. Host nation South Africa lost to the West Indies by four runs.
(Getty Images/Touchline Photo)

Youthful prodigy at the 1992 World Cup, Sachin Tendulkar was named Player of the Tournament in South Africa in 2003. The 'Little Master', seen here in action against Sri Lanka on 10 March 2003, when he provided another exhilarating batting master class, is widely regarded as the greatest batsman of his generation. *(Getty Images/Touchline Photo)*

The genius of Lara. Compact and increasingly confident as his innings progressed, Brian Lara took the West Indies from crisis to stability to win the opening match against South Africa in the 2003 World Cup tournament. *(Getty Images/Touchline Photo)*

During South Africa's group match against Kenya in Potchefstroom in 2003, star fielder Jonty Rhodes fractured a finger. When it was announced that he would be out of action for three weeks, Graeme Smith was called up as a replacement batsman. Part of the team since South Africa's re-entry into international sport, Rhodes's spirited enthusiasm was sorely missed by the home side.
(Duif du Toit/Touchline Photo)

In Canada's group match against the West Indies at the 2003 World Cup, Canadian batsman John Davison made history when he scored the fastest century in World Cup history – it took him just 67 balls.
(Getty Images/Touchline Photo)

To the delight of an enthusiastic flag-waving crowd of Kenyan cricket fans, their team comprehensively defeated Sri Lanka in their group match in Nairobi in the 2003 World Cup. The shock defeat, and the fact that New Zealand forfeited their points by not playing in Nairobi, ensured the East Africans a place in the Super Six stage of the tournament.
(Getty Images/ Touchline Photo)

South African captain Shaun Pollock is a picture of dejection as he waits to find out whether South Africa's rain-shortened group match against Sri Lanka in Durban in the 2003 World Cup will resume. In the event, the match was abandoned as a tie and South African hopes died a slow and painful death.
(Getty Images/ Touchline Photo)

Salute from the sky. Thirty-one thousand pairs of eyes at the Wanderers Stadium gazed in awe at the fly-past in formation of three South African Airways passenger jets during the lunch break of the 2003 World Cup final.
(Getty Images/Touchline Photo)

Victory in Johannesburg, 23 March 2003. Australia beat India by 125 runs in the World Cup final, retaining their world championship status and becoming the first country to win the World Cup three times. The squad huddled on the field under a threatening sky as the realisation dawned that their planning, hard work and plain Aussie guts had been duly rewarded.
(Getty Images/Touchline Photo)

Chapter Eleven

The Seventh World Cup

It was perhaps unfortunate that the Cricket World Cup should return to England at a time when, following the lead of a new government, the English people were being encouraged to disown their traditions and heritage, and embrace a cultural phenomenon known as 'Cool Britannia'. In the spirit most famously embodied by the Millennium Dome, political correctness became all the rage.

So the organisers of the 1999 World Cup declined to present anything similar in mood and decorum to the tournaments so neatly staged in 1975, 1979 and 1983, and instead tried to be so hip, hop and happening that their event ended up looking about as cool as a prime minister wearing jeans at official functions.

'Cool Britannia' was eventually exposed as a marketing sham, disappearing without trace, but by then both the ill-fated Dome and what unfolded as a generally underwhelming Cricket World Cup had been squandered in reverence of a false god.

The tournament did produce some unforgettable cricket, most memorably in two thunderous matches between Australia and South Africa, but the pitiably misguided presentation and marketing meant the event flopped in terms of its impact and legacy.

In truth, the general perception of the 1999 Cricket World Cup never truly recovered from perhaps the most embarrassing opening ceremony ever staged by any country, at any time.

The concept was weak, miserly and apologetic: a brief show squeezed into half an hour before the opening match between hosts England and defending champions Sri Lanka, incorporating a cheap day-time firework display, a parade of flags from competing nations, and a speech by Tony Blair to declare the event open.

In practice it was worse. A near-capacity crowd at Lord's sat and watched in bemused wonder as the fireworks sent pitiable puffs of smoke into a grey, soggy, overcast London morning. Blameless schoolgirls stood shivering in the cold, bravely clutching flags while the equally blameless Mr Blair made his speech, much of which was rendered inaudible because the microphone failed.

Members of the England team watched this debacle from their balcony in the pavilion and laughed.

This was 'Cool Britannia' in action; and, in their great wisdom, the organisers rejected as too traditional and too old-fashioned the simple, dignified act of assembling the players from 12 competing countries on the field in front of the Lord's pavilion. Deprived even of that enduring image, it was hard to imagine how the tournament could have started on a more deflating note.

'Welcome to the Carnival!' someone proclaimed.

Nobody seemed to be listening. The English Cricket Board had wanted the World Cup to revive the game in England, but misguided marketing undermined their best intentions.

They planned to increase revenue by securing eight frontline sponsors, rather than just one title sponsor, but then found no more than four companies prepared to join their carnival. They planned to spread the game by using 21 different venues, playing matches in every county plus Dublin, Edinburgh and Amsterdam, but the policy served only to dilute impact and awareness.

In fact, for much of the tournament, the cricketing showpiece was helplessly overshadowed, on television and in the newspapers, by Manchester United's march towards the treble.

Even the official song, 'Life is a Carnival' by Dave Stewart, hit a discordant note. It was only released into the shops the day after England was eliminated, although this may have been a blessing in disguise because the lyrics included no reference to cricket. Maybe the old game was considered just not cool enough.

This unfortunate state of affairs was all the more regrettable because, all things being equal, England remained ideally suited to host a successful Cricket World Cup. Outstanding transport and accommodation systems, small distances between venues, a broad and deep cricketing heritage, enthusiastic support for almost every competing nation: the ingredients were all there.

It was the artificial 'Cool Britannia' recipe that failed, creating the wrong mood and scenery for the entire event. As a result, when the greatest cricketers in the world did shine during the 1999 World Cup, they did so despite their circumstances.

This was such a pity. Even the weather had co-operated. As dire warnings of rain throughout May and June evaporated in warm, overcast conditions, only one match out of 42 was not completed, with one other spilling into a second day. Happily, the new-fangled Duckworth-Lewis equation for determining the winners of matches cut short by rain never needed to be invoked.

South Africa arrived as 11-4 favourites, followed in the betting by Australia and Pakistan, with England at 15-2. Scotland, Kenya and Bangladesh had qualified to join the nine Test-playing countries and make up the dozen in the draw, but the odds against the Scots becoming world champions were fixed at 3 000-1. Once again, dull and predictable mismatches seemed inevitable.

The International Cricket Council's response was to approve a brand new format for the World Cup, developed to maintain interest throughout while still giving the minnows their chance.

Twelve teams were again divided into two round-robin groups of six but, instead of eight qualifying for knockout quarter-finals as had happened in 1996, only the top three sides in each group would advance to a so-called Super Six stage.

Carrying points earned against the teams who also advanced from their group, these sides would then play three matches against the qualifiers from the other group. This process would leave a final all-played-all table, from which the top four countries would contest the semi-finals, with the winners playing the final.

It was complicated, and it became almost unfathomable when teams had to be separated by net run rates, but the new format did seem fair, and it would just about keep something at stake through all 38 days of the longest Cricket World Cup ever.

England's campaign lasted only 15½ of those days. Whatever the shortcomings in its presentation, a competitive performance by the home team could still have set the tournament buzzing. In this respect, at least, the organisers were unlucky.

Alec Stewart's squad began the tournament on the crest of a mishandled pay dispute with the ECB, but they seemed to have put these problems behind them with an emphatic eight-wicket win over Sri Lanka in the opening match at Lord's.

They then beat Kenya, but defeat against South Africa at the Oval hinted at the team's soft centre. Nonetheless, they returned to form when overhauling Zimbabwe's 167 for eight. 'We thought that was enough to reach the Super Six,' Darren Gough recalls. 'We had won three out of four, and that seemed that.'

It wasn't. One obscure equation in the complex mathematics before the last round of group matches indicated that, if Zimbabwe secured a shock win over South Africa, it would still be possible for England to be eliminated if they lost heavily enough to India. Since this scenario seemed so remote, nobody worried.

There was still no concern when the home team restricted the Indians to 232 for eight at Edgbaston, nor even when it was learned that Zimbabwe had made 233 for six at Chelmsford. Then the news filtered through that South Africa had collapsed to 40 for six. All of a sudden, England were under pressure. Now they would have to beat India to survive, and dark clouds were gathering.

When rain stopped play, the home team still needed 160 runs with seven wickets standing and two of their best batsmen, Graham Thorpe and Neil Fairbrother, at the crease. Nerves frayed overnight, and, resuming on a grey Sunday morning, Thorpe got a harsh LBW decision and Fairbrother ran out of partners. Amid unbridled misery, England subsided to 168 all out and was eliminated.

Their dressing room now resembled a morgue, but England's humiliation was not complete until they had joined the other teams at a reception with Queen Elizabeth II at Buckingham Palace. 'We felt like spare parts,' Gough recalls grimly.

David Lloyd, the England coach, swiftly confirmed his decision to resign, and while he departed centre stage, it seemed ironic that another English coach, Bob Woolmer, should be thriving in charge of the South African team at the top of Group A.

Woolmer, a former England opening batsman settled in Cape Town, had nurtured a strong relationship with team captain Hansie Cronje since taking over as coach of the national team; and, rarely seen without his laptop computer, he had become renowned for his diligence, judgement and careful preparation.

He took these virtues to new lengths in South Africa's opening match, against India at Hove, by introducing a microphone/earpiece system to communicate with Cronje on the field. The idea of a coach conveying instructions from the pavilion shocked traditionalists, and at the first drinks break ICC match referee Talat Ali asked Woolmer and Cronje immediately to dismantle their equipment.

The sport's governing body subsequently outlawed the use of such remote captaincy, but Woolmer was unrepentant, a champion of innovation, and his team started to emerge as a confident blend of hard work, professionalism and clinical efficiency.

Jacques Kallis made 96 and Jonty Rhodes an unbeaten 39 in a successful chase against India. Once Daryll Cullinan had rescued the innings from 24 for three against Sri Lanka, Kallis then removed the top three Slankies in nine balls. Organised and motivated, they then skittled England for 103 at the Oval, overcame Kenya, and booked a place in the Super Six with the minimum of fuss.

Even a startling defeat in what seemed a dead group match against Zimbabwe at Chelmsford, when not even the hard-hitting of all-rounder Lance Klusener could rescue them, scarcely dented their growing reputation. Unlucky with the rules in 1992, unlucky to find Lara in form four years later, the South Africans looked in the mood to make it third time lucky at their third World Cup.

India's campaign had been disrupted by the death of Sachin Tendulkar's father, but after flying home for the funeral the master returned to England and immediately crashed a magnificent 140 in 101 balls against Kenya. The decisive victory over England in their last group match enabled Azharuddin's gifted team to squeeze into the Super Six by virtue of a superior net run rate.

Surprisingly, the third qualifier from Group A was Zimbabwe, a side combining exceptional fielding, indomitable spirit and inspired batting by Neil Johnson. Moreover, with wins over India and South Africa, they not only advanced to the Super Six but also carried the maximum four points forward and headed the table.

Sri Lanka had mounted a disappointing defence of their title, winning only one match, with Sanath Jayasuriya, the hero of 1996, managing to score only 82 runs in five innings.

After the batting glut on the sub-continent, the grey, overcast conditions and responsive pitches seemed to turn the tide towards the bowlers. The nature of the contest had changed. In 1996, with pinch-hitters blazing, teams planned to score at least 90 runs in the first 15 overs. In 1999, with the ball seaming and swinging, teams were content to survive the first 15 overs, and keep wickets in hand for a traditional assault at the end of the innings.

Group B followed a curiously similar path to Group A, with the calculators again being required to separate the teams.

Pakistan matched South Africa's excellent early form, surging to four consecutive wins on the back of some explosive batting and the electrifying fast bowling of Shoaib Akhtar, and then losing what seemed an irrelevant last group match. This shock defeat, against Bangladesh at Northampton, aroused suspicions of match-fixing, but a later investigation failed to find any evidence.

So, with Pakistan topping the final Group B table with eight points, Australia, New Zealand and the West Indies were left locked together on six points; and it was the team from the Caribbean that suffered the fate of elimination by net run rate.

Lara's team had wasted a winning position against Pakistan, but then reeled off three victories in a row: beating Bangladesh, as hot soup kept them warm on a shivering day in Dublin; winning a crucial toss, and the match, against New Zealand; and needing only three hours to hammer Scotland in what was declared the shortest one-day international match ever played.

However, they then tried to manipulate their qualification for the Super Six by stretching the regulations against the Australians on an infamous afternoon at Old Trafford, Manchester.

First, the West Indies were dismissed for 110, then calculators were produced to work out how quickly the Australians should score the runs to ensure that not only their own net run rate, but also the West Indian net run rate, would stay above the net rate of the other team likely to finish with six points, New Zealand.

When the number crunching was done, the Australians slowed to a shameless crawl and the West Indian bowlers went through the motions. The last 19 runs were scored off 13 overs and, as appalled spectators booed and left the ground in disgust, it seemed somehow appropriate that a no-ball should yield the winning run.

Both captains later denied collusion, but the spirit of the game had been corrupted and the World Cup became a farce.

New Zealand had the last laugh. They had started by beating Australia, and ended by sufficiently raising their net run rate against Scotland to snatch third place from the West Indies.

For their part, the Australians were mightily relieved to seize second place and remain in the competition. They had started their campaign with an untidy win over Scotland, when the very first ball of the match was crashed to the boundary by an estate agent from Ayr, and Steve Waugh called their fielding 'atrocious".

Their attack was then humiliated by Roger Twose and Chris Cairns in defeat against New Zealand at Cardiff, and they were soon in trouble against Pakistan at Headingley. Steve Waugh appeared to be guiding his side through a tense run chase but, when his stumps were sensationally rattled by Shoaib Akhtar in the Leeds gloom, the Australians swiftly slipped to another defeat.

Confronted by the unthinkable prospect of elimination at the group phase, the captain gathered his players in the dressing room and laid the situation on the line. 'Every game is a final for us now,' Waugh declared. 'If we lose again, we're gone."

Bangladesh was beaten with Adam Gilchrist and Tom Moody finding form with the bat and, at last, Glenn McGrath being given a chance to open the bowling. Australia suddenly looked a new team, and the world-class paceman again made a difference in the crucial game against the West Indies, claiming five for 14.

So, Waugh's side scrambled into the Super Six, and the World Cup started to gather pace, even if the complex machinations of the format had by now lost anyone who was less than totally committed to understanding the various permutations. For them, it was enough to savour the spectacle and accept the outcome.

As Australia and India prepared for the first match of the new phase, both teams knew that, since neither was carrying any points from their group, defeat would effectively end their hopes. The Oval was buzzing and, yet again, McGrath found the rhythm and pace to swing the game decisively in Australia's favour.

Set 283 to win, India looked towards Tendulkar, a centurion in each of his three previous one-day innings against Australia, to lead the chase, but he flailed at a fine outswinger from McGrath and was caught behind without scoring. The Indians collapsed to 17 for four, and never truly threatened to reach their target.

For much of the next day at Trent Bridge, South Africa looked as though they were being blown away by a magnificently explosive Pakistan display. Moin Khan hit 63 off 62 balls as he carried his side to a decent 220 for seven in 50 overs, then Shoaib Akhtar stormed in and reduced Cronje's team to 58 for five.

Klusener stepped into the crisis and smashed his way to glory, placing his foot to the pitch of the ball and, without fuss, swinging his oversized bat through the line. Nicknamed 'Zulu' because he grew up in KwaZulu-Natal and so spoke that African language fluently, short and fair, the all-rounder led a stirring chase and finished with 46 from 61 balls, including the winning runs.

As the South Africans celebrated, the enormous contingent of expatriate Pakistan supporters in the ground fell quiet for probably the first time in the day. Shrouded in green flags, they had cheered, chanted, clapped and whistled in support of their team, creating an invigorating atmosphere only equalled in the World Cup by the vast number of anglicised Indians following their side.

This madly enthusiastic 'Asian' contribution to the tournament seemed to take the organisers by surprise. At one point, the public address announcer at Trent Bridge asked spectators to refrain from making 'excessive noise"; he was loudly jeered.

Opposing teams didn't much appreciate either the unrelenting cacophony of noise, or the fans' tendency to invade the field at the end of the match. This prompted the Australians, among others, to complain about the threat to their players' safety, but there were no serious incidents amid all the hustle and bustle. Even the potentially dangerous clash between these two animated armies of spectators, in the Super Six match between India and Pakistan at Old Trafford, passed with only three arrests and nine ejections.

On the field, the Indians won the third meeting in a World Cup between these bitter rivals, just as they had won the previous two matches. Tendulkar, Rahul Dravid and Mohammed Azharuddin each contributed to a total of 227 for six and, despite Saeed Anwar's fast start, Pakistan tetchily fell short of their target.

The sprint to the semi-finals was taking shape.

Australia continued to thrive on their spirit of raw desperation, overwhelming Zimbabwe at Lord's on the 16th anniversary of their historic World Cup defeat against the same opposition, and South Africa built from an opening stand of 176 between Gary Kirsten and Herschelle Gibbs to steamroller New Zealand.

Pakistan rediscovered their form to demolish Zimbabwe at the Oval, securing their berth in the last four when off-spinner Saqlain Mushtaq finished the match with only the second hat trick in World Cup history.

New Zealand ensured their progress when the in-form Twose led a typically resourceful chase to beat India.

So the tournament wound its way to Headingley, and the last match of the Super Six phase: Australia, who once again needed to win the game to stay alive in the competition, would play the South Africans, already sure of a semi-final place and now relishing a 'free' opportunity to send Steve Waugh's side home.

Gibbs, the fluent, richly gifted opening batsman, went straight for the jugular. Bursting with confidence after a splendid 91 against New Zealand, he cut and drove his way to an admirable 101. Shane Warne briefly stemmed the flow of runs, but the batsmen regained their momentum and crashed 88 in the last 10 overs. Rhodes made 39 in 36 balls, Klusener struck 36 in 21, and South Africa totalled a commanding 271 for seven. Australians gasped.

Their team was in trouble, and the situation got worse when Gilchrist went cheaply and Mark Waugh was needlessly run out. At 48 for three, the match appeared all but over.

Steve Waugh arrived in the middle and he, at least, would not go down without a fight. The defiant captain reached 56, but then clipped a ball from Klusener to mid-wicket, where Gibbs grabbed the catch. The South Africans cheerfully wrapped up the Australian tail, and advanced to win the World Cup at Lord's . . .

That could have, should have, happened.

It didn't happen.

Rewind the tape.

. . . to midwicket, where Gibbs grabbed the catch and, cockily, inexplicably, tried to throw the ball skywards in celebration but only succeeded in dropping it to the turf. Several of his team-mates later suggested the catch would have been given if the young fielder had casually ignored the ball and celebrated. Instead, he scrambled and appeared distraught, and Waugh was reprieved.

He had been walking towards the pavilion, but he returned to the crease and mercilessly relished his good fortune. 'Heh, Hersch,' Waugh chirped, as the young fielder jogged across the pitch at the end of the over, 'you just dropped the World Cup."

It's a tough game, and one of its toughest icons brutally took control of the situation. All class and determination, Waugh knew he had been given a life and he grimly resolved to make the very most of it. Memorably, he pulled Steve Elworthy, in for the injured Kallis, into the crowd at mid-wicket, and then cut Donald with such timing that the ball ricocheted off the advertising boards.

He added 126 with Ricky Ponting, who scored 69, and then picked up the pace with Michael Bevan, relentlessly moving towards an amazing win. As Donald and Shaun Pollock tightened the attack in the closing overs, 30 runs were required off five, 15 off two and still eight from the last over of a dramatic day.

Waugh was beginning to suffer leg cramps and Cronje urged his team to make one more effort, but Tom Moody settled the issue by slashing a priceless boundary past point. The batsmen scrambled the winning run with two balls to spare, and the habitually reserved captain then released his pressure and tension by celebrating like a footballer who had scored a goal, punching the air.

His innings of 120 not out, in 110 balls, included ten fours and two soaring sixes. It may have been only his second century in 266 one-day internationals, but it was performed on the grandest stage, scored against top-quality opponents, in demanding circumstances, and bears comparison with any in World Cup history.

Spectators wandered away from Headingley aware that they had seen something special: a match, and an individual performance, to remain undimmed and unfading in the memory.

By then, Waugh was already looking to the future. Victory had catapulted Australia above the South Africans in the final Super Six table, setting up a momentous semi-final between the same teams to be played at Edgbaston just four days later. 'This result will give us confidence going into that game,' he said, smiling.

Just down the corridor, Cronje and his players sat quietly in their dressing room, convincing one another that their campaign remained on track, working to persuade themselves it had been just another game and not further evidence of any psychological barrier between them and the reality of beating these Australians.

Gibbs, youthful and light-hearted by nature, started coming to terms with the scale and effect of his error, and the thought of what he might have denied his more experienced team-mates; but there was no turning back, and no grudges were kept.

Perhaps, in the final analysis, the team that had desperately needed to win at Headingley had defeated the side that only wanted to win. It was going to be different at Edgbaston, Cronje warned his team, where both sides would approach the game with the intensity of knowing there would be no second chance.

In the meantime, Pakistan and New Zealand were scheduled to contest the first semi-final at Old Trafford, a match played amid a deafening din of whistles, hooters and firecrackers.

The Kiwis batted first and, although they never came to terms with the scorching pace of Shoaib Akhtar, 'the Rawalpindi Express', Twose, Cairns and Fleming all passed 40, and there were some who believed a total of 241 for seven could be sufficient.

Any suggestions that the Pakistanis might choke on the chase, as they had against India at the same ground, were swiftly dispelled by their openers. Saeed Anwar and Wajahatullah Wasti saw off the threat posed by the tournament's leading wicket-taker, Geoff Allott, and advanced to 194 without loss, establishing a new record for the highest opening partnership in World Cup history.

Their excited supporters cheered every run and it was no real surprise when, with Pakistan still six runs short of their target, 25 of their fans could contain themselves no longer, invaded the field and delayed play for ten minutes. The security situation was not helped by the inopportune coincidence that saw the Old Trafford stewards wearing fluorescent bibs that looked similar to the pea-green replica shirts preferred by many Pakistani supporters.

Chaos threatened, but this was happy chaos, especially when Saeed Anwar drove the winning runs, booked Pakistan's place in the final, and prompted thousands of delirious fans to swarm across the field. The New Zealanders, beaten by nine wickets with almost three overs to spare, dashed for the haven of the pavilion.

Akram's side could now unwind and join the rest of the cricket world in savouring the semi-final at Edgbaston.

Many observers anticipated a classic, and their expectations were magnificently fulfilled by what no less an authority than Wisden subsequently reflected as 'perhaps the finest of all the 1 483 official one-day internationals that went before'.

If the South Africans needed a boost after the disappointment of losing at Headingley, they received one when Kallis was declared fit to play in the semi-final. His stretched stomach muscles were not fully healed, but the team needed all their big guns on deck and the all-rounder was willing to play through the pain.

'We know we can beat these guys,' Cronje told his team after winning the toss and electing to field first. 'We all know we can win this World Cup.

Let's not let ourselves down.'

Donald roared in as though the estimation of his entire career hinged on this game (in terms of medals on his mantelpiece, maybe it did), and young Pollock matched his senior partner for accuracy, aggression and raw pace. Forced onto the back foot, the Australians lost wickets and, at 68 for four, they were in trouble.

Waugh and Bevan steadied the innings, but Kallis seized the ball and maintained the pressure, heroically bowling through his full complement of ten overs at a cost of only 27 runs. Rhodes kept the players on their toes, clapping out an infectious rhythm, and Cronje kept a firm hand on his bowlers and field placings.

It was clinical, and it was professional. The Australians gamely wriggled on the hook, but they could not produce any late onslaught and their 213 all out in 49.2 overs appeared inadequate. Pollock had finished with five for 36, while Donald seized four for 32. In thought and deed, South Africa had taken complete control.

Cronje wasn't smiling. 'It's not done yet,' he insisted between innings. 'Keep concentrating. Let's finish the job.'

Kirsten and Gibbs launched the pursuit with conviction, racing to 48 without loss. They seemed so assured that South African fans began taunting Australian fielders on the boundary. The game billed as a battle of the giants had become a procession.

Waugh called for Warne.

The genius spinner had suffered considerable criticism for his early performances at the World Cup, but at Edgbaston he found a pitch with real bounce and, with the semi-final swiftly drifting away from his team, he discovered a desperate cause. Cometh the hour, cometh perhaps the greatest spinner of all time.

Warne's ninth ball of the day pitched outside the leg stump, leaped, turned and flicked the top of the off-stump. Gibbs turned and looked down in horror. The opener, so keen to atone for his error in Leeds, had been bowled by an unplayable delivery.

Gleefully in the groove, in his next over the Australian bowled Kirsten on the sweep and dismissed Cronje, who was unfortunate to be sent on his way after being caught off his boot.

'Bowled, Warney,' bawled Gilchrist behind the stumps.

The spinner had taken three wickets in the space of eight balls without yielding a run. When he finished with three for 29 in his ten overs, he had turned the game. In the twinkling of his blue eyes, in the twirling of his spinning fingers, he had transferred the pressure away from his team-mates and onto the opposition.

That was his genius.

South Africa's run chase had almost completely stalled, and it needed the classically correct Kallis and the scurrying Rhodes to get the scoreboard moving again. Nudging singles, nicking twos, always looking to punish a bad ball, they edged ever closer.

There was nothing between two great teams. No sooner than an accurate over or a clambering stop had put Australia back in the ascendancy, a boundary would set South Africa back on course. As the pressure mounted, the overs ticked away.

Exactly 70 runs were needed from the last ten overs with six wickets standing. Then, they required 38 runs from five overs with four wickets left. The semi-final was perfectly poised, and with two overs remaining South Africa still needed 18 runs.

The peerless McGrath eased into his run-up, bowled and took Mark Boucher's middle stump out of the ground; then Paul Reiffel's rocket throw caught Elworthy short of his ground. The game finally appeared to be swinging Australia's way. Only eight balls remained, and still 16 runs were needed with one wicket to fall.

Yet, where there was Klusener, there was hope. The biggest hitter of the tournament took guard, and steadied. McGrath bowled, Klusener swung straight and hard, and connected, and the ball flew straight towards Reiffel at long-off, and up, and passed through the fielder's upstretched hands and over the ropes.

Six! Was it? Yes! Six!

South African flags that had fallen limp were proudly unfurled around the ground. Klusener's grim expression did not change. This was his time, this was his moment, and an astutely prodded single ensured he kept the strike for the last over of the innings. While the excitement and tension fizzed around him, the all-rounder appeared the personification of calm and focused resolve.

One over left, one wicket left, nine runs required. Waugh gave the ball to Damian Fleming. The fast bowler's mind had drifted back to an almost identical situation in Chandigarh at the last World Cup, where he had been required to bowl the last over of an equally tight semi-final against the West Indies, and where he had won the game for Australia by clean-bowling Courtney Walsh.

Now, in Birmingham, he concentrated on the job at hand, and on

Klusener, already waiting in his broad stance, staring intently at the bowler, tapping his bat on the crease. The crowd hushed. At the end of a fantastic duel, everything came to this.

Fleming bowled the first ball, straight, fast, fractionally short of a length, nothing wrong; Klusener drove hard, connected sweetly, and the ball sped through the off side, past extra cover, beating the sweeper on the boundary, and over the ropes.

Amid pandemonium in the stands at Edgbaston, and in front of televisions the length and breadth of South Africa, Klusener took guard again. Fleming bowled again, and the all-rounder drove again, remarkably, unerringly and unforgettably. Again the sweeper tried to intercept, and again he failed, and the umpire signalled another boundary. Fleming stood, hands on hips, aghast.

That seemed that.

Klusener had reached 31 in only 14 balls, and all of a sudden he now needed only one more run from four balls to emerge as the hero of a game that would be indelibly engraved in sporting history. For him, in fact for anyone, it seemed a doddle.

Waugh called his fielders into a tight cordon, in what seemed a hopeless attempt to prevent the winning single. One well-directed nudge, any lofted shot, any cut or deflection: that was all that stood between South Africa and a place in the final.

Fleming moved in again, and bowled a little fuller. Klusener drove for the third time, but the ball jarred at the bottom of his bat and dribbled straight to Lehmann. Donald was backing up too far at the non-striker's end, Klusener yelled 'no' and the No. 11 batsman frantically scrambled back into his ground. If Lehmann's throw had hit the stumps, the decision would have been tight.

Three of the South African players watching from the pavilion had their heads in their hands, hardly able to watch.

One run was still required, from three balls. Where they might have consulted and reassured each other, the two batsmen stood at their respective ends, wide-eyed and unblinking. Where some might have stretched muscles to relax, they stood still.

Waugh gestured for a couple of his fielders to move, clapped his hands and told his players to keep it tight. Amid feverish excitement in the stands, the Australian captain stayed alert.

So, Fleming ran in for a fourth time. Klusener drove again, off the bottom of his bat, and the ball ran towards mid-on.

'Yes, yes,' the all-rounder screamed as he ran. He was going for the run, straining every muscle to make his ground.

Donald didn't hear the call. In all the noise and activity at the ground where he had shone so often for the Warwickshire side, the legendary fast bowler didn't hear the call. In the space of just a few frozen, frenetic seconds, his eyes followed the ball and he grounded his bat; then he dropped his bat before turning back to find, to his horror, that Klusener had doggedly continued to run.

He immediately started to run himself.

It was too late.

Mark Waugh adeptly flicked the ball to Fleming, who quickly assessed the situation, noted that Klusener had almost made his ground, and calmly rolled the ball down the pitch to Gilchrist, who broke the stumps and ran out Donald by several metres.

The Australians leaped in delight, arms aloft, dancing, hugging, smiling. Apparently doomed, they had battled to the end and shown the famous Aussie virtues of simple guts and self-belief.

Klusener, still wide-eyed and unblinking, kept running without looking back, finding a path through the crowd to the pavilion, only too aware that he had taken his nation to the brink of glory only for the dream to slip like water through the fingers. Donald stood in the middle of the pitch, red-eyed, an image of disbelief.

South Africa had been dismissed for 213, matching Australia's score and ending the first tied game in the history of the World Cup, but it was the Australians who advanced to the final by virtue of the fractionally superior 'net run rate' that enabled them to finish above South Africa on the final Super Six league table.

Almost to a man, the South African players wept in the dismal silence of their dressing room, struggling to understand how or why they should have been fated, twice within six days, to lose dramatic matches to Australia with two balls to spare. After the misfortune of 1992 and 1996, they had expected their luck to change. Instead, at Edgbaston, they felt more cruelly denied than ever.

'We haven't reached the World Cup final,' said Cronje, brave and dignified, afterwards, 'but I suppose that was about as close as you can get. We had a chance, but we faltered . . .' and the captain's voice trailed away. There were no more words.

Warne was christened Man of the Match, and Australia headed to Lord's, to play Pakistan in the World Cup final.

In the wake of these two remarkable matches, at Headingley and Edgbaston, many people remarked that either would have been fit to grace the final. For that the organisers soon had cause to be grateful, because the actual final was a damp squib.

Notoriously unpredictable, Pakistan appeared as lethargic and ineffective in the final as they had seemed explosive and irresistible in the semi-final against New Zealand. Nobody could offer any easy explanation as to why such a talented group of players could look so awe-inspiring and, a few days later, so awful.

Wasim Akram won the toss and decided to bat, maybe paying more attention to his team's preference for chasing a target than to damp early conditions that could assist the bowlers.

Saeed Anwar had scored centuries in his two previous innings, and he cut the third ball of the day for four, but from that moment of fleeting pleasure it was all downhill for Pakistan.

First Mark Waugh held a fantastic slip catch to dismiss Wasti, then Warne bowled Ijaz with another unplayable ball.

The Australians had seized the final by the scruff of the neck and, like an eager lioness, would not let go. True, they were fortunate to see the back of Inzamam, caught off his pad, but the innings swiftly lurched from severe trouble at 69 for three to much worse. Not long after Ponting clutched an outstanding catch to end Saqlain's stay at the wicket, the Pakistanis were dismissed for 132.

Spectators who had paid several thousand pounds for a ticket from a tout angrily looked at their watches. Measured in pounds per minute, it was becoming an expensive occasion.

The Australians batted, in the well-worn phrase, as if they had a plane to catch. Occasionally riding his luck, Gilchrist unleashed an astonishing barrage of strokes and reached his 50 in 33 balls, and it was all over by half-past four in the afternoon. Lehmann struck the winning runs, taking his team to 133 for two.

Considering the start of play had been delayed by 30 minutes following overnight rain, the seventh World Cup final ended with what added up to five playable hours remaining.

Waugh and his team, of course, were not concerned, and they gathered on the pavilion balcony to receive the trophy and pose for photographs marking their second World Cup win.

Australia were the world champions again because, in winning seven matches on the trot, when one defeat would have eliminated them from the tournament, they had proved their amazing mental toughness under pressure. For all the talents of Waugh, Warne and McGrath, it was their minds that set them apart.

Thus, the tournament that had started with just a few puffs of smoke and a faulty microphone ended with the welcome realisation that, for the first time since 1979, the team generally recognised as the strongest on the planet had become world champions.

One-Day Hero

Steve Waugh

One measure of Steve Waugh's immense contribution to Australian cricket is that, at one stage during the late 1980s, his admired twin brother Mark was teasingly nicknamed 'Afghanistan'.

Why?

Afghanistan, of course, was the forgotten war.

Mark, incidentally, was one of the outstanding batsmen in the world, on his majestic way to amassing 8 029 runs in 128 Tests. If, as a joke, he was forgotten, it can only have been in comparison to one of the toughest, sharpest cricketers of all time.

Steve Waugh will be remembered for his talent and his guts, but maybe his greatest quality lay not in his genes nor in his heart, but in his mind. Yes, he outplayed his opponents in 1-1 battles and as captain, but more often he out-thought them.

He made his one-day international debut in January 1986 at the Melbourne Cricket Ground against New Zealand. In those years, limited overs cricket was generally played on impulse and instinct, without an inordinate amount of planning.

Through the 16 seasons that followed, perhaps more than any other individual, Waugh proved instrumental in the evolution of the one-day game to the scientific, specialist code, entirely distinct from first-class cricket, that it has become today.

In almost every game, almost every situation, scornful of just doing the same as everyone else, Steve Waugh set himself to find a better way. For him, year after year, 'it'll do' never did.

This world-famous resolve was forged in Bankstown, a gritty working-class suburb south-west of Sydney. On summer Saturdays the twins played age-group games in the morning and worked the scoreboard for the senior side in the afternoon. Aged 12, they paid a dollar each to watch Tony Greig play for Waverley: 'I didn't have the guts to ask for his autograph,' Steve recalls.

Guts was rarely a problem thereafter. Both were selected to play for New South Wales as 19-year-olds, and barely a year later Steve was in the Australian squad as an all-rounder: a middle-order batsman and aggressive medium-pace bowler.

Soon established as the second name on the team sheet after Allan Border, he set about creating his own World Cup legend.

At the 1987 tournament his disciplined, economical bowling in the closing overs became a major feature of Australia's triumph, prompting his team-mates to call him 'Iceman'.

In 1996, with the West Indies at 165 for two and coasting to victory in the semi-final, it was Waugh who ingeniously bowled Lara and prompted a Caribbean collapse to 202 all out.

Still a match-winner three years later, it was his courageous and unbeaten 120 that saved his side from elimination in the Super Six match against South Africa at Headingley.

Twice a world champion, the image of Waugh that endures is the trophy scene on the Lord's balcony in 1999, where, typically, far from standing alone and hogging the limelight to himself, this loyal, modest captain is surrounded by his beaming team.

His Test career has included its own highlights – 200 against the West Indians in 1995, a partnership of 385 with Greg Blewett in Johannesburg, and a fine century versus England at the SCG in the game that many thought might be his last Test – but the flow of runs and wickets has been relentlessly consistent.

Even through inevitable bare patches, Waugh has never been less than a competitor feared by the opposition.

As captain of Australia's one-day side from December 1997 till he was controversially overlooked in February 2002, and as captain of a super-confident, all-conquering Test team since February 1999, a period when his side had often been lauded as the best of all time, he has always set a resolutely professional example.

Through 10 039 runs in 156 Tests, and 7 569 in 325 one-day internationals, when his teams have won, and won, he has ensured that this is one Waugh that will never, ever be forgotten.

Chapter Twelve

Broken Trust

For more than three decades, the relationship between the one-day game and its enthusiastic public was affectionate and trusting. Then, in April 2000, this bond was exposed as an illusion.

In the minds of spectators across the globe, from Melbourne to Mumbai, London to Lahore and Cape Town to Queenstown, it had seemed absolutely inconceivable that any individual player might be accepting bribes and selling the game short. The word 'cricket' had long been synonymous with a sense of decency and fair play; the authenticity and honesty of the contest through hundreds of one-day internationals and seven World Cups had always been taken completely for granted.

Then, the game lost its innocence.

When Hansie Cronje woke on the morning of 4 April 2000 he appeared to be at the pinnacle of an illustrious career. The established captain of South Africa, he was respected across the world, revered as a national hero, disciplined, successful, a winner.

Then, out of the blue, Cronje found himself cast as the central figure in a Shakespearean tragedy. Hamlet may have been brought down by his indecision, and Macbeth by his boundless ambition, but Cronje's fatal flaw was his hunger for wealth . . .

5 April 2000: rumours abound that Indian police have a recording of a mobile phone conversation between the South African captain and a representative of a betting syndicate made during the one-day series between India and South Africa in March 2000.

The voice alleged to be Cronje's offers information about his team, including a suggestion that off-spinner Derek Crookes would open the bowling later in the series. The two men also arrange that Herschelle Gibbs will not score more than 20 runs.

History records that, to his own surprise, Crookes had indeed been told to open the bowling later in the series, conceding 53 runs in six overs; and Gibbs was out for 19. It looks bad.

7 April: *'I am stunned,' Cronje declares indignantly. 'These allegations are completely without substance.'*

11 April: *Tormented by guilt, curled on his bed in the foetal position, at three o'clock in the morning the captain finally decides to telephone Dr Ali Bacher, MD of the United Cricket Board of SA, to concede he has not been 'entirely honest'.*

He confesses to having received around US$15 000 from an Asian bookmaker, for what he describes as 'forecasting' results, but he denies match-fixing or ever trying not to win. The UCBSA quickly sacks the captain and launches a public inquiry.

10 June: *The King Commission opens, and hears a litany of evidence, conjuring up an overall picture of regular contact between top players and bookmakers since the mid-1990s. Often appearing to shoulder the blame for widespread corruption in the sport, Cronje eventually admits to having been paid a total of US$140 000 and, in tears, promises to 'redress the wrongs I have done'.*

11 October: *Cronje is banned from cricket for life, but after a drawn-out appeal, which frequently turns nasty and personal, he is given permission to coach in a private capacity and to work in the cricket media. Cautiously, he launches the process of rehabilitating his name in a country that, since emerging from a divided past, has turned forgiveness into a national pastime.*

1 June 2002: *Flying from Johannesburg to his home on a golf course estate near George in the Western Cape, Cronje is killed when the light cargo plane crashes into a mountain. Aged only 32, he leaves a wife, no children and many, many memories, good and bad.*

Perhaps history will judge that, in his death, Cronje took away not only his own remorse and guilt, but also the collective penitence and shame of a sport that seemed to have lost its way.

For, if anything is certain, it is that the South African was not the only prominent cricketer to take money from Asian bookmakers for manipulating matches. Indeed, the weight of evidence suggests the practice was rife, a cancer at the heart of one-day international cricket played around the world during the 1990s.

Cronje simply got caught red-handed, condemned as the fall guy. A man of many fine qualities and great achievements, this was his fate. First he was banned in order to restore a veneer of purity, then his tragic death seemed to mark a point when cricket could draw a line in the sand, put corruption in the past, and move on.

In fact, rumours of match-fixing had been swirling around the underworld of the game for almost two decades.

Back in 1982, after Australia had beaten the West Indies in a World Series group match, an article appeared in the Melbourne *Age* suggesting the Caribbean team had 'thrown' the match for financial reasons. Clive Lloyd, the captain, brought a libel action against the newspaper, and the court found in his favour, awarding damages of US$100 000 plus costs against the *Age*.

These particular allegations may have been settled, but other situations provoked more whispering until February 1995, when two Australians spoke out loud. Shane Warne and Mark Waugh declared that Salim Malik, the Pakistani batsman, had offered them money not to try during Australia's tour of Pakistan in 1994.

Various investigations and judicial inquiries probed the issue for months, and years, and the issue was further spiced when it was disclosed, in December 1998, that Warne and Waugh themselves had been secretly fined by the Australian Cricket Board during the same tour to the sub-continent four years earlier.

Amazingly, the two Australian players had admitted to being paid £2 600 each by an Indian bookmaker for supplying information over a six-month period about the weather and the pitch conditions. This seemed a large sum to pay for facts that were readily available to television viewers. As time went by, 'information about the weather and pitch conditions' appeared to become a coded term for insider tips more obviously useful to bookies.

The plot thickened but, through all the hearings and appeals, somehow, nobody appeared transparently and unequivocally guilty of anything . . . until Cronje was caught on tape.

'I never gave anything less than 100 per cent to win any match for South Africa,' the captain repeatedly protested, and he was almost certainly telling the truth. The mechanics of cricket corruption were far more sophisticated than just fixing the result.

Babbling bookies in Asia were eager to accept bets on almost anything in the game: how many runs would a team score between the 10th and the 15th over, who would open the bowling, how many runs would any individual batsman score? The options were endless, and mobile telephones buzzed back and forth.

In a part of the world where betting was officially legal only at a few racecourses, the Asian gambling industry thrived underground, and, in the absence of regulation, the hounds were loose.

Spread betting, sometimes known as split betting, became all the rage. Syndicates scarcely cared who won or lost, but they were eager to pay large sums of money to anybody who could make sure a less obvious, equally lucrative bet came through.

For example, having placed a large bet on Team A taking their score to 100 in the 17th over, representatives of the syndicate would approach the captain of Team B and offer him, say, $30 000 to control his bowling changes to ensure the opposition did indeed reach the nominated target during the 17th over.

The corrupted captain would then monitor the innings, taking any measures required to ensure the syndicate won its bet without substantially affecting the course or result of the match. Perhaps, if Team A had reached only 86 for two after 15 overs, he would know they needed 14 off the next two overs and would, inconspicuously, bring on a spinner or leave a few gaps in the field, just to give away the runs needed, and then proceed with the contest.

Within the world of sport, captains of cricket sides are ideally, almost uniquely, placed to control the flow of the game. Certainly their counterparts in rugby or football are not able to manage their matches in the same way. So, the betting syndicates moved in on cricket, and introduced themselves to captains.

Other players could squeeze their snouts into the trough, most obviously by controlling how many runs they scored, but it was the skipper who held the trump cards and it was not surprising that no fewer than eight international captains were subsequently linked to the scandal that began to engulf the game.

The International Cricket Council responded to this crisis of confidence by appointing Sir Paul Congdon, a former Commissioner of Britain's Metropolitan Police, to lead a new Anti-Corruption Unit, created to identify guilty men and clean up the game.

Congdon travelled the globe, interviewing players, spreading the ACU's net wide, and gathering names, addresses, bank accounts and mobile phone records to build a data base that would support the drive to track down those individuals who had betrayed the ethics of the game.

Various household names were mentioned in the scandal but, all said and done, only five players were given life bans: Mohammad Azharuddin and Ajay Sharma, both from India; Ata-ur-Rehman and Salim Malik, both of Pakistan; and Cronje, the South African.

Other top players – perhaps many others – kept their heads down, said nothing, quietly thanked their lucky stars, and continued their careers on the treadmill of international cricket.

The ACU eventually presented a detailed report, containing 24 proposals, all of which were duly implemented by the ICC. 'This is a blueprint to put match-fixing in the past,' Congdon stated. 'The ICC will be in a stronger position to deal with this problem if it continues to develop from its origins as a loose, fragile alliance into a modern, regulatory body whose transactions are transparent.'

After Malik, Waugh and Warne, after Cronje, after Congdon, is it possible to say one-day international cricket is clean?

Everybody hopes so.

Nobody knows for sure.

Broken trust is not easily repaired.

Chapter Thirteen

The Eighth World Cup

It was going to be the best Cricket World Cup ever.

Everyone said so. From Ali Bacher, the tournament director, to each of more than 3 000 volunteers, nobody seemed to have any doubt that the 2003 event would set new standards.

South Africa appeared the ideal host country: smart, modern stadiums, excellent transport, world-class hotels, hours of sunshine and, above all, an eager, energised cricketing public.

Whether it's simply in the genes, or whether it's the legacy of 20 years in international isolation, South Africans remain fabulously enthusiastic and passionate about their sport. Cynicism and apathy may be the norm in other countries, but, at the foot of Africa, there is an innocent, even naïve readiness to get excited.

'This is our World Cup,' declared one volunteer. 'The world is coming, and we're going to make it great.'

Bacher certainly shared these sentiments, but this perceptive administrator also recognised that, for the tournament to be judged a success within South Africa's social and political realities, it would have to be palpably pan-African in shape and style.

In 2003, nine eventful years on from the end of apartheid and the joyful transition to democracy, it was no longer enough to shout for unity, wave the flag and ride the rainbow fever, as a triumphant, nation-building Rugby World Cup had done in 1995.

If the Cricket World Cup was going to engage the emotions of the black majority, and indeed the black government, it would have to demonstrate through solid actions that this was not just a festival being played out in a white cocoon for white cricket lovers, but that it was an event with its heart and soul in Africa.

This was the challenge, and Bacher's missionary response was to carry the tournament north, deep into Africa. It was agreed that Kenya would host two group matches in Nairobi, and that Zimbabwe would play three games in Harare, and three in Bulawayo.

'This will be an African World Cup,' he declared.

In theory, the plans looked excellent, maybe even inspired. In reality, sadly, the idea proved unfortunate because it unleashed the hounds of politics. As a result, as the event drew near, far too often, far too few people were focused on the cricket.

The build-up was dominated by other issues: would England agree to play Zimbabwe in Harare, and would the New Zealanders fulfil their group match against Kenya in Nairobi?

These problematical questions arose as soon as the draw was made, but, inexplicably, the ICC, the tournament organisers and the two national Boards concerned said and did nothing. It was almost as if the game was strapped to railway tracks, determined to ignore a political express train that was fast approaching.

Officials took no action. Robert Mugabe burgled an election, tortured his political opponents and constructively starved millions of people, and the world's cricket administrators stood by, plainly proclaiming their matches would be played as scheduled.

Determined to safeguard the tournament's African dimension, the organisers turned a blind eye to Mugabe's tyranny. As morality fled, the issue drifted into 2003. If the paralysed ICC hoped it would somehow go away, they were disappointed.

Eventually, following an embarrassing series of meetings, and statements, and appeals, and press conferences, through which the English Cricket Board displayed an incredible lack of leadership and clarity, it was left to Nasser Hussain and his players, themselves, to decide they would not play cricket in Harare.

Uncertainty and frustration filled the vacuum of leadership, as blameless young cricketers sat through marathon discussions about complex security arrangements and anonymous death threats when they should have been practising in the nets. Little wonder, Hussain revealed some of them had been reduced to tears.

Absurdly, disgracefully, the final decision was reached only 48 hours before the match was supposed to start.

With less furore and fanfare, the New Zealanders decided they would not play in Nairobi. Only nine months before, this same group of players had hastily abandoned their tour of Pakistan after a bomb exploded in the street outside their hotel. Supported by their Board, they were simply not prepared to take any risks in Kenya, a country that had already suffered major terrorist attacks.

The net result of this shambles was the decisive distortion of the contest. As the tournament unfolded, the effect of these forfeits was that Zimbabwe, not England, progressed from the group stage and Kenya, not New Zealand, reached the semi-final.

What could have been done?

The ICC could have assumed control of the situation one year before the tournament by holding a meeting of all the stakeholders, analysing security and moral issues, and reaching a final consensus either to play games in Zimbabwe and Kenya, or move the matches to South Africa. Instead, they dithered and dallied.

Relief from these mind-numbing machinations finally came at the opening ceremony at Newlands in Cape Town.

After the bungling in Calcutta in 1996, and the damp squib at Lords in 1999, the eighth Cricket World Cup was launched by a tidy, bright, enjoyable show beneath Table Mountain. Musicians and dancers in animal costumes entertained the capacity crowd, and players from 14 competing nations formed a happy parade.

President Thabo Mbeki opened the tournament, and, in broad tone and mood, the occasion struck the right note. Even the English players, taking a break from their deliberations over whether to play in Harare, appeared to be enjoying themselves.

So, the close-knit community of international cricketers stood shoulder to shoulder on the turf at Newlands. Friendships forged on the relentless merry-go-round of the Test circuit were renewed, and, in sideways glances, opponent sized up opponent.

The Australians had arrived as favourites. So strong that they had left Steve Waugh at home, replacing the 37-year-old icon with the as yet unfulfilled talent of Andrew Symonds in the middle order and with Ricky Ponting as captain, they had no clear weakness.

In Gilchrist, Hayden, Ponting, Martyn, Lehmann and Bevan, the batting looked dynamic and powerful. In McGrath, Warne, Gillespie and Lee, their bowling appeared explosive and balanced. So, on a balmy, late summer evening in Cape Town, this massively confident squad marched into view, all power and resolve.

Their main challengers drank deep from the cup of hope. The relentlessly marketed South African side was thunderously cheered at Newlands, almost as if the patriotic masses were trying to create the emotional wave to carry their team to victory. The Indian squad smiled, their quiet ambition founded on Tendulkar, Sehwag, Dravid, Ganguly and Kaif, a thrilling battery of batting class.

Shoaib Akhtar spearheaded a Pakistan side capable of beating anyone on their day; Nasser Hussain led an England squad that had shown improved form and, pending the fitness of key players, could mount a genuine challenge; and Stephen Fleming walked out at the head of his gutsy, competitive New Zealand team.

The West Indians seemed to be heading in the right direction under Carl Hooper, but perhaps not fast enough; and few reckoned the Sri Lankans would emerge from their recent indifferent form on tour to Australia and pose any serious threat.

Beyond these eight major nations, the other six teams looked set to enjoy the sights and sounds of the World Cup, but not much more. Zimbabwe could surprise, but such ambitions seemed beyond Bangladesh, Kenya, Canada, Holland and Namibia.

The diverse cricketing world had gathered, and keen amateurs excitedly rubbed shoulders with polished professionals. Through 54 games in 46 days, the teams would compete for an unprecedented total prize money of US$5 million, of which a cheque for US$2 million would crown the new world champions on 23 March.

Tiger Woods might hardly have blinked at these numbers, but they represented genuine riches for cricket. At the high point in the sports rights market, the brazen Global Cricket Corporation, backed by Rupert Murdoch, had agreed to pay US$550 million for rights to the Cricket World Cups in 2003 and 2007. All of a sudden, the bank manager was laughing all the way to the ICC.

Suspicions that GCC had paid a grossly inflated price seemed to be confirmed when they secured only four main sponsors for the 2003 World Cup, and the draconian measures introduced to protect these companies' interests smacked of desperation.

A man named Arthur Williamson took his children to watch a World Cup match at Centurion, but was forcibly ejected from the stadium for drinking a can of Coca-Cola. This everyday act had been prohibited because Pepsi was an official sponsor.

The young Williamsons watched in disbelief as the business of modern cricket took its course; so, perhaps, from another place, did W.G. Grace, Jack Hobbs and Donald Bradman.

As the host country, South Africa had been scheduled to play their first group match, against the West Indies, under floodlights at Newlands the day after the opening ceremony; and the tournament was launched by a dramatic and thrilling contest.

Brian Lara, now 34, had arrived almost unnoticed at the World Cup. Recovering from injury, the genius batsman had not played a truly competitive innings since 14 September 2002, and he looked in trouble when he walked to the crease with his country, sent in to bat, struggling at 7 for two after seven overs.

He fended tentatively at the very first delivery he faced, from Makhaya Ntini, and the ball flew just wide of Jacques Kallis's grasp at third slip. Lara had made his first, and last, mistake.

Compact and increasingly confident, he proceeded to produce a master class of sweet drives and cuts. Skilfully dismantling South Africa's fragile confidence, he scored 116 runs in 134 balls and took his team from crisis to stability at 215 for five.

Two of the new generation West Indian batsmen, Ramnaresh Sarwan and Ricardo Powell, excelled on this platform, thrashing 64 runs in 28 balls, and the upbeat Caribbean side accelerated to post a highly competitive 279 for five in 50 overs.

Shaun Pollock was taken aback. The determined South African captain had conceded only 20 runs in his first eight overs, but been bashed for 23 in his ninth. His team had lost their discipline towards the end of the innings, bowling their overs too slowly, and they now faced the daunting challenge of batting under lights and scoring 270 to win in a reduced complement of 49 overs.

The chase often seemed to gain a winning momentum, but at crucial stages wickets kept falling. Gibbs and Dippenaar went in the 20s, Kirsten's anchor was raised at 69, Boucher made 49.

As the possibility of unthinkable defeat dawned upon amazed Capetonians in the stands, the West Indians warmed to their task, and by the time Lance Klusener strode to the middle, the required run rate had increased towards ten an over.

Surely it was too much to expect the talismanic all-rounder to pick up where he had left off at the 1999 World Cup in England? No, it wasn't. Amid gathering delirium at Newlands, he bludgeoned five sixes and hauled his team back into the game.

Eventually, eight runs were needed from the last four balls. In form, in the eye of the storm again, two blows from glory, his score on 57 from only 47 deliveries, Klusener steadied.

However, just as he had fallen at the final hurdle in the World Cup semi-final at Edgbaston in 1999, so he would come short in the opening match at Newlands four years on.

Then as now, his magnificent efforts had taken South Africa to the brink of victory; then as now, the fates conspired to deny him at the last. Then, he joined Donald on a suicidal single. Now, he pulled a full toss towards Hooper on the deep-mid-wicket boundary and, as he saw the ball falling to the fielder, he inexplicably headed towards the pavilion instead of crossing with his partner.

This simple discipline would have left the established batsman Nicky Boje on strike, still with three balls to face, still with a decent chance of getting the runs. Instead, with Boje stranded at the other end, the tail-ender Ntini had to walk in and take guard.

He missed his first delivery, and was caught off the next ball, although this time at least the batsmen did remember to cross, and Boje was back on strike. It was now too late. He hit the final ball of the innings to the boundary but the West Indies had secured a fine, extraordinary, spectacular victory by four runs.

Newlands fell silent, stunned, but, as Pollock correctly pointed out, the home team would live to fight another day. The wider view held that, following the feel-good opening ceremony, it was difficult to imagine a better start to the 2003 World Cup.

Meanwhile, in Harare, two established Zimbabwean cricketers were planning to leave their mark on the tournament. Andy Flower, the team's outstanding player for a decade, and Henry Olonga, the first black man to play for Zimbabwe, had decided they would not participate in the World Cup without at least recognising the social, economic and political crisis in their country.

They settled upon a simple gesture – wearing black armbands during Zimbabwe's group match against Namibia – but it is difficult to exaggerate the scale of their bravery. In Mugabe's Zimbabwe in February 2003, to criticise the government publicly in any way was to risk ostracism, persecution and even a beating.

By issuing a statement in which they 'mourned the death of democracy', these men sent themselves into exile.

The official response was predictable. Mugabe's spokesperson denounced Flower as a 'racist' and a 'bitter man because he saw his father being forced to share vast tracts of land he once owned with landless black Zimbabweans'. In fact, Flower's father Bill, a retired Harare businessman, had never owned a farm.

Olonga was branded an 'uncle Tom' and 'a black man with a white mask', and swiftly expelled from his club in Harare, which, by a quirk of fate, Bill Flower had worked hard to launch.

The players' protest had been quiet, dignified and extremely effective. While the ICC tried to dance on eggshells again, warning the players against 'blurring the line between politics and cricket', substantial sections of the crowd at subsequent matches involving Zimbabwe were seen wearing black armbands.

As the World Cup unfolded, the issue rumbled on. Olonga was unaccountably dropped from the side when, with the selectors split 3-3, Ali Shah, the chairman of selectors well known for his political sensibilities, cast his vote for another player. Flower was laughably accused of not trying his best, but he responded by scoring a gutsy 62 against the rampant Australians in Bulawayo.

At the end of the campaign, Flower announced his retirement from international cricket, and planned to divide the rest of his most distinguished career between playing for the Essex county side and South Australia. Then he flew to safety in England, where, as a wise precaution, he had already sent his wife and children.

Olonga's future seemed less certain. He went into hiding after Zimbabwe's last match, apparently dodging attempts by Mugabe's secret servicemen to drag him back to Zimbabwe. It seemed likely that he too would continue his career overseas.

Whatever the future may hold, the names of Andy Flower and Henry Olonga have been engraved in World Cup history, not for the runs they scored or the wickets they took, but for their quiet, simple courage in standing up to a regime that had inflicted huge suffering and pain upon, in their words, their 'beloved country'.

The hosts had been beaten on Sunday; the Zimbabweans had made their protest on Monday. What could this remarkably eventful World Cup deliver for the headlines on Tuesday?

WARNE TESTS POSITIVE FOR DRUGS.

It defied belief.

The Australian spinner, perhaps the most celebrated player in the tournament, was flying home to defend himself after it emerged that a drugs test, conducted in Sydney on 22 January, had shown a positive result for fluid-reducing diuretics.

Shane Warne appeared at a press conference in Johannesburg and vehemently denied he had ever used illegal substances, but the cricketing community was already dividing into those who believed his side of the story and, bluntly, those who didn't.

Either people accepted Warne's explanation that he had taken the diuretic pills from his mother because he wanted to lose weight and that, at worst, he had been foolish and careless in not checking the legality of the tablets before swallowing them.

Or they stood back from the sentiment and assessed the plain facts: Warne had been working hard to recover from a torn shoulder muscle to get fit for what would be his last World Cup; steroids are thought to accelerate the healing process; diuretics have frequently been used as a masking agent for steroids.

Promptly, the Anti-Doping committee of the Australian Cricket Board met to weigh the balance of probability and suspended Warne for one year, a sentence that would cost the player nearly £600 000 in lost playing and sponsorship contracts.

Warne continued to protest his innocence, a claim backed by his team-mates who insisted his recently improved physical condition owed everything to sweat in the gym, and nothing to drugs, but he declined to appeal and accepted the judgement.

'My life is a soap opera,' the blond, blue-eyed icon is fond of saying and, through epic performances, match-fixing and drugs, this gifted, lively character has starred in every episode.

Nonetheless, he remains resolved to play Test cricket for five or six more seasons, and to overtake Courtney Walsh and become the leading Test wicket-taker of all time. In this regard, however, he may finally be foiled by Muttiah Muralitharan, the prolific Sri Lankan spinner who, three years younger, has time on his side.

The 2003 World Cup moved on.

In early matches, New Zealand seemed strangely subdued in losing to Sri Lanka, a result that, combined with their refusal to play in Kenya, meant Fleming's highly rated team all of a sudden needed to keep winning to remain in the tournament. Andrew Symonds hit a wonderful 143 not out as Australia put the Warne situation behind them and posted 310 for eight against Pakistan, but the victory was soured when Gilchrist accused

Rashid Latif of racism, and a number of players angrily refused to shake hands at the end.

While the professionals snapped at one another, the amateurs were loving every minute of the experience. A sharp, dreadlocked plumber from Toronto named Austin Codrington claimed five for 27 as Canada defeated Bangladesh in Durban.

The tournament was buzzing. Volunteers in mauve tracksuits smiled as they manned car parks, offered directions and vigorously oiled the cogs of Bacher's smooth organisation.

However, every venture needs an element of good luck, and, having waved goodbye to Warne, the World Cup could hardly afford to lose another of its most popular faces. Yet during South Africa's win over Kenya in Potchefstroom, Jonty Rhodes fractured his finger in the field, and was subsequently driven to hospital.

Once pins had been placed in his hands, doctors declared that the infectious, inspiring personality at the heart of the home side would be out of action for three weeks. Never mind, people thought, Jonty would be back towards the end of the Super Six.

Some South Africans sensed echoes of the 1995 Rugby World Cup when the Springbok fullback Andre Joubert had shattered his hand in two places but bravely overcame the pain and was allowed to remain in the team, playing his full part in the semi-final and the final, and sharing in the ultimate glory at Ellis Park.

Regrettably, such thoughts did not cross the closed minds of the cricket officials, and they sent Rhodes home. Inflexibly insisting that it was necessary to summon a replacement batsman, they unwisely overlooked the veteran's gargantuan value to the squad in terms of offering uncon-ditional support to the captain, encouraging younger players, and keeping the dressing room upbeat.

Occasionally in sport, special players merit special treatment, and Rhodes should have been permitted to stay with the squad, and contribute, and encourage, and recover. Instead, small men made a small-minded decision and, by all accounts, the positive atmosphere within the home camp soon began to evaporate.

Decent to the last, Rhodes equitably announced his retirement from international cricket and shuffled off the stage.

Notwithstanding these empty seats in the front row, the World Cup bus ploughed on regardless, continuing to generate high-quality entertainment for healthy, enthusiastic crowds.

Chaminda Vaas, Sri Lanka's premier fast bowler, woke up with a sore back on the morning of the match against Bangladesh. Thank goodness, he wasn't fully fit. Running in to bowl the first over of the day, he took a wicket with each of the first three balls, then bowled a dot ball, then conceded four runs past point, then bowled a wide, and captured another wicket with the last ball.

After one over in placid Pietermaritzburg, Bangladesh stood at four wickets for five runs. Everyone was home for tea.

India's title aspirations faced a rigorous examination in their game against Australia at Centurion, but the outcome was humbling for Saurav Ganguly and his players. Bowled out for 125 in only 41.4 overs, they were soundly thrashed by mid-afternoon.

The outrage at home was amazing, even by Indian standards of cricketing fanaticism and fervour. The young Mohammad Kaif was told his house had been smeared with tar and, if Ganguly was upset to learn a newspaper columnist had called for him to be replaced as captain, he would have been more disturbed to know the newspaper columnist in question was his own brother.

Sachin Tendulkar stepped forward to ask for calm. 'We realise what we have to do,' the batsman told supporters in a special radio interview. 'Be patient and we won't let you down.'

Another team feeling the pressure was New Zealand, but they kept their heads above water by defeating the West Indies, fielding like tigers in defence of a vulnerable total and running out Lara with an amazing telegraph throw from the boundary, and they moved on to a crunch match against the South Africans.

The losers would face elimination. As a capacity crowd passed through a tight security cordon around the Wanderers Stadium, the stakes could hardly have been higher. Both New Zealand and South Africa were playing to stay alive in the tournament.

Herschelle Gibbs appeared to thrive on the pressure, crashing an extraordinary 143 as the home team reached a commanding 306 for six in 50 overs. The traditionally demanding Johannesburg crowd appeared to relax, content that their team's supposedly predestined march to the final, at least, was back on track.

Stephen Fleming and Nathan Astle took a different view, and the Kiwi batsmen launched the pursuit with calm purpose. The runs began to flow, and flow. Anxiety seeped into the stands.

When they should have been closing out a crucial victory, the South

Africans began to flounder because, firstly, too many of their key bowlers, most notably Allan Donald and Jacques Kallis, failed to exert pressure on the batsmen, and, second, because this particular team unaccountably kept making basic mistakes.

Mark Boucher was a consistent, admired wicketkeeper and he would most probably have caught the basic, regulation catch edged by Fleming 999 times out of a thousand. However, on this particular day, the ball escaped from his gloves, and the New Zealand captain, on 53, advanced to play maybe the innings of his life.

An almost paternal figure, Fleming had earned the respect of his players when he stood resolutely at the forefront of a tense pay dispute with the Board. Even when the squad effectively refused to play from the start of October 2002 until mid-November, this most impressive captain remained solid, unflinching.

Now, he demonstrated the same resolve in the middle. From his ideally poised, perfectly still stance, through his classic, powerful strokeplay, Fleming developed an irresistible momentum. Even after the match was interrupted for an hour by rain, shrinking the target by the Duckworth-Lewis method to around seven runs per over, the captain concentrated and kept his team on course.

With an ease that had seemed unimaginable between innings, New Zealand cantered to victory, completing the job at 229 for one, of which Fleming had scored 134 not out in 132 balls.

South Africans drifted quietly away into the northern suburbs of Johannesburg, battling to accept their hyped-up team would now have to rely on other results if they were to reach the Super Six. On this solemn Sunday, huge roadside billboards eulogising Pollock and his team seemed to taunt them on their way home.

The following morning, Gibbs chose to make an extraordinary contribution to the situation. As his team hovered on the brink of a humbling disaster, the opener attended the launch of his authorised biography and let it be known that he believed Shaun Pollock 'had a lot to learn about captaincy'. With friends like that . . .

However, even as Gibbs was holding court among the media, South Africa's luck appeared to be changing.

Constant rain was falling in Potchefstroom, forcing the match between the West Indies and Bangladesh to be abandoned. It was only the second time the Asian underachievers had avoided defeat in 29 one-day internationals, both times because of rain. In despair, the West Indians were forced to share the points.

This outcome put South Africa's fate back in their own hands. Three wins in their three remaining group matches would, after all, send them scrambling gratefully into the Super Six.

The event flowed on, but it had become an inexorable stream of one-sided matches between professionals and part-time players who had had neither the funding nor the time to prepare properly, and who came from countries where perhaps 99 per cent of the population didn't know a Cricket World Cup was taking place.

Unfortunately, latest news of the tournament was not buzzing on the streets of Amsterdam and Toronto.

Now and then, an outstanding individual performance would break the tide – Jan Berry Burger hit a brave 85 off 86 balls for the Namibians against England, and John Davison thrashed the fastest century in World Cup history, from 67 balls, for Canada against the West Indies – but there was only one true shock.

Of the major teams, Sri Lanka seemed one of the least likely victims because they appeared to have perfected the art of beating ICC associate members, ruthlessly dismissing the Canadians for 36, the lowest-ever total in a one-day international, and then requiring only 28 balls at the crease to complete a 10-wicket victory.

However, it was Jayasuriya's experienced side that faltered at the colonial Gymkhana Ground in Nairobi.

The mood in Kenya was still optimistic two months after the unpopular President Moi had been defeated in democratic elections, but few people expected much from their national side in the World Cup. The veteran Steve Tikolo led a mix of familiar names and youthful talent, but Kenyan cricket appeared hamstrung by internal politicking and ongoing allegations of corruption.

Nonetheless, Kenya's home match with Sri Lanka was eagerly antici-pated, particularly after the other game had fallen away when the New Zealanders cancelled their visit to Nairobi. An enthusiastic, flag-waving group of cricket fans made their way to the ground and seemed to be enjoying the occasion, even when their team cobbled together an unremarkable 209 in their 50 overs.

The Sri Lankans looked strangely diffident in the field, content to leave the work to Muralitharan, who had claimed four for 28, and complacency surfaced in the run chase as well. Once Jayasuriya had checked a lofted drive and been caught at mid-wicket, their middle order was routed by a

21-year-old leg-spinner.

Collins Obuya had always been more interested in training to become a doctor than in playing cricket, but he had followed his elder brothers into the game and had recently signed a part-time contract with the Kenya Cricket Association worth £600 per month. Living at home with his brother David, he supplemented this meagre income by helping out at his mother's vegetable store.

Now, suddenly, the tall, upright spinner found himself hopping in to bowl before a worldwide television audience of millions, and, to his beaming delight, he seized five wickets for 24 runs. Jayasuriya watched in disbelief as his team was rolled for 157: 'This has been the worst day of my career,' the captain said later.

The thrilled Kenyans celebrated a wonderful occasion, just as they had celebrated their famous triumph over the West Indians at the 1996 World Cup, but the difference this time was that, combined with their points from the New Zealand forfeit, this upset win would have a significant bearing on the tournament.

Indeed, out of the blue, the arithmetic now indicated that, by winning their final group match against humble Bangladesh, Kenya would be able to secure a place in the Super Six.

'You're joking,' one leading Test cricketer said to another.

'Look at the group table,' came the reply.

Silence confirmed the fact.

Meanwhile, far more established, better-equipped sides were struggling to progress from their groups. The likes of England, the West Indies, Pakistan and South Africa would have thrashed Kenya nine times out of ten, but that meant nothing now.

England had seemed to be making progress, producing a tidy performance to defeat Pakistan. In the space of five months, James Anderson had risen from the third team of the Burnley Cricket Club via the National Academy into England's World Cup side. Now, the 20-year-old seamer took four frontline Pakistani wickets for 29 runs and inspired his country to a 112-run victory.

Shoaib Akhtar and his team-mates were bewildered by another defeat. The fast bowler had tried everything against England, even managing to bowl the first ball ever irrefutably registered at a speed in excess of 100 miles per hour. 'I wanted to cross that barrier and finish it for the rest of my life,' he said later. 'Unfortunately, I didn't bowl very well today, so I am not that happy.'

The stakes were rising as the groups reached their conclusion, and each of the four major sides threatened with elimination in turn faced a crucial match to make or break their World Cup.

The West Indies had to defeat Sri Lanka, Pakistan had to beat India, England had to overcome Australia, and only victory over Sri Lanka would keep the South Africans in their own tournament.

Lara, Gayle, Hooper, Shoaib, Waqar, Wasim, Vaughan, Trescothick, Flintoff, Pollock, Gibbs, Kallis, Kirsten and Donald: many of the biggest names in the sport had packed into the Last Chance saloon; and, in their dire situation, there was nothing to be gained by propping up the bar and complaining about the format, the politics or the weather. These were the realities and there was still a World Cup to be won.

'There's no room for error,' Hooper told his team, after losing the toss and facing the prospect of batting second, under lights, against Sri Lanka at Newlands. 'This is our last chance.'

The fast-improving West Indies had played consistently competitive cricket since arriving in South Africa, bowling and fielding with purpose, and, after running out Atapattu in the fourth over, they held the Sri Lankans in check by restricting their totem, Jayasuriya, to a scratchy 66. Only a late onslaught from Russell Arnold and the tail eked Sri Lanka to 228 for six in 50 overs, and Hooper's side seemed in control.

Chaminda Vaas had other ideas. Confidence soaring, the fast bowler glided in, removing Hinds for nought and Lara for one. Sarwan then ducked into a Dilhara Fernando bouncer. After lying motionless on the pitch for five minutes, amid hushed concern, he was stretchered away to hospital by paramedics.

Hooper fell LBW soon afterwards, but the innings was watchfully revived by Gayle and Chanderpaul until the irrepressible Vaas seemed to have turned the match when he returned for a second spell and, swinging the ball at will, transformed Caribbean optimism at 121 for three into despair at 122 for six.

Chanderpaul remained, nudging and chipping away at the target and, as the evening churned towards a dramatic conclusion, word began to spread around Newlands that Sarwan had returned from hospital and was willing to resume his innings. This seemed far-fetched but, when the seventh wicket fell, with his side needing 60 runs from 47 balls, the bruised batsman emerged from the pavilion.

With a gentle tug at his helmet and an unwavering gaze, Sarwan joined Vasbert Drakes in the middle and set about creating one of the most extraordinary stories in cricket history.

Vigilantly at first, he kept the scoreboard rotating with singles and twos but, when Drakes was caught in the deep, with 42 runs still required from the last four overs, the West Indian hero struck out for glory. A firm flat six over long-off, a brilliant straight drive for four and a lofted three: it was happening, and, when he was dropped by Atapattu at backward square leg, events seemed to be falling in his favour.

Only 16 runs were needed from the last two overs, but then Muralitharan stepped forward and conceded only two runs from a cold-blooded penultimate over. Pulasthi Gunaratne was called upon to bowl the 50th over and, amid great tension, the opening bowler held his nerve. Sarwan was left stranded and unbeaten on 47 off 44 balls, denied the emotional triumph his courage had surely deserved.

The West Indies ended six runs short and, their pride intact, were cruelly eliminated from the tournament they had launched with such style only 19 days before on the same ground.

'There is no room for error,' Waqar Younis told his team at Centurion Park, aware that, more than ever, Pakistan needed to defeat their greatest rivals. Three times they had played India in a World Cup; three times they had lost. Now, before a frenzied capacity crowd, Waqar's side needed to stand tall.

They batted first on a belter and, with Saeed Anwar making a century, scored a formidable 273 for seven in 50 overs. The elegant opener had seemed unlikely to play in the World Cup but he was persuaded to change his mind by family, friends and religious scholars, and now he set the green flags waving.

Enter Sachin Tendulkar, in his pomp.

Shoaib roared in to bowl, and all India's hero imperiously whipped the ball off his hips to the square leg boundary. Then Waqar roared in, and the adored 'little master' merely pushed an impeccably straight bat with such sweet timing that the ball fizzed past the bowler for four. The genius was picking the length of every ball with ease; the finest batsman of his generation was setting the World Cup alight.

In the first five overs of the innings, in tandem with Virender Sehwag, he launched an onslaught of such ferocity that Pakistan's celebrity pace attack was made to look like park amateurs. Even when Sehwag was out, swiftly followed by Ganguly for nought, Tendulkar maintained his majestic form.

On the back foot, on the front foot, through the off-side, through the leg-side, compact and splendid: at one point he played a drive of such pure beauty that he had to be forgiven for indulging himself, and the eager Press photographers, by holding a posed follow-through for a few extra seconds.

In partnership first with the increasingly impressive Kaif and then the rock-solid Rahul Dravid, Tendulkar raced towards the century that seemed the inevitable prize for his flawless clean hitting. However, in sprinting for a quick single, he aggravated a long-standing thigh injury and, having called for a runner, was surprised by an express delivery from Shoaib that flew from his bat and into grateful hands at gully. Out for 98 from just 75 balls, borne by applause to the pavilion, Tendulkar had played a magical innings.

And yet the match was not over. With India stalled at 177 for four, the Pakistanis sensed the chance to stage another of their trademark fight-backs, but their hopes were mercilessly extinguished by Dravid and the calmly assured Yuvraj Singh, who finished unbeaten on 44 and 50 respectively, and safely guided their side to an emphatic, satisfying six-wicket victory with more than four overs to spare.

The match had been played in an excellent spirit, belying the endemic hostility between the two nations, but the disappointed Pakistanis had been bundled out of the tournament and the players knew precisely what to expect on their premature return home. An official inquiry was established and, within days, Waqar Younis was offered for sacrifice, dropped from the side and replaced as captain by Rashid Latif.

'There is no room for error,' Nasser Hussain told his team, after deciding to bat first against Australia on a slow pitch at St George's Park, Port Elizabeth. 'We know we can beat these guys.'

England was playing under pressure after suffering the worst of the conditions against India and folding under the lights in Durban, but, aware how they had almost beaten their old rivals in the recent VB series, they genuinely believed they could upset Australia and thereby advance to the Super Six.

Ponting's team was bidding for a 12th successive victory, which would establish a new world record in one-day international cricket, but they were caught cold by the English openers. Trescothick and Knight carried the fight to the tournament favourites, and hurtled to 66 in just nine overs.

England's loyal, long-suffering travelling supporters, the Barmy Army, were beginning to find their voice but, as ever, one of the Australians stepped up and helped the team out of trouble. Andy Bichel was rated as a relative journeyman alongside his more celebrated team-mates, and the fair-haired all-rounder was only playing in the match because Jason Gillespie was injured, but this turned out to be his day.

He bowled with intelligence and accuracy, and took a remarkable seven wickets for 20 runs in 10 overs, reducing England first from 66 without loss to 74 for four, and then, after Flintoff and Stewart had rallied the innings to respectability, from 177 for 5 to an eventual total of 204 for eight.

Hussain gathered his team again. His standing as captain had been enhanced by his emphatically decent and principled stand during the protracted debate over whether or not to play in Zimbabwe, and he implored his players to believe in themselves, defend the total and stay in the tournament.

Andy Caddick heard the call and dramatically sent four frontline batsmen back to the pavilion with only 48 runs on the board. England were holding their catches and firing.

Lehmann and Bevan weathered the storm, and cautiously took the score to 111 for five in the 29th over, but another flurry of wickets appeared to put England decisively back in control. Floundering at 135 for eight, apparently on the skids, the Australians would surely find no way back.

In fact, the 2003 World Cup was proving the Australians always found a way back. Gradually, with care and application, Bevan and Bichel steadied and edged towards their target. Maybe Hussain could have kept his frontline bowlers in the harness and, with eight down and only McGrath to come, gone for the kill. Perhaps, at the death, he erred by asking the youthful Anderson to bowl the penultimate over.

Whatever the 'ifs', the two Australian batsmen kept their nerve and completed the counter-attack when Bevan pulled the fourth ball of the last over for four. Unbeaten on 74, he walked down the pitch and cheerfully clicked clenched fists with Bichel, who had added 34 not out to his heroics with the ball.

The English players trooped slowly back to the pavilion, obviously battling to understand quite how they had not won the match. They had not played badly at the World Cup – in fact, at times, they had looked like a reasonable outside bet – but they now faced the grim reality that the combined effect of two defeats and their decision not to play in Harare would send them on an early flight back to London.

In many respects, approaching the end of the third week, the tournament was struggling to maintain its early momentum. Kenya and Zimbabwe were advancing, but the West Indians, Pakistan and England were on their way home. It was hard to avoid the sense that something had gone wrong.

The unkindest cut was still to come.

South African summers are well known for the long hours of sunshine, but less famous for their equally reliable late-afternoon rainfall and, unfortunately, two Englishmen by the names of Frank Duckworth and Tony Lewis were starting to emerge as significant players in the World Cup. It was this pair who had developed the ICC's latest approved method for determining the result of matches affected by rain.

The system may have been clever but, to most followers of the game, both in the stadiums and watching on television, it seemed so complicated that it was hardly worth trying to understand. Like inexpert motorists listening to any mechanic explaining what needs to be repaired in their broken-down car, most people found it easier to accept the official verdict, ask no questions, and move swiftly on.

Even established, experienced players, armed with D/L charts folded in their pockets whether they were batting or in the field, seemed frequently confused by the method's machinations.

When England was fielding against Namibia, Marcus Trescothick had been detailed to keep the stand-in captain, Alec Stewart, informed about the ongoing D/L situation, but it later transpired that he had misread the figures and been unaware that, for 12 overs, his side was in a losing position.

Even the Australians were battling to get to grips with the system. Batting first under dark clouds against Holland, Martyn and Lehmann agreed to play carefully towards the end of the innings, and scored only 47 runs in 48 balls, because they believed that, according to the D/L method, in the event of rain, their wickets in hand would substantially increase the target set for the Dutch. They were wrong. In fact, D/L rules state the number of wickets lost only enters into the equation for the team batting second.

The fact that rigorously professional teams such as England and Australia did not completely understand the system should put in some sort of context, and perhaps a more forgiving light, the straightforward mistake that, on a melodramatic night in Durban, sent South Africa out of the World Cup.

'There is no room for error,' Shaun Pollock told his team as they sat in the dressing room at Kingsmead, desperately wanting to set aside the burden of a nation's expectation, to overcome the nerves and produce the kind of competitive, high-intensity cricket for which they had become known.

However, yet again, for the third time in three matches against established opposition, the South African bowling attack proved incapable of consistently restraining top-class batsmen. Having won the toss and opted to bat first, the Sri Lankans seemed to be wobbling at 90 for three, but Marvan Atapattu and Aravinda de Silva expertly consolidated the innings, took control, and then let loose. The talented opener scored 124 in 129 balls, the crafty veteran made 73 in 78 balls: together, they added 152 for the fourth wicket.

Sri Lanka eventually finished with 268 for nine, more than the home team would have wanted to chase, and yet, but for a cascade of late wickets, the target would have been nearer 300.

Gibbs and Graeme Smith appeared at the head of a rejigged, but perhaps fatally unsettled, batting order and launched the pursuit with an impressive stand of 65 in 11 overs, but Jayasuriya's initiative to summon his spinners into the attack earned swift rewards. Smith was caught on the mid-wicket boundary, pulling De Silva's first ball, Kirsten was bowled behind his legs, sweeping, and Kallis was castled.

Still all seemed well while Gibbs remained, excitedly unfolding his full repertoire of attacking strokes, but the fluent opener tried to sweep Muralitharan and was bowled for 73. When Dippenaar fell LBW to Jayasuriya in the next over, the home side looked in trouble at 149 for five in the 30th over.

Pollock walked to the middle, applauded all the way by his home crowd, his fellow Natalians. If ever the captain needed support, it was now. Appointed in the wake of Hansie Cronje's fall from grace, he felt he had never been given adequate authority over the team by officials who were cautious of allowing any captain the kind of absolute control granted to Cronje, with such disastrous consequences.

He had endured criticism to his face and behind his back, from inside and outside his team. Some said he was remote and obstinate, others suggested he was weak and ineffective. Nobody denied he had always given his best for his country, and few could point a finger at his record over three years.

However, the captain dared not fail in this home World Cup and, together with Boucher, his vice-captain, Pollock pulled his team back on track, shrewdly adding 63 runs in 13 overs. He appeared well set but, when a freakish back-flick by Muralitharan caught him short of his ground, he was run out for 25.

In many of his plays, William Shakespeare used stormy weather as a portent of tragic events, and on this increasingly frenzied night in Durban, the first drizzle of rain began to appear in the floodlights just as Klusener emerged to join Boucher. If the weather held, only 47 runs were needed off 45 balls.

'If the weather held' . . . that was by no means certain.

Cool heads were required.

Jayasuriya, secure in the knowledge his team had already secured their place in the Super Six, appeared calmly in control as he regularly checked the D/L chart in his pocket, working to ensure that his bowlers kept South Africa below the listed score at the end of each passing over.

Neither Boucher nor Klusener was in possession of a chart, and both batsmen displayed a strange lack of urgency in the 43rd and 44th overs, with the usually aggressive all-rounder blocking seven of the eight balls he faced. As Muralitharan prepared to bowl the next over, Boucher received an urgent message from the dressing room telling him that South Africa needed to reach 229 by the end of the 45th over.

Boucher checked the scoreboard, saw 219 for six; he then glanced at the soft rain falling and recognised that the time had come to take a few risks and score some runs. After four wides had provided a welcome gift, the wicketkeeper drove the fifth ball of Murali's over into the stands for a magnificent six.

Believing he had done what was required, the wicketkeeper guardedly prodded the last ball of the over into the leg side: no run, no matter. He had been asked to guide the score to 229 for six by the end of the 45th over and, in what seemed the most clinical fashion, he appeared to have done exactly that.

By now, the rain had become appreciably heavier, and umpires Bucknor and Venkat were starting to get wet. They consulted briefly in the middle, and at 9.52 pm reluctantly agreed they had no option but to take the players off the field. At that moment, even the television commentators were uncertain what would happen if it was not possible to resume play before the cut-off time at 10.45 pm.

However, it soon became clear that, if the rain did continue, the match would be declared a tie, and two points would not be enough for South Africa. Boucher had been misled. In checking their D/L charts, the home team had read '229 for six' and calamitously forgotten that the batting side needed to be ahead of that score to win the match. In reality, South Africa had required 230 for six after 45 overs.

Pollock was aghast. Now aware that his team would be eliminated unless play resumed, the captain suddenly cut a pitiful figure, sitting alone, head in his hands, staring out of the dressing room window at the steady rain that was now starting to gather on the covers. As the minutes ticked away to the cut-off time when the match would be abandoned as a tie, South African hopes died a slow and painful death.

If only the captain had not been run out, the target would have been lower . . . if only Boucher had been given the correct information, he would surely have scored a single off the last ball of the 45th over. These would be 'if onlys' to last a lifetime for every member of the squad, but they offered no solace.

Unthinkably, against every prediction, South Africa had suffered the same fate as Australia in 1992 and England in 1999, cast as a host nation failing to advance past the group stage.

The manner of their elimination prompted headlines in local newspapers such as 'JINXED' and 'CURSED', and it was strange how South Africa's experience in 2003 had incorporated all the elements that had befallen them in their three previous World Cups: they had suffered in a rain-adjusted game, as in 1992; they had been cut to pieces by Lara, as in 1996; and they had gone out after a tied match, as in 1999.

However, the inescapable facts remained that, firstly, their bowling and fielding had been so indifferent against major sides that they hardly merited a place in the Super Six, and, second, the fatal, probably foolish misunderstanding of the D/L status against Sri Lanka was entirely self-inflicted.

Within two weeks, the under-pressure selectors had sacked Pollock as captain and named Graeme Smith, a self-assured 22-year-old with eight Tests to his name, to lead the side at the one-day tournament in Sharjah, from which South Africa later decided to withdraw in light of the ongoing war in Iraq. Contemplating his enormous challenge, it may have been some relief for Smith to know he would not have to captain the home team in a World Cup, at least not for the next 16 years.

All that remained of the group stage was the game between Zimbabwe and Pakistan in Bulawayo, where the home side needed to win to confirm their passage to the Super Six. In keeping with the pall that seemed to have descended upon the tournament, a drenching downpour forced the match to be abandoned, a result that suited Heath Streak and his team, who happily rode their luck and advanced.

By now, the Super Six was not looking particularly super at all.

The six qualified nations each carried points forward from their group matches, according to yet another unfathomable formula, and one glance at the table confirmed that, even before a ball had been bowled in this phase, Australia, India and Sri Lanka were already well set for the semi-finals.

These teams were obviously eager to keep winning and maintain their form, but the actual competitive function of the Super Six, of the next nine fixtures, appeared restricted to determining which country from New Zealand, Kenya and Zimbabwe would secure the other position in the semi-finals. After all the excitement and impassioned drama of the previous week, the prospect seemed humdrum.

The Australians and the Indians were unconcerned, and they clinically confirmed their growing status as the two strongest teams, easing to wins over Sri Lanka and Kenya respectively.

If anybody believed the defending champions would be significantly weakened by the loss of two world-class bowlers, Warne and Gillespie, this illusion was shattered at Centurion. Ponting's century enabled his team to post an imposing 319 for five, and the dynamic, pumped-up Brett Lee then literally blasted the Sri Lankans out of contention. Enjoying the chance to take the new ball, the fast bowler drilled a rising ball into Jayasuriya and generally cut an impressive figure, heart on his sleeve, all rhythm and power.

India also appeared to be gaining in confidence with each passing match. They wobbled in pursuit of 226 to win against the Kenyans, slipping to 24 for three at one stage, but Ganguly steadied the pursuit, chewing his lip in deep concentration, and his innings of 107 laid the foundation for victory.

Everyone knew how Tendulkar and their other outstanding batting guns were beginning to fire, but few had predicted that the veteran opening bowler Srinath would be so magnificently supported by the two young left-arm-over-the-wicket seam bowlers, Zaheer Khan and Ashish Nehra.

Perhaps above all, Ganguly's side was playing with a degree of spirit and support for one another that was almost unprecedented in Indian teams. Each time they took a wicket, all eleven players would sprint and form a tight circle, arms linked and bound around shoulders, urging one another to greater efforts.

New Zealand kept their hopes alive with a competent victory against Zimbabwe, but very few citizens of Bloemfontein bothered to come and watch, and, as Nathan Astle's century enabled the Kiwis easily to overhaul a target of 253, the lack of atmosphere at Goodyear Park was almost embarrassing.

Predicting results was becoming an easy game in the Super Six.

People expected India to defeat Sri Lanka at the Wanderers, and they did. Tendulkar provided another exhilarating batting masterclass, sharing in a 156-run opening stand with Virender Sehwag, before once again falling just short of his century. The master's pleasing innings of 97 helped India to reach 292 for six, and this proved beyond the Sri Lankans, who were dismissed by the Indian seamers for 110.

People also expected Australia to overcome New Zealand in Port Elizabeth, and they did, although their victory was not achieved without some alarm. Shane Bond, the bold young Kiwi fast bowler with the smooth, textbook action, ran in and claimed six wickets for 23 runs in his 10 overs. With Australia in trouble at 84 for seven, Bevan and Bichel staged the recovery, just as they had against England on the same ground, reaching 208 for nine; and that proved sufficient when the Black Caps collapsed to 112 all out.

Just when the tournament seemed to be running on autopilot, the smiling Kenyans reappeared, evidently enjoying every minute of their adventure. Under normal conditions, they would have expected to battle against the famously competitive Zimbabweans in Bloemfontein, but these were not normal times for Heath Streak and his players, whose morale had been sapped by politically motivated selections.

Streak won the toss and elected to bat first, but only the steadfast Andy Flower emerged with any credit, scoring 65 in an otherwise humiliating total of 133 all out in 44.1 overs. The buoyant Kenyans had bowled well and once again brimmed with unlimited energy in the field; then Maurice Odumbe joined Thomas Odoyo and briskly secured the historic seven-wicket win with fully 24 overs to spare.

The next morning's front page headlines in Harare lamented 'Zimbabwe's worst performance ever', but the losing team's dismay should not detract from Kenya's achievement in following their wins against Sri Lanka and Bangladesh with a third victory over a Test-playing nation. The result gave the East Africans 14 points on the Super Six table and, amazingly, assured them of a top four finish.

'Now you're in the semi-final!' the MC told Steve Tikolo at the post-match ceremony.

'Yes,' replied the animated Kenyan captain, grinning. 'People said we didn't belong in the Super Six, but we got there. Now, I suppose they'll say we don't belong in the semi-final either. Maybe, they will soon be saying we don't belong in the final.'

Kenya's fairytale voyage of discovery may have been launched by New

Zealand's decision to forfeit their match in Nairobi, but their earnest, unfettered approach to the game billowed like a spring breeze through the familiar blooms of what remains a relatively insular international cricket community. The likes of Collins Obuya offered something new, something hitherto unseen and something unpredictable.

Nobody suggested their progress signalled the emergence of a brand new power, but it did bring colour and romance to the tournament and, as such, was widely welcomed.

Cricket was long established in East Africa. Introduced by the English during the age of Empire and then sustained for many years by the resident Asian population, the game has more recently been eagerly adopted by indigenous Africans, specifically members of the Luo tribe in western Kenya.

'Our common background keeps us together,' Martin Suji explained during the tournament. 'Luo people are often known for eating fish, which they say makes you bright. You can tell a Luo because it is probable that his name will start with an 'O', like Odumbe, Obuya, Odoyo, Otieno and Ongondo.'

In spite of this spirit, little was expected of Kenya at the 2003 World Cup. They seemed out of touch and out of their depth, having played no more than 18 one-day internationals in the previous four seasons. Yet, the appointment as coach of Sandeep Patil, a World Cup winner with India in 1983, instilled belief into a squad that blended youth with seven veterans from the epic win over the West Indies in 1996.

Kenya's continuing success left New Zealand needing to defeat India at Centurion to move past the Sri Lankans and reach the semi-finals, but Fleming's side made an appalling start, losing McMillan and Astle to the second and third balls of the day. From 0 for two, they scampered and scratched their way to 146 all out in the 46th over, setting an apparently inadequate target for the in-form Indian batsmen.

Any faint hopes rested on Bond's broad shoulders, and the young fast bowler quickly dismissed Sehwag and Ganguly in one of the most devastating opening bursts of the tournament. When Tendulkar was caught at point, the New Zealanders sensed an opportunity with India at 21 for three. Bond steamed in again, tempting Dravid to drive outside the off-stump and nick a simple catch to the wicketkeeper.

'Howzaaaa . . .' the bowler yelled, before his voice suddenly trailed away.

McCullum spilled the chance. The combined screeches of anguish from Bond on his follow through, and Fleming at first slip, effectively signalled the end of New Zealand's campaign. Dravid made the most of his 'life', and, together with Kaif, took India to a seven-wicket win with ten overs to spare.

The Kiwis would still have advanced if Sri Lanka had failed to defeat Zimbabwe the following day in East London, but Atapattu contributed another superb century to a total of 256 for five and, once Aravinda de Silva had been fortunate to have Andy Flower judged LBW for 38 in what the batsman had announced would be his last international appearance, Zimbabwe was swiftly dismissed for 182.

Not one match during this low-intensity Super Six had produced anything resembling a close finish, and the last game of the phase, played between Australia and Kenya in Durban, was not going to be any different once the irrepressible Brett Lee had captured a World Cup hat trick at the start of the Kenyan innings. His third victim was clean-bowled by a virtually unplayable delivery, fast and full, fired in at the base of the stumps. The outsiders did not roll over, but Australia duly secured a ninth win in nine matches.

This marathon tournament was now moving into its fifth week and, with the semi-finals imminent at last, even Dr Ali Bacher, the refreshingly blunt tournament director, was prepared to concede the 2003 World Cup had been too long. 'That is probably true,' Bacher concurred. 'I met Bob Hawke, the former Australian prime minister, at the Olympic Games in Sydney and, when I told him the World Cup would last for 44 days, I recall he replied by saying: "Well, that's an event of biblical proportions". He was right.'

Whether the ICC decides to condense future tournaments by reducing the number of competing teams or by revising the format, there should be no question at all that some action needs to be taken. Notwithstanding the generally smooth organisation, hassle-free transport and comfortable accommodation in South Africa 2003, there was scarcely a player, journalist, television commentator, supporter or even administrator who was not ready, by the second week of March, to agree the tournament had been too long.

They could not all have been wrong.

For the four teams still involved, at least, the real business was just beginning. The two semi-finals both pitched overwhelming favourites against dangerous outsiders with no fear of losing.

Australia and India had seemed the most probable finalists for several weeks, but the Australians could not be completely confident of overcoming Sri Lanka in Port Elizabeth, and the Indians had not forgotten how Kenya had given them some anxious moments earlier in the tournament.

At St George's Park, the Sri Lankans took confidence from the knowledge that they had won each of the past four competitive knockout matches against Australia, a run of success that started at the 1996 World Cup final and continued through to the semi-final of the ICC Champions Trophy in 2002.

Ricky Ponting was also aware of the statistics but, an increasingly assured figure at the forefront of the Australian campaign, he seemed positive his team would perform on the slow, low-scoring Port Elizabeth pitch, where they had already beaten England and New Zealand. Winning the toss, the yellow-clad captain elected to bat first and set his mind on scoring anything in excess of 210 in 50 overs.

Gilchrist and Hayden provided their familiar fast start, with the former launching his body into a mighty pull for six over mid-wicket. Then, well set at 34 without loss, Gilchrist went on the sweep. The ball looped into the air and was taken by wicketkeeper Kumar Sangakkara, who appealed.

Umpire Rudi Koertzen seemed to mouth the words 'not out' but, to general amazement, Gilchrist was already heading back to the pavilion. He was 'walking', giving himself out in a World Cup semi-final, apparently reviving a noble tradition that most people assumed had withered in the modern game.

Some cynics immediately doubted the authenticity of the gesture, least of all from a player representing a country in which successive captains had almost banned 'walking', and Ponting later suggested Gilchrist hadn't seen Koertzen say not out. 'He knew he had got a bat on it, and he didn't bother looking at the umpire,' said the captain, adding that he wouldn't be encouraging any of his players to walk.

The Sri Lankans had established a foothold in the game and, when Ponting and Hayden had been safely caught inside the circle, the Australians were struggling at 51 for three. Andrew Symonds may have gone soon afterward, but Sangakkara missed the stumping chance, and the hard-hitting middle-order batsman set about rebuilding the innings in partnership with the dependable Darren Lehmann.

Jayasuriya gamely pegged the Australians back again when, with the score on 144, he bowled Lehmann and had Bevan caught behind off successive deliveries, but Symonds remained, at one point smashing the ball out of the ground with not much more than a forearm jab. And, with the tail chipping in, he finished unbeaten on an excellent 91 as the tournament favourites posted a total of 212 for seven.

Any hopes of an upset seemed to rely on one of the top Sri Lankan batsmen coming good, but the three headliners were gone with only 51 on the board. Atapattu was bowled by one of Lee's trademark full deliveries, rocketing into the stumps at 95 miles per hour; having clipped Lee over mid-wicket for six, Jayasuriya checked a pull against McGrath and was caught; then De Silva was run out by Bichel's direct hit.

A team where prima donnas were not tolerated, where everybody worked towards common goals, where players constantly encouraged one another: the Australians looked unstoppable.

By the time the rain arrived, forcing the semi-final to be abandoned, Sri Lanka was limping along at 123 for seven after 39 overs, out of contention and now out of the World Cup. The embarrassment in Nairobi aside, Jayasuriya and his team had performed reasonably well and it was no surprise when, at home in Colombo, the captain's humble offer to resign was firmly rejected by the selectors.

Two days later in Durban, the assembled ranks of Indian supporters were hoping their team would match Australia's professionalism in securing a place in the final. Ebulliently in form with bat and ball, Ganguly and his players were not lacking confidence but a consensus had emerged that their task at Kingsmead would be made easier if they could avoid the burden of batting second, under floodlights.

The Indians had become dangerously obsessed by the perceived importance of the toss in Durban, even asking the ICC to switch the semi-final from a day-night match to a day match because they believed any side batting second would be placed at an unfair disadvantage. In fact, over the years, conditions at the Kingsmead ground had always been variable, hingeing on the tide, wind and much else, benefiting the side batting first on one day, and the side batting second the next week. It was part of the game. India's application was rejected, but Ganguly could not hide his pleasure when he called correctly, and opted to bat.

Tikolo had amiably described the occasion as the career highlight of all his players, and the Kenyans did not lack for effort, but they proved unable to contain India's batting princes. Once Sehwag had established the tone with an impeccable cover drive in the first over, the runs flowed.

Sehwag made 33, and Tendulkar again played beautifully, but again fell short of a century, dismissed for 83 from 101 balls. Ganguly pressed on, reaching three figures for the third time in the tournament and ending unbeaten on 111, as his team posted a pedigree 270 for four in 50 overs.

Kenya lost two early wickets with 21 runs on the board, and their run chase started to seem in vain when Odumbe became the impressive Zaheer Khan's third victim at 63 for five. Stress-free and focused, the Indian bowlers demonstrated exactly the kind of tight discipline they would need to show against far more dangerous opponents in the final, and effectively strangled the Africans' ambitions.

Tikolo tenaciously gave nothing away, appropriately finishing as the highest scorer with 56, as his side's innings drifted gently to a creditable conclusion at 179 all out in the 47th over. Kenya's adventure had come to an end in Durban, but the financial and commercial windfall from the side's success will give the national body the opportunity to take the game to the next level. Hopefully, that chance will be seized.

So, the circus moved to its final stop, and the extended family of international cricket duly gathered at the Wanderers Stadium in Johannesburg on Sunday 23 March 2003.

Whatever anyone said about the length of the tournament, about results distorted by rain, about all the mysterious inner workings of Duckworth and Lewis, about the number of predestined mismatches, about the ICC's heavy-handed mishandling of political matters, nobody could deny that, somehow, the 2003 World Cup had found its way to a 'dream final' between, clearly, the two strongest teams.

Australia had not played India in a one-day international since losing a three-match series 2-1 in March 2001, but the defending champions approached the World Cup final as clear favourites.

Perhaps their top-order batting had not scored as heavily as they might have hoped, but the pluses far outweighed the minuses in the Australian camp. Ponting had emerged as an outstanding captain, generating a spirit within his squad that broadcast a strong work ethic, a contagious self-confidence, and a visible self-belief that, no matter what crises developed, somebody would emerge to win the day.

The early loss of both Warne and Gillespie had been a blow to their bowling plans, but Lee had stormed in with pace and enthusiasm, McGrath had remained a genuine class act, Bichel had emerged from obscurity to produce match-winning performances, and Hogg had maintained a tight and tidy line.

Gilchrist and Hayden headlined the batting, more often than not launching the innings in a blur, and the self-assured, rigorously prepared likes of Ponting, Martyn, Lehmann and Symonds maintained the pace. On the few occasions when the specialist batsmen failed, Michael Bevan stood prepared at No. 7, mentally resilient and technically strong, every inch the ideal stopper primed to salvage the situation.

The team's high standard of fielding was such that any dropped chance was likely to draw more comment than just another one-handed wonder in the slips or a determined swoop in the outfield.

'Do you think the Australians are unbeatable?' someone asked Ganguly on the eve of the final.

'Of course not,' replied the combative Indian captain.

India's hopes of winning a second World Cup, to set beside the achievement of Kapil Dev's team in 1983, were founded on two premises: first, the enchanting, though uncertain, prospect that their wonderful in-form batsmen would be able to weave their magic against the accurate, aggressive Australian attack; second, that their gifted young seamers would be able to contain the powerful, ruthless batting. The final boiled down to a contest between relentless Australian science and unpredictable Indian art.

Most of the capacity 31 000 crowd had made their way through the lush, tree-lined streets of Illovo and settled in their seats inside the Wanderers by the time the two captains emerged for the toss, but the exercise was academic because Ponting was planning to bat, and Ganguly wanted to field.

In Australian eyes, the pitch was hard, true and full of runs, but the Indians had arrived at the ground to find staff using a portable hairdryer to draw moisture out of the wicket. Heavy rain had fallen in Johannesburg the previous evening, and another shower early that morning had prompted Ganguly to conclude that the ball could move in the air and off the seam for, perhaps, the first hour.

As the coin fell, India won the toss, and Ganguly invited Australia to bat. His decision quickly prompted debate around the ground: some people said his strategy was bold, indicating a desire to carry the fight to the Australians; others said it showed fear, because he was scared to bat first and run the risk of being dismissed cheaply, as was the case when Ponting's side thrashed them in the group match.

Either way, the two teams lined up for the national anthems and, as soon as the last note died away, the Indian players dressed in light blue fanned out across the outfield, raring to go. For these young men, idolised by several hundred million supporters across the sub-continent, this final represented an opportunity for them to inscribe their names in history, even to touch a kind of sporting immortality.

Far, far more then just another game of cricket, this particular contest offered them the chance to reflect glory on their parents, on their extended families and friends, and to bring delight and pride to their immense, seething, cricket-mad country. The stakes could not have been higher, and, as many millions of people paused to see the television or listen to the radio, Ganguly tossed the ball to Zaheer Khan.

The 24-year-old left-arm seamer from Shrirampur had emerged as India's most effective strike bowler in the tournament, and now, heart pounding, hands sweating, Khan moved in to bowl . . .

His first ball is called a no-ball by umpire David Shepherd. His second ball rises outside the off-stump and tempts Gilchrist to play and miss. Khan offers a few words to the batsman, indicating India's determination to give as good as they get in the verbal battle. Third ball, he oversteps again, and the no-ball brushes Gilchrist's thigh and runs down to fine leg, where Srinath misfields. Final nerves are everywhere.

Fourth ball, Gilchrist guides a single to third man. Fifth ball, Khan produces a superb outswinger, beating Hayden, who plays and misses. The ball is moving around. Ganguly's decision to field looks inspired. Sixth ball, Hayden plays into the covers, and Khan again offers his opinions to the batsmen.

Seventh ball, Khan strays down the leg side, the ball swinging away from Dravid and accelerating to the boundary. Shepherd signals four wides. Calm down, the bowler tells himself, calm down. Eighth ball, it's a half-volley outside the off-stump and Hayden sends an impeccable drive fizzing past extra cover for four. Ninth ball, another wide, as the ball curves away past leg-stump where Dravid makes a fine stop. Tenth ball, full and on middle-stump, Hayden gets in line and plays quietly into the off side.

Australia – 15 for nought after one over: Gilchrist 4*, Hayden 1*, Extras 10.

In some respects, as a genuine contest, the 2003 World Cup final lasted one over.

Whether he was overwhelmed by the big occasion or was simply trying too hard, Zaheer looked stunned by what had happened, and his disastrous start set the tone for the rest of the day: the Australian batsmen got off to a flyer from which they never looked back; Zaheer's confidence was fatally undermined, putting pressure on Srinath who also then failed to bowl with any kind of discipline or control. Before long, the body language of the Indian players had translated from excited and positive to gloomy and negative.

Ganguly stood impassive and powerless at slip. His bowlers had pitiably let him down. They wasted the helpful conditions. They failed to take early wickets and place the Australians under pressure simply because, with the possible exception of Nehra, they proved incapable of putting the ball in the right places, and instead fed Gilchrist and Hayden a steady diet of loose deliveries asking to be hit.

After ten overs, Australia had raced to 80 without loss.

Quickly running out of options, Ganguly tried to stem the tide by calling Harbhajan Singh into the attack much earlier than he would have liked, but the tactic worked when Gilchrist pulled the spinner hard and high, only to be caught by Sehwag in the deep for an explosive 57 in only 48 balls.

India's only hope of restraining the runaway innings was to keep taking wickets, and when Hayden was caught behind off Harbhajan for 37, at 125 for two in the 20th over, the raucous Asian supporters in the ground roared their approval. Briefly, the underdogs looked as if they might get back into the final.

The illusion didn't last long. Ponting, 29, settled cautiously in partnership with Martyn, who had seemed unlikely to appear in the final after fracturing the index finger of his right hand eight days before. However, the right-hander had missed the World Cup final in 1999, and was eager to play at the Wanderers. Taking no risks, finding their rhythm, working the ball into the gaps, running brilliantly between the wickets, latching onto bad deliveries, the pair moved smoothly through the gears at five or six runs an over.

Ganguly shuffled his bowlers, searching for the trump card to turn the game, and he found some success with Dinesh Mongia, but, as the runs flowed, one dot ball felt like a major achievement for the fielding side and two dot balls was a triumph. In 50 overs, the Indians would manage not one maiden.

The Australian captain was patiently biding his time, content to hit just one boundary in his first 50 runs, but towards the 38th over he suddenly unleashed a blistering assault. One moment he was dancing down the wicket and heaving Harbhajan into the third tier of the Unity Stand. Next he was crouching on one knee, using one hand to thrash the ball square, powered for six over cover point. Minutes later, two quick steps put him in position to send another extraordinary drive soaring up and up, out of the ground.

One moment Ponting resembled Tiger Woods, effortlessly clipping a nine-iron 95 metres into the green; the next, he looked like Barry Bonds, clubbing a low full toss into the bleachers for a home run. By the end, he had struck a meagre quartet of boundaries and no fewer than eight breathtaking sixes, more than any batsman from any country in any innings played during any Cricket World Cup.

Martyn was hardly holding back, most memorably giving himself room outside the off-stump, rocking on his back foot and magnificently lifting Nehra inside out for six over extra cover.

Ponting completed the innings in ruthless fashion, sending Javagal Srinath into retirement by striking the last two deliveries of his long, distinguished international career for six over long on and four past fine leg. The two batsmen embraced at the end, partners in an episode of cricketing history.

They had taken Australia to a remarkable total of 359 for two in 50 overs ... the eighth-highest total ever scored in a one-day international, the highest score of the 2003 World Cup, the highest score of any Australian team at any World Cup, the highest score in any one-day international played at the Wanderers, the highest score ever conceded by an Indian side in a one-day international. And this awe-inspiring total had been built upon a record-breaking third-wicket partnership that yielded 234 runs in 181 balls.

Martyn finished with an outstanding 88 not out from 84 balls, but the greatest praise had to be reserved for Ponting, who had faced 121 balls and ended unbeaten on 140. Gathering more than 80 per cent of his runs on the leg side, he had eclipsed Viv Richards as the highest scorer in the great showpiece.

Like Clive Lloyd's century in the first World Cup final at Lord's, Ricky Ponting's innings in the eighth World Cup final at the Wanderers will remain forever enshrined in the history of the game. The writing that appeared on the wall when India conceded 15 in the first over was now writ large for posterity.

'So, tell me,' one of the television presenters asked as three South African Airways jets executed a daring fly-past over the stadium during the lunch interval, 'can India get 360 to win?'

'Well, Tendulkar will need to get a quick double century,' came the expert reply.

Accustomed to dealing with pressure every time he picks up his bat, the Indian hero walked out at the Wanderers, contemplating a task that, for anyone else, would have been considered impossible. The fact that experts even discussed 360 to win reflected the unique esteem in which he is held.

McGrath prepared to bowl, and Tendulkar left the first ball of the innings as it moved appreciably away from the right-hander. He played no stroke at the second ball either, but this time the Australian brought the ball back in to the Indian and it only missed the off-stump by inches. Perhaps unsettled, the little genius asked for the sightscreens to be adjusted. He let the third ball pass harmlessly by as well.

An unreasonable murmur rumbled around the ground. If India was to have any chance, Tendulkar would need to destroy the Australian pace attack exactly as he had obliterated the Pakistani fast bowlers at Centurion earlier in the tournament. People quietly urged him to bid for glory, and attack.

McGrath bowled again, fractionally short, scarcely short. Tendulkar swivelled and pulled, and although his timing was not perfect, the ball ran away from the fielder and bobbled over the rope. The Wanderers erupted in joy and excitement. Was this the start of something special, something unforgettable?

The Australian bowled again. Tendulkar swivelled into position, aiming to pull again, but the ball was too far up, much too close to him, and it flew off the top of his bat, straight up in the air. McGrath ran into position, held the catch, and promptly disappeared beneath a jubilant maul of yellow shirts.

In near silence, Tendulkar walked slowly away towards the dressing room, dismissed for four in the first over, and India's hopes for a miraculous run chase seemed to disappear with him.

Sehwag and Ganguly, of course, would not meekly surrender, and once they had bravely reaped 19 runs from McGrath's third over, they took the score to a competitive 58 for one in the tenth over. Out of the blue, out of the tournament's infamous rule book, India suddenly found new hope.

Dark, threatening clouds had started to mass over Johannesburg, raising the nightmarish possibility that Messrs Duckworth and Lewis could yet have a more significant impact on the 2003 World Cup final than Messrs Ponting and Martyn. The weather forecast had identified a 60 per cent chance of rain during the afternoon, and, as the air suddenly seemed to turn cold, two specific scenarios seemed possible.

First, if persistent rain forced play to be abandoned before India had faced 25 overs, the rules said the teams would have to return on Monday and start a completely new match. It seemed inconceivable that one of the greatest innings of all time would suddenly be erased, but these were the rules.

Second, if the rain forced the Indian innings to be abandoned at any stage after the 25th over, then the World Cup final would be decided by the Duckworth/Lewis method and, so long as they didn't concede more wickets, this equation seemed likely to favour the team batting second.

For example, if the match was abandoned after 26 overs, India would need to have scored no more than 126 for one to be declared the new world champions. For Ganguly, this looked promising. In order to get ahead on the D/L charts, he and Sehwag needed only 68 runs in the next 15 overs; their strategy thereafter could be simply to keep their total ahead of the D/L chart for so long as the innings continued.

A appalling entry in the history books loomed in the mind's eye: *2003 WORLD CUP FINAL: Australia – 359 for two in 50 overs; India 126 for one in 25 overs. India won by D/L method.*

Just as such horrendous prospects were starting to demand attention, Ganguly tried one premeditated pull too many and, on 24, lobbed a straightforward catch to Lehmann at mid-on. Four balls later, Mohammad Kaif was caught behind by Gilchrist off McGrath without scoring, and India had quickly slumped to 59 for three in the 11th over. Now even their potential D/L targets were slipping out of reach.

Still the possibility of a washed-out match remained, and Ponting reacted promptly to the threat, bringing two spinners, Hogg and Lehmann, into the attack and asking them to hustle through the 14 overs that still had to be bowled for the match to be declared valid. Sehwag gleefully seized upon the opportunity to cash in some cheap runs, audaciously striking Lehmann for three successive boundaries.

The rain finally arrived during the 17th over and, while the umpires did remain in position until the end of that over, with India at 103 for three, they then briskly led the players from the field.

Several groups of Indian supporters watching from the grassed bank in front of the dressing rooms at the Wanderers chose this exact moment to stand, cheer and wave their flags, probably excited by the thought that the rain might stay and literally wash away everything that had happened so far.

If this was indeed the motivation for their bizarre behaviour, they were surely Indians who had travelled from the Asian sub-continent specially to watch the cricket World Cup, rather than the descendants of migrant workers who had made precisely the same journey early in the 20th century.

For anyone living permanently in Johannesburg would know that afternoon showers towards the end of summer invariably tend to be short and sharp, quickly clearing to leave cool, fresh blue skies until evening. So, the covers were rapidly pulled over the middle, and within 15 minutes the shower had passed and the covers were being dragged back to the boundary in preparation for the resumption of play.

It had become clear that, to everyone's relief, the 2003 World Cup final would reach its conclusion within the day intended and without the unwelcome assistance of Duckworth/Lewis; and, as perilous rulebooks were put away, it was also obvious that Australia would deservedly win the World Cup.

Sehwag bravely sustained the struggle, guiding his team to 122 for three after 20 overs, only four runs behind the Australians at the same stage, but the fluent opening batsman was eventually caught half a metre short by Lehmann's direct throw, dismissed for a spirited 82 in 81 balls.

It appeared as though a noble dressing room decision had been reached that the team should go down blazing, and batsmen such as Rahul Dravid and Yuvraj Singh came, kept scoring at a healthy rate of around six runs per over, and went; and the end was not petulantly or pointlessly delayed.

Zaheer Khan, with whom the story of this high-quality final had so dramatically begun earlier in the day, found himself standing in the spotlight again. McGrath moved in to bowl, and Zaheer tried to pull but could only sky a simple catch to mid-on where the catch to win the match was safely held by Darren Lehmann, curiously the same man who had hit the runs to win the final at Lord's four years before.

Australia had dismissed India for 234 and won by 125 runs, becoming the first country to win the World Cup three times and the first back-to-back world champions since the West Indies in 1979. Tears flowed amid the hugging and backslapping as the squad huddled together on the field, coming to terms with the realisation that all their planning, hard work and plain Aussie guts had been duly rewarded.

'Everything went really well for us,' said Ponting, man of the match and the winning captain of a team that had just magnificently extended its unprecedented winning streak to 17 one-day internationals. 'I'm lost for words at the moment, but this has been an outstanding effort by every-one.'

And, with those words, he took the World Cup and raised it aloft.

The tournament had been a success: it had demonstrated South Africa's capacity to host a global sports event in safety; it had further enhanced the brand of World Cup cricket; it had been borne through its schedule by a consistently high standard of play; and, at the last, most importantly, it had produced great champions.

One-Day Hero

Sachin Tendulkar

It would be easy to have watched Sachin Tendulkar bat during the 2003 World Cup, or indeed at almost any stage of the international career he launched at the age of 16 in 1989, and conclude that the greatest batsman of his age was a born genius.

It would be easy, but only half the truth.

Of course, this short, round-faced, soft-spoken man, this idol to hundreds of millions of people in India and right across the globe, entered this world with a unique talent. His special ability to assess both the pace and length of a cricket ball hurled towards him from a distance of 20 yards has set him apart.

Yet this natural gift would have withered like a red rose in the desert had it not been relentlessly nurtured by the fertiliser of hard work. Yes, it sounds dull and predictable, but Tendulkar's superstar status today owes as much to many years of unrelenting, unseen application as it does to his inherent genius.

As a small boy – small even for his age – in Mumbai, the vast city then known as Bombay, he would typically make his way down to Shivaji Park, one of those dusty brown open expanses of ground where thousands of people regularly gathered to indulge their love of cricket in hundreds of games, side by side.

And, having waited for his turn to bat, just as Vivian Richards used to wait to bat on the beach at Antigua, Tendulkar often found a smiling man named Ramakant Acherkar stepping forward to place one single coin on the top of his middle-stump.

'OK,' the coach would say. 'Anyone who can get Sachin out, and knock that coin off his stump, can keep it. If nobody can knock it off, Sachin gets to take home the money.'

So, the challenge was set and the small boy would adopt his compact, perfectly balanced stance and he would play, taking care to fend away the accurate balls, relishing the opportunity to stroke into the distance anything wide or short.

To this day, the greatest batsman in the world still keeps 13 of these coins safely in his possession at home.

At the age of 12, he was generally practising for more than 10 hours in every day, sometimes batting while his elder brother, Ajit, bowled, other times taking part in match after match, the next one beginning as soon as the last one had finished. 'One day, I played 24 matches in a row,' he remembers fondly.

Two years later, he was invited by Dilip Vengsarkar, then one of India's finest batsmen and the captain of Bombay, to come along for a net, not with Bombay, with the national side.

At that time, the 14-year-old was playing most of his cricket for Shardarsham School and averaging a meagre 1 034. Up to that point in the term, he had played five innings: 27 not out, 125, 207 not out, 346 not out and the last of them in the crucial school final, 329 not out in an unbroken first-wicket partnership of 664 with his friend and future Test team-mate, Vinod Kambli.

He played his debut for Bombay in the next season, scoring a century against Gujarat. Indeed, he soon became the only player in the history of Indian cricket to score a ton on his first appearance in each of the three main domestic competitions, the Irani Trophy, the Ranji Trophy and the Duleep Trophy.

The next year, aged 16, after his father had signed a contract with the Board of Control of Cricket in India because Sachin himself was still too young to do so, the prodigy was selected in the Indian team to play the first Test against their arch-rivals, Pakistan, in Lahore.

'It was a green wicket,' he recalls, 'and Waqar Younis, Wasim Akram, Imran Khan and Aqib Javed were in great form. We were 30 for four and battling to save the Test when I came in. Waqar hit the bridge of my nose – I still have the scar now – but I hung on, made 59 and, somehow, we got away with a draw.'

Since then, he has batted quite beautifully on a regular basis, breaking records, captaining India through two challenging periods before deciding to focus on his batting, and becoming so revered that his image dominates Indian life, appearing on billboards, radio and television so often that his annual income from endorsements has risen to nearly US$5 million, more than three times the amount earned by the world's second most popular cricketer.

His status is most accurately reflected in every perfectly timed prod for four, every blistering hook, every uncomplicated back-foot drive bisecting the cover cordon on its way to the boundary, but it is also perforce measured in his unmatched statistics.

On the day he was named Man of the Tournament at the 2003 World Cup, a month short of his 30th birthday, Tendulkar had played in 105 Tests, scoring 8 811 runs at an average of 57.58, including 31 centuries. While shying away from personal goals, preferring to focus on the team, he admits the target of 15 000 runs and 40 Test centuries continues to linger at the back of his mind.

The so-called 'little master' has also flourished in limited overs cricket, scoring a remarkable 12 219 runs, at an average of 44.43, in 314 one-day international matches for India.

So many figures blur into one another, and impact is lost, but during the course of the World Cup in South Africa he scored 673 runs from a total of 754 balls, storing more wonderful memories in the hearts of a billion Indians, and in the minds of anyone who has been fortunate enough to sit back and marvel at his batting.

So much done, so much still to do: it'll be worth watching.

Chapter Fourteen

Days to Come

The crowds keep coming, sponsors join the queue, and the value of television rights continues to rise . . . some people say the only threat facing one-day cricket in 2003 is complacency.

They could be right, for now.

However, nothing stays the same for long, particularly in the highly competitive world of popular entertainment, which is where, in many ways, this 'product' has pitched its tent.

In Australia, South Africa, New Zealand and, increasingly, in England and the sub-continent, watching the limited overs game is being projected as more fun than spending time in the cinema or at the shopping centre. People pay their money not so much to delight in a balanced contest and classic strokeplay as to share the vibe with their mates, enjoy a drink, and have a party.

This marketing approach has worked tremendously well, to a point where a typical one-day crowd embraces the core cricketing public (many of whom still prefer the first-class game but faithfully attend the one-day matches), usually sitting in the members' area, and the younger party-people in the public stands.

Sport as entertainment keeps the cash tills ringing, but trends in entertainment are precisely that: trends. By definition, they come and go. The appeal is broad, but perilously shallow.

'In' today can easily become 'out' tomorrow.

A sport such as cricket often inspires deep, enduring affection that runs from generation to generation. However, when the game is tricked up as light entertainment, there is a risk that the public's affection turns out to be more superficial. Time will tell.

In the meantime, those administrators charged with running the one-day game, with ensuring this golden goose continues to lay golden eggs for many glory days to come, could perhaps focus their attention on addressing two specific areas of concern.

The first is the continuing increase in the number of one-day internationals being played around the world. The golden goose has been working overtime. How much can she take?

Ten ODIs were played during 1978. This increased to 66 in 1983, then 89 in 1992, and 127 in 1996. The glut reached a peak in 1999, when the world watched no fewer than 154 ODIs, of which 37 featured Australia and 41 involved India.

Indeed, over the past few years, on average, the Indians have appeared in a one-day international every nine days.

Geoffrey Boycott has rung the alarm bells. 'As the roundabout of one-day cricket gathers momentum, more and more is demanded from the top players,' the former England batsman believes, 'and it is possible that these guys will become jaded.

'The body is more resilient than people think, but the mental pressure is silently debilitating and a few major players are starting to calculate that, if they can skip a few one-day games, they could extend their careers for many years to come.'

Nasser Hussain and Shane Warne are prime examples of the emergent phenomenon whereby leading players retire from one-day international cricket to prolong their Test careers. In the fickle world of light entertainment, the spectacle of box office superstars moving away from centre stage is not a promising sign.

Another of the sport's big names has expressed concern about the mounting number of one-day internationals.

'I am not a great admirer of one-day cricket because it is not a true test of ability,' says Brian Lara, the West Indian genius. 'I do recognise the need for it because it attracts large crowds and brings in much-needed revenue but, when it starts to take over and actual Test cricket is cut back to accommodate more one-day matches, the time has come for the authorities to act.

'In my view, it is the ICC who should be tackling this problem in the interests of the game. The highest form of cricket is still Test cricket, and that needs to be protected at all costs.'

There appears little doubt that the relentless desire for more and more revenue will lead to more and more one-day international series being scheduled. The only question is whether administrators will move to restrict this number before the spectators lose interest, before the players totter off the treadmill, before that golden goose eventually collapses, exhausted, abused and spent.

Perhaps the second issue requiring consideration is the format of the game's prized showpiece, the World Cup.

For all the admirable intentions and outstanding efforts of the respective organising committees, it can scarcely be denied that the past four tournaments have not worked as sporting events.

Time and again, in-form teams have fallen foul of complicated regulations or ill-conceived formats, and bewildered spectators have been left to wonder what on earth has happened.

The events have been distorted by politics and security fears: firstly in 1996, when Australia and the West Indies decided not to travel to Colombo and gave two wins to Sri Lanka, who went on to win the World Cup. Then, in 2003, the refusal of England and New Zealand to play in Zimbabwe and Kenya respectively paved the way for the latter two nations to reach the Super Six.

And the competition has been too easily ruined by rain, most notably in 1992 when a ten-minute shower reduced the semi-final between South Africa and England from the brink of a memorable finish to farce, and in 2003 when the West Indians were effectively eliminated because rain meant they collected only two points from an abandoned match against lowly Bangladesh.

The ICC should learn from these unsatisfactory scenarios and make the necessary changes to ensure that they are not repeated at the 2007 World Cup in the West Indies and USA.

Four straightforward measures can effectively repair the pure sporting credibility of what now seems a damaged event.

First, the contortions caused when play is interrupted by rain, and all the awful equations to revise targets, could all be eliminated by a binding ICC resolution that every 50-over World Cup match will be allowed to run its full length, 50 overs per side, even if the game must be allowed to run into a second day.

The provision of so-called 'rain days' is most strongly opposed by broadcasters because the planning of their logistics, allocation of facilities and their TV schedule becomes horribly complicated by the possibility that matches will run into extra days.

It is tempting to say stuff the broadcasters ... this is a sporting event and nothing is more important than the even-handedness and authenticity of the contest, yet it is these broadcasters who fund the World Cup by paying millions of dollars in rights fees.

Perhaps the ICC needs to sit down and explain to the television executives that reserve days are required to safeguard the integrity of the competition, to ensure the success of the tournament and, as a result, guarantee a return on their investment.

Everyone needs to recognise the bigger picture. Reserve days will unavoidably make a dent in the tournament profits, but this will be a small price to pay for a fair and just contest.

Second, the Super Six innovation in 1999 and 2003, whereby teams carry weighted points forward from their group matches, has failed because it proved too complicated. Everyone, from players to spectators, will appreciate a far simpler system.

The measure of any format is its capacity to carry the quality teams to the latter stages. Through its unfathomable equations, the Super Six experiment has patently failed, twice.

Perhaps the most logical option is for 16 nations to play four round-robin groups of four, from which the winners and runners-up advance to two further round-robin groups of four. The winners and runners-up of these second round groups qualify for the semi-finals, and these lead to the climactic World Cup final.

'There will be changes to the format,' declares Chris Dehring, head of the 2007 World Cup organising committee, positively. 'The strongest teams in the world must go forward.'

Third, the ICC must work harder to avoid the political potholes that tripped up the tournament in 1996 and 2003.

There remains a profound racial fault line within the cricketing world, with both the 'white' and 'non-white' countries scurrying back to their trenches at the slightest controversy, but the ICC must be bold and proactive in identifying and resolving potential conflict.

Mercifully, with the vast majority of matches due to be played in the Caribbean and perhaps four in the United States, maybe even at Disneyland, the 2007 World Cup should be free from any political problems dressed up as player security concerns.

Fourth, again notwithstanding any marketing considerations, the ICC should prevent any matches being played in conditions that will inordinately and unfairly favour one team. The day-night matches in Durban in 2003 were a case in point: yes, they generated a magical atmosphere and a wonderful vibe, but the playing conditions made batting so difficult after nightfall that the result of the toss too often appeared to determine the result of the match.

With these measures in place, and an eye on evolving trends, there is no reason why the one-day game should not build upon its outstanding progress over the past 40 years, and delight spectators around the globe for at least another 40.

There are, all going well, many glory days to come.

References

Agnew, Jonathan *Over to you Aggers* Victor Gollancz, 1997
Benaud, Richie *On Reflection* Willow Books, 1984
Bird, Dickie *Not Out* Arthur Barker Ltd, 1978
Bird, Dickie *That's Out* Arthur Barker Ltd, 1985
Blofeld, Henry *Cricket and All That* Hodder and Stoughton, 2001
Boon, David *In the Firing Line* Pan Macmillan, 1993
Border, Allan *A Peep at the Poms* Arthur Barker Ltd, 1987
Border, Allan *Beyond Ten Thousand* Swan Publishing, 1993
Bose, Mihir *All in a Day* Robin Clark Ltd, 1983
Botham, Ian *Botham* Harper Collins, 1994
Boycott, Geoffrey *Boycott* Macmillan, 1987
Boycott, Geoffrey *On Cricket* Ebury Press, 1999
Chappell, Ian *Cricket in Our Blood* Stanley Paul, 1996
Cork, Dominic *Uncorked* Richard Cohen Books, 1996
Cricket's Clash of the Titans Andre Deutsch, 1999
Crowe, Martin *Out on a Limb* Reed Publishing, 1995
Denness, Mike *I Declare* Arthur Barker Ltd, 1977
Donald, Allan *White Lightning* Collins Willow, 1999
Engel, Matthew, ed *The Guardian Book of Cricket* Pavilion, 1986
Gatting, Mike *Leading from the Front* Queen Anne, 1988
Gooch, Graham *Gooch* Collins Willow, 1995
Gough, Darren *Dazzler* Penguin Group, 2001
Gower, David *A Right Ambition* Collins, 1986
Hartman, Rodney *Hansie and the Boys* Zebra Press, 1997
Jones, Dean *Deano, My Call* Swan Publishing, 1994
Lara, Brian *Beating the Field* Partridge Press, 1995
Lloyd, Clive *Living for Cricket* Stanley Paul, 1980
Richards, Viv *Hitting Across the Line* Headline, 1991
Swanton, E.W. and Woodcock, John *Barclays World of Cricket* Collins, 1980
Thomas and Harris *Great Moments in Cricket* Queen Anne, 1976
Wisden (1955-2002)

Index

Hilditch, Andrew 45
Hinds, Wavell 189
Hobbs, (Sir) Jack 57, 180
Hogg, Brad 203, 209
Hogg, Rodney 45, 46, 83
Holder, Vanburn 25, 27, 29,
Holding, Michael 32, 39, 48, 52, 58, 70, 72
Hookes, David 65
Hooper, Carl 111, 179, 181, 189
Houghton, Dave 60, 63, 64, 114, 115
Howarth, Geoff 50, 66
Hudson, Andrew 111, 121, 142
Hughes, David 82
Hughes, Kim 45-47, 59, 61, 62, 64, 65
Hurst, Alan 45
Hussain, Nasser 177, 179, 191, 192, 217

Ijaz Ahmed 166
Illingworth, Raymond 9, 11, 141
Illingworth, Richard 123, 141
Imran Khan 47, 49, 57-59, 66, 67, 90-93, 96, 111, 115-118, 122-128, 130, 214
Inzamam-ul-Haq 111, 118, 123, 139

Jadeja, Ajay 141
Javed Burki 126
Javed Miandad 46, 49, 67, 90, 93, 113, 115, 116, 118, 119, 123, 139, 141
Jayasuriya, Sanath 130, 139, 141, 143, 146, 147, 155, 187-189, 194, 195, 197, 201, 202
John, Vinothen 66
Johnson, Neil 155
Jones, Dean 95, 97, 100, 108, 109
Jordaan, Alan 121
Joubert, Andre 184
Julien, Bernard 25, 29

Kaif, Mohammad 179, 185, 191, 200, 209
Kallicharran, Alvin 21, 23, 24, 29, 48, 51
Kallis, Jacques 155, 159, 161-163, 180, 186, 189, 194
Kaluwitharana, Romesh 139, 141, 143, 146, 147
Kambli, Vinod 112, 214
Kanhai, Rohan 8, 24, 25, 29
Kapil Dev 59, 62-64, 69-78, 89, 90, 93-95, 130, 204
Kapoor, Aashish 144
King Commission 172
King, Collis 48, 51, 52
Kirmani, Syed 62, 63, 70, 72, 76
Kirsten, Gary 139, 158, 162, 180, 189, 194
Kirsten, Peter 109, 112, 121
Klusener, Lance 155, 158, 159, 163-165, 180, 181, 195
Knight, Nick 191
Knott, Alan 10, 21, 22, 45
Koertzen, Rudi 201
Kuiper, Adrian 121

Laker, Jim 17
Lamb, Allan 59, 67, 91, 94, 97, 115, 123, 127
Lara, Brian 107, 111, 113, 130, 137, 138, 142, 155, 156, 170, 180, 185, 189, 196, 217
Larkins, Wayne 50, 51, 53
Larsen, Gavin 107
Larwood, Harold 35
Latham, Rod 107
Laughlin, Trevor 45
Law, Stuart 144
Lawry, Bill 10
Lee, Brett 178, 197, 200, 202, 203
Lees, Warren (Wally) 50, 106

Lehmann, Darren 164, 166, 178, 192, 193, 201, 203, 209, 210
Lewis, Chris 114, 120, 123
Lewis, Tony *see* Duckworth/Lewis method
Lillee, Dennis 17-19, 21, 23-27, 31, 45, 64, 65, 131
Lloyd, Clive 11, 17, 19, 23-25, 28-32, 39, 48-51, 53, 57, 58, 62, 68, 71, 73, 80, 130, 144, 173, 207
Lloyd, David 154
Logie, Gus 131

Madan Lal 63, 70, 71
Mahanama, Roshan 143
Majid Khan 12, 43, 46, 49, 126
Major, (Prime Minister) John 105
Mallett, Ashley 21
Mandela, Nelson 105
Maninder Singh 88, 94
Manjrekar, Sanjay 143
Marner, Peter 2
Marsh, Geoff 93, 95, 109, 110
Marsh, Rodney 21, 22, 24, 25, 45, 59, 62, 65, 81, 83
Marshall, Malcolm 32, 58, 70, 72, 108
Martyn, Damien 178, 193, 203, 206-208
Matthews, Greg 83
May, Peter 4
Mbeki, (President) Thabo 178
McCosker, Rick 21, 22, 25
McCullum, Brendan 199
McDermott, Craig 88, 93, 97
McGrath, Glenn 144, 157, 163, 167, 178, 192, 202, 203, 208-210
McKechnie, Brian 50, 81
McMillan, Brian 121, 122
McMillan, Craig 199
Mendis, Duleep 20
Meyer, Barry 72

Mohsin Khan 67
Moi, President 187
Moin Khan 109, 118, 123, 157
Mongia, Dinesh 206
Moody, Tom 108, 157, 160
More, Kiran 113
Mudassar Nazar 49
Mugabe, (President) Robert 177, 181, 182
Muralitharan, Muttiah 146, 183, 187, 190, 194, 195
Murdoch, Rupert 179
Murray, Deryck 19, 25-27, 29, 48
Mushtaq Ahmed 123

Nawab of Pataudi 6
Nehra, Ashish 197, 206
Neser, Umpire 81
Ntini, Makhaya 180, 181
Nugent, Lord 6, 7

O'Donnell, Simon 96
O'Reilly, Bill 38
Obuya, Collins 188, 199
Obuya, David 188
Odoyo, Thomas 138, 198
Odumbe, Maurice 138, 198, 203
Old, Chris 22, 51, 53
Olonga, Henry 132, 181, 182
Oslear, Don 68

Packer, Kerry 6, 36-39, 41-44, 104
Patel, Dipak 106-108
Patil, Sandeep 68, 70, 199
Pele 95
Pollock, Graeme 6
Pollock, Shaun 160, 162, 180, 181, 186, 189, 193-196
Ponsford, Bill 79
Ponting, Ricky 144, 146, 160, 166, 178, 191, 197, 201, 203, 204, 206-210

Powell, Ricardo 180
Pringle, Derek 113, 122
Pringle, Meyrick 110, 111
Procter, Mike 109
Pycroft, Andrew 60

Rajab Ali 138
Raju, Venkatapathy 108
Ramiz Raja 117, 123
Ranatunga, Arjuna 114, 115, 141,
    144-147, 150
Randall, Derek 45, 47, 50-53
Rashid Latif 141, 184, 191
Rawson, Peter 60, 63
Reeve, Dermot 114, 120, 141
Reid, Bruce 93, 97
Reiffel, Paul 163
Rhodes, Jonty 111, 112, 121, 130,
    132, 142, 155, 159, 162, 163,
    184
Rice, Clive 109
Richards, (Sir) Vivian 25, 26, 29, 32,
    39, 48, 49, 51-53, 55-58, 62, 63,
    67, 70, 71, 77, 88, 91, 92, 113,
    207, 213
Richards, Barry 57
Richardson, Dave 110, 121, 132
Richardson, Richie 111, 113, 138,
    142, 144, 145
Roberts, Andy 19, 27, 29, 32, 48, 49,
    58, 62, 69, 70, 72

Sadiq Mohammad 18, 49, 76, 77
Saeed Anwar 139, 141, 161, 166,
    190
Saleem Jaffer 91
Saleem Raza 140
Salim Malik 141, 173, 175
Salim Yousuf 90
Salve, N.K.P. 85-87, 89, 98
Sandhu, Balwinder 70
Sangakkara, Kumar 201

Saqlain Mushtaq 158, 166
Sarfraz Nawaz 19
Sarwan, Ramnaresh 180, 189, 190
Sehwag, Virender 179, 190, 198,
    199, 202, 206, 208-210
Shahid Afridi 131
Shakoor Rana 98
Sharma, Ajay 175
Shastri, Ravi 94
Shepherd, David 113, 205
Shoaib Akhtar 157, 161, 179, 188-
    191
Sidhu, Navjot 89, 141, 143
Simpson, Bobby 6
Singh, Harbhajan 206
Skelton, Tony 38
Small, Gladstone 121
Smith, Brian 33-36
Smith, Graeme 194, 196
Smith, Ian 81, 89
Smith, Robin 113, 115
Snow, John 6, 22
Sobers, (Sir) Garfield 6, 8, 57, 130
Spencer, Charles 1
Spencer, Tom 26, 27
Split betting see Spread betting
Spread betting 174
Srikkanth, Krishnamachari 68-70
Srinath, Javagal 108, 143, 197, 205,
    207
Statham, Brian 2
Stewart, Alec 114, 115, 123, 153,
    192, 193
Stewart, Dave 152
Streak, Heath 196, 198
Suji, Martin 138, 199
Swanton, E.W. 7, 9
Symonds, Andrew 178, 183, 201, 203

Talat Ali 155
Tariq Ali 138
Tavare, Chris 67